Millie Snyder

Headline Books, Inc.
Terra Alta, WV

This book is dedicated to: Allison Rebekah Snyder, Jackson Noah Briant, Holden Mathew Briant, Aubrey Paige Snyder, Hunter James Mize,
(in the order of their ages)
From Bubbe BaBa (one and the same), Millie Snyder, A Proud Grandmother!
And to my children: Jennifer, Howard, Craig and Margie
for making them possible! Thanks Guys and Gals!

Lean and Luscious and Meatless

by Millie Snyder

This book has been adapted from the Lean & Luscious series, originally co-authored by Bobbie Hinman and Millie Snyder.

Important

This compilation of recipes is not intended as a promotion or recommendation for any specific eating program. It's always recommended to share these recipes with your health care professional. Eating healthfully to include a wide variety of fruits, vegetables, grains, all varieties of beans, utilizing the right combination of seasonings and spices is the goal of ***Lean and Luscious and Meatless***. For our vegetarian friends who choose a strictly vegan lifestyle, in using the recipes in this cookbook, please make the necessary additions, deletions or applications to take the finished recipe to your highest vegan standard.

To order additional copies of this book or to contact the author:

Headline Books, Inc., P O Box 52, Terra Alta, WV 26764
www.HeadlineBooks.com 800-570-5951
www.Millie Snyder.com
Photo credit: Danussa

ISBN-13: 9781882658428

Library of Congress Control Number: 2015949783

Meatless / more than 300 Lean & Luscious recipes
from Chef and author Millie Snyder
p. cm.
Includes index.
1. Vegetarian cooking. 2. Healthy eating / living tips.

ISBN 9781882658428

PRINTED IN THE UNITED STATES OF AMERICA

Foreword

by Rabbi Victor Urecki

B'Nai Jacob Synagogue, Charleston, West Virginia

Why am I writing a foreword for this cookbook? Granted, this book you are lucky enough to now own has some of the healthiest and most delicious recipes you will ever find. Terrific. Tasty. Tantalizing.

But what do I know? I am a rabbi. I don't cook. I can't tell you the difference between simmering and boiling. My dear wife will use this cookbook regularly and, yes, I will reap the benefits, enjoy each sampling. As for me? The recipes might as well have been written in Mandarin as far as I am concerned (there actually may be a recipe or two using those kind of oranges, but what do I know?).

Why am I writing a foreword for a book from a woman who has built a successful health empire from the ground up, who has built a reputation as an incredible employer, who understands small business, who has had a lifetime of outstanding accomplishment and continues to mentor and inspire?

I am a rabbi. True, we both try to mentor and inspire but I can't even balance my checkbook without, again, my wife (sense a pattern?). So I can't cook. And I am not a successful business person who has improved the lives of countless individuals. But I am thrilled to write this foreword because I know the importance of healthy eating. For years, I was "horizontally challenged." Not quite obese but "husky," "chubby," "fluffy," fill in the politically correct wording.

Then I started exercising. More importantly, I began eating right. No fad diets. No denial of good living and eating. Just smart eating. Like what you will find in this book. And I lost weight. I have kept it off for years because of the sensible recipes and wise advice found in this book.

I am writing this foreword because I may not know how to cook and I don't know how to run a business, but I do know how to eat and still keep the weight off and that type of eating is found here.

And I know Millie. For over 30 years, I have been friends with this remarkable woman who has helped people make positive changes in their lifestyles. Responsibly. Carefully. Smartly. I have seen how this woman has taught people how to eat healthy, dramatically improve their lives and enjoy the benefit of good living.

Her books have been in my . . . er . . . wife's kitchen for years. I could probably learn how to make these recipes if I really wanted to but I am more than happy to let my wife, who is a maven in the kitchen, enjoy preparing them. I will be more than content to simply savor these magnificent dishes and continue to rejoice in an active and fulfilling lifestyle.

This cookbook is a celebration of eating and healthy living. I know a lot about the former and I can attest to the benefits of the latter. And with Millie's guidance, you can, too.

L'chayim!
Rabbi Victor Urecki

Contents

Introduction

Meatless Meals Are Healthy

Meatless meals are an expression of the expanding knowledge of many health professionals in our country. It seems that everywhere we turn we read about more and more scientific evidence supporting the benefits of a meatless diet. In our society, where people are suffering from diseases that health experts feel are the result of eating too much fat and too little fiber, meatless meals can provide the answer.

It's important to note that meatless" does not *always* mean "healthy." A meatless diet that relies heavily on eggs and high fat dairy products can still contain large amounts of fat and cholesterol and even though eggs have been vindicated, moderate usage is a smart step. Because of this, my recipes use only egg whites—the cholesterol is in the yolk—and only lowfat dairy products, both of which have been kept to a minimum. Also, a meatless diet consisting largely of "junk food" obviously is not a healthy way of eating.

A well-balanced diet, consisting mainly of whole grains, fruits, vegetables and legumes, can supply *all* of the vitamins, minerals, protein and fiber that we need. These meals can be prepared with a minimal amount of fat and they are filling and delicious. So, with the mounting medical evidence pointing to the importance of reducing our intake of fats, cholesterol and sodium and increasing our intake of fiber, I have responded to the challenge.

Meatless Meals Are Delicious

People are continually amazed at how tasty a meal can be – without the meat. A few years ago, at a holiday dinner, a relative was overheard saying, Everything else is so delicious, I forgot to eat the meat." That's when I realized that I wasn't the only one who loved the wonderful flavors and vast variety available in the other" parts of the meals. I started serving larger portions of vegetables, grains, pasta, beans, potatoes and smaller portions of meat – both to my family and guests. The comments were more than favorable! Soon my meatless meals became my family's favorite meals. Popular foods such as pasta, pizza, stir-fries and enchiladas can be made from wholesome ingredients, with a minimal amount of fat and lots and lots of flavor.

Meatless Meals Are Economical

Our recipe testers were amazed at the drop in their grocery bills when they began testing my meatless recipes. They all found that they could feed their families nutritious, filling meals for a fraction of what they were used to spending. Just compare the price of a box of pasta or some canned beans to a family-sized package of meat and you'll see the difference.

Making your own whole-grain desserts and breads will also save on your grocery bills. Your family will benefit from better flavor *and* better nutrition.

Meatless Meals Are Easy

Yes, they certainly are! Most of my meals can be prepared in less than an hour – from start to finish. After all, there's no need to wait for meat to defrost. Many of my most commonly used ingredients are ready-to-eat, such as fruits, vegetables, and canned beans which are ready-in-a-flash such as pasta, tofu and grains. If you stock your pantry with a variety of grains, pastas and beans and have plenty of fruits and vegetables on hand, you can whip up a hearty meal with a minimum of fuss in a minimal amount of time.

Lean and Luscious and Meatless is not a diet book. It is a collection of recipes that will allow you to enjoy wonderful meals without adding unnecessary calories and fat. It will give you delicious, filling, meatless entrees, many wonderful meatless side dishes, soups made without the added fat of meat broth, and many delectable lowfat desserts.

Most of these new recipes are my own, a result of countless hours of cooking and tasting. I have also included meatless versions of some traditional favorites, such as Chickenless ala King," and other recipes that have been graciously given to me to adapt" by loving friends and family members.

So, whether you're a vegetarian or just looking for some interesting new ways to prepare delicious, low-fat meals and desserts, you've come to the right place!

Our Use Of Sugar

In all my recipes, I have kept the use of sugar to a minimum. I found that you can greatly reduce the amount of sugar in a recipe and still, by increasing the vanilla extract and by adding fruits and spices, achieve delicious, sweet results. I have also found that by using a liquid sweetener, such as honey, molasses, or Agave, we can cut down on the amount of oil in desserts, thereby greatly lowering the fat content of our recipes. Newly arrived for consumer usage is Stevia. Grown in tropical areas that support heavy green growth, these leaves provide a natural sweetness and can be found under leading brand and store-brand packaging. I also have learned of Monk fruit which carries a zero calorie marker but is a natural sweetener. Stevia is being found in many products in the supermarkets.

In general, I have found that foods made with artificial sweeteners often do not have as pleasant a taste and texture as those made with sugar, and wanting my recipes to be as wholesome as possible, I have chosen not to use any artificial sweeteners in these recipes. It is the opinion of many health experts that it is the excess fat that is the main problem in our diets, more than the sugar, so I have turned my attention to lowering the fat content and adding fiber to my recipes. By doing this and by keeping the sugar to a minimum, I have achieved a balance of flavor and nutrition.

Are You Familiar With These Ingredients?

The following is a list of the most commonly used ingredients in our recipes. Some of them may be new to you, so I have included a very brief description of each one along with hints for buying and using them:

- All-purpose flour – Available in grocery stores, this is one of the most commonly used flours. It has been milled, so unlike whole wheat flour, it has been stripped of the bran and germ. For added vitamins and fiber, I like to use it in combination with whole wheat flour.
- Bamboo shoots – This vegetable is used in many Oriental recipes. Look for it in cans in the Oriental section of most grocery stores.
- Barley – A whole grain available in most grocery stores, barley is commonly used in soups and stews.
- Black beans – These beans appear in many Southwestern-style recipes. They are available in grocery stores and health food stores in dry form and are also available canned and ready to use.
- Bran (wheat) – This refers to the outer layer of the wheat. It is high in fiber and is often used in breads, muffins and breakfast cereals.
- Bread crumbs – Available in most grocery stores, commercial bread crumbs are usually made from white bread. For added nutrition, you can make your own crumbs by toasting whole wheat bread in the oven until crisp and then crushing it.
- Brown rice – This refers to the whole grain of rice with the outer layer, the bran, still intact. It is higher in vitamins and fiber than white rice or converted rice and has a nutty flavor.
- Bulgur – Also known as cracked wheat, this form of wheat has been partially cooked and then ground. It cooks in a short amount of time and is commonly used in soups and pilafs. Bulgur is available in most grocery stores.
- Buttermilk – Made from cultured milk, buttermilk can be made from whole milk or skim milk. I prefer the one made from skim milk. An easy substitute for buttermilk is to add lemon juice to skim milk and let it stand for one minute before using. Use 1 tablespoon of lemon juice to one cup of skim milk. This will also work with soy milk.
- Carob powder – Made from the ground pods of a tree common in Mediterranean regions, this sweet powder is often used to replace cocoa in cakes and muffins. Unlike cocoa, it contains no caffeine.
- Cheddar cheese – In all of our recipes I use the lowfat variety. It is available in grocery stores and contains less fat than the regular cheddar

cheese. For those who prefer, Cheddar-flavored soy cheese will also work in my recipes.

- Chick peas (garbanzo beans) – Widely used in Middle Eastern recipes, these legumes are often called for in soups, stews, and meatless burgers. They are available in dry form or canned and are found in most grocery stores.
- Cider vinegar – This tangy vinegar is made from apple juice. It is available in grocery stores and has a unique flavor that adds variety to salads.
- Cocoa – In my recipes I specify unsweetened cocoa rather than the presweetened beverage mix. Look for it in most grocery stores.
- Coconut, shredded – I choose unsweetened coconut available in health food stores, and because it is high in saturated fat, I use very small amounts. I make up for the flavor by adding coconut extract.
- Cornmeal – Made from corn that has been dried and ground, cornmeal adds flavor and texture to breads and muffins and is used to make spoon breads and tortillas. Look for stone ground whole cornmeal available in most grocery stores and health food stores.
- Cornstarch – Available in grocery stores, cornstarch is used as a thickener for sauces and pies.
- Cottage cheese – In all recipes that call for cottage cheese, I choose the low fat variety. For a non-dairy cottage cheese substitute, crumbled tofu will work in many recipes.
- Couscous – Authentic couscous is made from wheat that has been crushed. The type that is available in most grocery stores and used in my recipes is actually a semolina product similar to tiny bits of pasta.
- Dijon mustard – Available in grocery stores, this is a tangy, French-style mustard made with white wine.
- Dried fruit – Most grocery stores carry the individual dried fruits such as figs, apples, apricots, prunes, pears and peaches. Many also carry mixed chopped fruits. Most health food stores carry dried fruits that do not have chemicals such as sulfur dioxide, added as a preservative.
- Egg whites – In all of my recipes, I use egg whites in place of whole eggs since the cholesterol is found in the yolk. (Two egg whites are equivalent to one whole egg.) Egg substitutes can also be used, but in many cases it is more economical to buy the whole eggs and just use the whites. In most breads, cakes and muffins, a three-ounce piece of tofu will also work in place of one egg. (Place the tofu in the blender with the liquid ingredients and blend until smooth.)
- Evaporated skim milk – This condensed form of skim milk comes in cans. It is available in grocery stores and is not to be mistaken for sweetened condensed milk. It is ideal to use in place of cream.

- Garlic – Once available only in fresh form, garlic is now also sold in jars and already chopped. Look for it in the produce section of most grocery stores.
- Great Northern beans – These white beans are available in grocery stores and health food stores in dry form and are also available canned and ready to use.
- Green chilies – A favorite in Mexican recipes, these chilies are available fresh in many grocery stores. I prefer the ease of the canned ones. They are available either hot or mild.
- Honey – Found in grocery stores and health food stores, honey is available in many varieties. I usually choose a mild-flavored one such as clover honey.
- Kasha – Also known as buckwheat groats, this grain has a distinctive toasty flavor. It is available in grocery and health food stores and is found in several sizes or granulations. In my recipes, I use the medium-size kasha.
- Kidney beans – This versatile legume is available in grocery and health food stores in dry form and is also available canned and ready to use. It is most commonly used in soups and chili.
- Lemon juice – Freshly squeezed is my favorite with the average lemon yielding about 2 tablespoons of juice.
- Lemon peel – What I use in my recipes is often called the lemon zest. It is the outermost yellow part of the lemon and does not include the white part of the peel.
- Lentils – A relatively fast-cooking legume, lentils are available in dry form in grocery and health food stores. Often used in soups and stews, lentils also make great meatless burgers and loaves.
- Maple syrup – In my recipes, I specify pure maple syrup rather than the maple-flavored variety. It is available in grocery stores.
- Margarine – Margarine has the same amount of calories as butter but is lower in saturated fat and contains no cholesterol. Because it is still relatively high in fat, I use margarine sparingly and choose one with a liquid oil as the first oil listed on the label. Reduced-calorie margarine has been whipped with water, thereby reducing the amount of fat in each serving.
- Mayonnaise – When mayonnaise is used, choose the reduced-calorie mayonnaise that is whipped with water, which cuts the calories and fat by half. For those who prefer, many grocery and health food stores also carry egg-free and tofu mayonnaise.
- Millet – This pleasant-tasting grain is available in health food stores. It can be used in place of rice in soups, pilafs and desserts.
- Miso – Miso is a thick paste made from soybeans. It has been used by the Japanese for centuries. It is available in health food stores and makes delicious soups, gravies, and salad dressings.

- Molasses – This sweetener, available in grocery and health food stores, has a wonderful, distinctive flavor. If you like a very strong molasses flavor, try blackstrap molasses. It's also a good source of iron.
- Mozzarella cheese – I choose the part-skim variety and use it in all recipes that call for mozzarella cheese. For those who prefer, most health food stores carry a mozzarella-type soy cheese that may be substituted. Recently, fresh mozzarella has appeared on the shelves and can be used in recipes calling for a white, mild flavored cheese product. Always remember to drain the liquid if purchased in containers.
- Non-fat dry milk – This economical, dried form of skim milk can be reconstituted by adding it to water. Available in grocery stores, it is convenient to keep on hand for baking.
- Noodles – Traditionally made with whole eggs, yolkless" noodles, which do not contain cholesterol, are now available in most grocery stores. Also available in health food stores are eggless whole wheat noodles and whole wheat noodles made with the yolk of an egg.
- Nuts – I like the flavor and crunch nuts add to many dishes, but because they are rather high in fat, use them sparingly in your recipes. In other recipes calling for a cup of nuts, I have found a few tablespoons will do.
- Oat bran – The outer covering of the whole oat, this is the part that contains most of the fiber. It can be cooked with water for a nutritious breakfast cereal or added to breads, cakes and muffins. Oat bran can be found in the cereal section of most grocery stores.
- Olive oil – Olive oil is high in monounsaturated fat, a quality many health experts believe can help lower blood cholesterol levels. It has a distinctive flavor and is often used in Italian and Middle Eastern recipes. It is available in grocery stores.
- Orange peel – Often referred to as the orange zest, this is the outermost skin of the orange. It does not include the white part of the peel.
- Orzo – Orzo is a tiny, rice-shaped form of pasta. It is found in the pasta section of most grocery stores.
- Parmesan cheese – This popular cheese gives many ethnic foods their distinctiveness. Because of its strong flavor, you can greatly reduce the amount called for in most recipes, thereby reducing the amount of fat without sacrificing flavor. There is a lowfat version found in many grocery stores and one made from soy milk in many health food stores.
- Part-skim ricotta cheese – Ricotta cheese is creamier than cottage cheese and is used in many Italian entrees and also in many desserts. This reduced-fat version can be used wherever whole milk ricotta cheese is called for.

- Pasta – Pasta is available in many sizes and shapes. It is also available made from grains other than wheat. Health food stores often carry corn, rice and buckwheat pasta as well as pasta made from other less familiar grains. Become familiar with other choices of pasta to broaden your tastes and cooking adventure.
- Peanut butter – I prefer peanut butter made from ground peanuts with no added fat or sugar. It is available in most grocery stores.
- Picante sauce – Found with the Mexican foods in most grocery stores, this sauce comes in a jar and is used as a condiment with many Mexican dishes. It is usually available hot or mild.
- Pimentos – Pimentos, or sweet peppers, come in jars and are usually found in grocery stores alongside the pickles.
- Pine nuts – Pignolias, or pine nuts, are often used in Spanish and Italian dishes. They are found in grocery, health food and specialty stores.
- Pita breads – These flat breads can be opened to form a pocket and filled with a variety of sandwich fillings. They are found in the bread section of most grocery stores. I prefer the whole wheat variety. In health-savvy locations that serve prepared foods, the pita fiber breads are chosen for the crust rather than made with enriched flours.
- Quinoa – This ancient grain is making a reappearance. It is high in fiber and can support a totally nutritious meal when used in place of other whole grains. Uniquely delicious!
- Reduced-sugar jam and marmalade – These are made with less sugar than regular jams and marmalades, hence they have fewer calories. Most grocery stores carry a variety of flavors.
- Rolled oats – These are the flattened out flakes many people refer to as "oatmeal." I prefer this type of oats to the "quick" or "instant" ones that are sometimes processed or sweetened. Most grocery stores carry rolled oats in the cereal section. Steel cut oats have not been milled or decreased in nutrition. When using for a breakfast choice, extra time is required in preparation.
- Salsa – This tomato-based sauce comes in jars and is found with the Mexican foods in most grocery stores. Used to top tacos and other Mexican dishes, it is available mild, medium, and hot.
- Sesame oil – Often used to give flavor to Oriental dishes, this oil is found in most grocery stores. The flavor is strong and a little goes a long way.
- Sesame seed – This versatile little seed has a nut-like flavor. Most grocery stores carry it in the spice section.

- Sherry – Buy an inexpensive medium or dry sherry rather than the specially bottled cooking sherry. Use it in moderation and find that just 1 or 2 tablespoons gives sauces a wonderful flavor.
- Skim milk – Skim milk or non-fat milk can be used in any recipe that calls for milk. It is lower in fat than 2% milk and higher in calcium since the fat is gone. (If you prefer a non-dairy milk, soy milk will also work in recipes, but it has a higher fat content than skim milk.)
- Snow pea pods – These bright green pods are available in most grocery stores, either fresh or frozen. They are most often used in Oriental dishes and the whole pod is eaten.
- Soy sauce – Made from fermented soy beans, this popular Oriental sauce is available in regular and reduced-sodium forms in most grocery stores.
- Sunflower seeds – Look for already shelled sunflower seeds in most grocery stores alongside the nuts. I prefer either raw ones or dry roasted, unsalted.
- Swiss cheese – In all of my recipes, I use the lowfat variety. It is available in grocery stores and contains less fat than the regular Swiss cheese.
- Tahini – Tahini is made from ground sesame seeds and has a texture similar to peanut butter. A Middle Eastern favorite, it is available in health food and specialty stores.
- Tapioca – This thickener for fruits, puddings, and pies is available in most grocery stores.
- Tofu – Made from soy beans in much the same way that cheese is made from milk. Its bland flavor gives it a remarkable versatility. Look for tofu in the produce section of most grocery stores, available in either soft, medium or firm textures.
- Tomatoes, canned – Salt-free canned tomatoes, found in most grocery stores, are lower in sodium than regular canned tomatoes. A variety of different tomato cuts are also available in grocery stores. The varieties have increased and can contain chilies, peppers, onions, and basil for added convenience and to enhance flavors.
- Tomato sauce – Most grocery stores carry salt-free tomato sauce, which is lower in sodium than regular tomato sauce.
- Tortillas – These Mexican flatbreads are made with either cornmeal or flour and can be topped with a variety of fillings and are often rolled. They are available, refrigerated or frozen, in most grocery stores. In all of my recipes, use the 6-inch size tortillas.
- Vegetable broth mix – A combination of soup-flavored spices, this mixture can be used in place of meat-based broths in soups and stews. It is available in health food stores or you can make your own (recipe is found in the Soup section of this book).

- Vegetable oil – Many health professionals recommend choosing a monounsaturated oil such as canola or olive oil. Look for sunflower or safflower oil as additional choices.
- Water chestnuts – Not really a nut, this starchy vegetable adds crunch to many Oriental dishes. It comes in cans and is available in the Oriental section of most grocery stores.
- Wheat germ – Sometimes called the "heart" of the grain, wheat germ is high in vitamins, minerals and protein. It resembles coarse crumbs and can be used in place of bread crumbs in many recipes. It can also be used to replace some of the flour in bread recipes. Wheat germ comes in jars and is available in the cereal section of most grocery stores.
- Whole wheat bread – This bread is made entirely, or at least predominantly, from whole wheat flour and is higher in vitamins and fiber than ordinary white bread. Look for the first ingredient to be 100% whole wheat flour. Once available only in health food stores, whole wheat bread is now sold in most grocery stores.
- Whole wheat flour – This flour is made from the whole grain of wheat. It contains more vitamins, minerals and fiber than all-purpose flour and adds a wonderful flavor and texture to baked goods.
- Wine vinegar – A mild-flavored vinegar made with wine, this is a delicious salad ingredient. I prefer the red wine vinegar, available in grocery stores.
- Yogurt – This cultured milk product can be used in place of sour cream in most recipes. The non-fat variety has the lowest fat content.
- Greek yogurt – This yogurt is available in plain and flavored varieties and has been used in a vast array of cooking. It is often used to replace mayonaise, adding a unique and surprising end result.

Spice It right

Over the years, through all of my cooking, I keep coming back to one basic truth – the spices and extracts are what make the difference between an ordinary meal and an extraordinary meal. I have removed a lot of the fat, sugar and salt from these recipes, but I still find that if the combination of spices is right, the dishes are delicious. Actually, foods taste better than ever because we are relying more on spices and extracts for flavor and less on the fat, sugar, and salt.

In most of these recipes, I used dried spices. If you wish to substitute fresh ones, you will need to use 2 to 3 times the amount called for.

Following are some hints for the most commonly used spices and extracts. Use these as a guideline and remember when trying a new spice to go easy. You can always add more.

- Allspice – Used in cakes, cookies, muffins, breads, pickles, and tomato-based sauces. Delicious in combination with cinnamon, nutmeg or cloves.
- Almond extract – Used to give a rich almond flavor to cakes, pies, sauces, puddings, breads, and muffins. Enhances the flavor of cocoa.
- Basil – Used in many Italian dishes and tomato dishes such as pasta sauce and pizza. Delicious in combination with oregano, garlic, and/or thyme.
- Bay leaves – Commonly used in soups, stews and sauces. Delicious in combination with oregano, garlic, marjoram, basil or thyme. They should be removed from the dish and discarded before serving.
- Caraway seed – Used in rye bread and often in cabbage recipes.
- Celery seed – Often used in slaws, pickles, and salads.
- Chili powder – Used mainly in Mexican recipes, such as chili, tacos and casseroles. Delicious in combination with cumin and garlic.
- Chives – Commonly used in salads, salad dressings, sauces, and vegetable dishes. They work well with garlic and lemon.
- Cinnamon – Used in breads, fruits, many types of desserts and vegetables such as carrots, winter squash, and sweet potatoes. Delicious alone or in combination with nutmeg, allspice and/or cloves.
- Cloves – Ground cloves are often used in cakes, breads, muffins, steamed puddings, and vegetables such as carrots and sweet potatoes. Delicious in combination with cinnamon, nutmeg, and allspice.
- Coconut extract – Used in cakes, pies, puddings and fruits to give the flavor of coconut without the fat. Delicious in combination with bananas and/or pineapple.

- Coriander – Used in soups, sauces, bean dishes, puddings, breads and muffins. Works well with cumin and chili powder; also works with vanilla and lemon in sweet recipes.
- Cumin – Used in many Middle Eastern and Mexican recipes such as chili and other bean dishes. Works well with chili powder and garlic; also works well with basil and oregano.
- Curry powder – A common ingredient in Indian dishes such as soups, stews and vegetables. It is actually a blend of spices.
- Dill weed – Used in pickles, salads and vegetable dishes. Delicious in combination with garlic; also works well with lemon.
- Fennel seed – Used in soups, stews and tomato-based sauces. Delicious in combination with garlic and thyme.
- Garlic – Commonly used in soups, stews, vegetables, salads, dips, pickles, and sauces. A favorite ingredient in foods in most parts of the world. Delicious when combined with onions and with most other spices.
- Garlic powder – Use 1/8 teaspoon to equal 1 clove of garlic.
- Ginger – Ground ginger is used in cakes, breads, steamed puddings, sauces, fruits and vegetables such as sweet potatoes and carrots. Delicious in combination with cinnamon; also combines well with garlic in Oriental dishes.
- Lemon extract – Used to give a rich lemon flavor to cakes, pies, puddings, fruits and sauces.
- Lemon zest – Lemon peel and it is the outermost yellow part of the lemon—does not include the white part of the peel.
- Marjoram – Used in soups, stews, vegetables, stuffing, and sauces. Works well with garlic and bay leaves.
- Mustard – Dry mustard is often added to give zip" to salad dressings, sauces and cheese dishes.
- Nutmeg – Used in cakes, breads, muffins, puddings, fruits, and sauces. Delicious in combination with cinnamon. Also works well with garlic in spinach and cheese dishes.
- Orange extract – Used to give a rich orange flavor to cakes, pies, puddings, fruits, sauces, and vegetables such as sweet potatoes, winter squash, and carrots.
- Orange zest – Orange peel and it is the outermost orange skin of the orange—does not include the white part of the peel.
- Oregano – Commonly used in tomato dishes such as soups, stews, chili, pasta saucc, and pizza; also used in salads and salad dressings. Delicious in combination with garlic, basil and/or thyme; also good with chili powder.
- Paprika – Used to add color to foods and to flavor soups, salad dressings, and stews such as goulash. Often used to top potatoes and cream sauces.

- Parsley – Used to add color and a mild flavor to soups, stews and vegetable dishes. Works well in combination with most other spices.
- Pepper – Used to add “zip” to almost any food.
- Pickling spice – Available already blended and commonly used in all types of pickles.
- Poultry seasoning – Used in soups, stews, stuffings, patés, and burgers. Delicious in combination with onions, garlic and thyme.
- Pumpkin pie spice – A blend of spices commonly used in cakes, breads, muffins, pumpkin pie, fruits, and vegetables such as sweet potatoes and winter squash.
- Rosemary – Often used in soups, stews, tomato-based sauces, and vegetable dishes. Combines well with onions, garlic, basil, oregano or thyme.
- Rum extract – Used to give a rum flavor to sauces, cakes, pies, breads, muffins, puddings, fruits, and vegetables such as sweet potatoes.
- Saffron – Used in many Spanish dishes such as soups, stews, and rice. Works well with onions, bay leaves, and garlic.
- Sage – Commonly used in soups, stews, casseroles, vegetables, and stuffing. Delicious in combination with onions, garlic, rosemary and thyme.
- Tarragon – Used in dressings and sauces, especially cream sauces. Works well with bay leaves.
- Thyme – Used in soups, stews, vegetables, and tomato-based sauces. Delicious in combination with garlic, basil and/or oregano.
- Turmeric – Used to add color and flavor to soups, pickles, sauces, salads, and many Indian dishes. Often used with cumin and curry powder.
- Vanilla extract – A favorite extract commonly used to enhance the sweetness of cakes, pies, breads, muffins, sauces, custards, pudding, fruit desserts, and vegetables such as sweet potatoes and winter squash. Delicious in combination with other spices. The pure vanilla extract has a much richer flavor than the imitation extract.

Menus For Meatless Meals

For many people, it is hard to get away from the stereotypical meal of meat, potatoes and a green vegetable. They may be afraid either that they will not get enough food to fill them up or not get enough of the nutrients necessary to sustain them. Well, they needn't worry. A balanced diet of fruits, vegetables, whole grains, and legumes contain all the necessary nutrients for a healthy life, including good-quality protein and lots of complex carbohydrates. If prepared correctly, this type of meal will contain very little fat. It's important to emphasize the term balanced "diet." By this, I mean a good variety each day of fruits, vegetables, whole grains, and legumes. The reason I emphasize this is because, theoretically, a person could eat meatless meals consisting of refined grains, high-fat dairy products, and few, if any, fresh fruits or vegetables. While he or she may consider this to be healthful because it is meatless, it certainly does not contain adequate nutritional value.

I have put together some sample menus to help you and your family enjoy delicious, nutritious meatless meals. These menus represent just a few of the many meals available using the recipes in this book. I invite you to be creative, try lots of varied meal combinations and discover a healthy lifestyle.

Enjoy!

(see index for page #s of recipes)

Breakfast Menus

Orange-Berry Fruit Cup
Gingerbread Raisin Pancakes
topped with
Vanilla Creme Sauce

* * * * *

Citrus Brulée
Scrambled Tofu Spanish Omelet
Whole Wheat Toast

* * * * *

Swiss Apple-Fruit-and-Nut-Muesli
Eggless Honey Wheat Muffin
with Orange-Fig Spread

Cooked Oatmeal
topped with
Spiced Peaches
Cinna-Muffin

* * * * *

Sliced Bananas topped with
Raspberry Melba Sauce
Toasted English Muffin with
Pineapple-Pepper Cheese Spread

* * * * *

Orange Prune Compote
Apple-Raisin Spice Bread
with Nut Butter

Lunch Menus

Lentil Paté on
Whole Wheat Pita Bread
with Lettuce and Tomato
Honey-Pear Waldorf Salad

* * * * *

Tossed Salad with
Miso Dressing
Eggless "Egg" Salad on
Whole Wheat Toast
Pineapple Slaw

* * * * *

Tossed Salad with
Lemon Vinaigrette
Black and White Bean Soup
Herb Biscuit

* * * * *

Miso Soup
Party Pasta Salad
Grape Nutty Baked Apple

Chunky Tomato Salad
Great Northern Mock Tuna Salad
on Toasted English Muffin
Bread and Butter Pickles

* * * * *

Bean and Cheese Wrap-Ups
Millie's Everything Salad
Fresh Fruit

* * * * *

Toasted Bagel with
Hot Pizza Dip
Fresh Fruit Salad

* * * * *

Fresh Vegetables with
Tofu Spinach Dip
Baked Sweet Potato

GOOD HEALTH ALERT:

Choose other cruciferous vegetables besides broccoli: cabbage, cauliflower, kale, collards, mustard greens and brussel sprouts. These all contain nitrogen compounds called indoles, which may protect against certain cancers. The dark green vegetables in this family are also good sources of cancer-fighting carotenoids notably beta carotene (the chlorophyll hides its orange-yellow color), and they all supply Vitamin C and fiber.

Dinner Menus

Cranberry Crunch Salad on
Bed of Lettuce
Shanghai Grilled Tofu
Brown Rice
Steamed Broccoli
Celestial Lemon Custards

* * * * *

Tossed Salad with
Cranberry Vinaigrette
Dinner in a Nest
Steamed Green Beans
Raspberry-Glazed Apple Pie

* * * * *

Convenience Vegetable Soup
Marvelous Meatless Mushroom
Cheeseburger
on Whole Wheat Bun
Pineapple Orange Tapioca

* * * * *

Lentil-Nut Loaf
Sweet and Tangy Cole Slaw
Baked Potato Onion Wrap-Ups
Spiced Peaches

* * * * *

Tossed Salad with
Cranberry Vinaigrette
Dinner in a Nest
Steamed Green Beans
Raspberry-Glazed Apple Pie

Tossed Salad with
Oriental Sesame Dressing
Chinese Vegetable Pasta
Razzleberry Crisp

* * * * *

Chick Peas Italiano over
Cooked Noodles
Steamed Broccoli and Cauliflower
Dreamy Orange Ice Cream Pie

* * * * *

Fresh Vegetables with
Mexicali Bean Dip
Tofu Fajitas
Orange n' Raisin Rice Pudding

* * * * *

Super Quick Chili
Acapulco Corn Bread
Fresh Fruit Salad with
Almond Yogurt Topping

* * * * *

Tailgate Picnic

Antipasto-Stuffed Hoagies
Pineapple Slaw
Fruit-to-Go
Sir Isaac's Fig Bars

Sunday Brunch

Fresh Fruit Cup
Tofu and Cheese Blintzes
Raspberry Melba Sauce
Rum n' Raisin Muffins

* * * * *

Veggie Quiche
Pears a l' Orange
Molasses-Raisin-Spice Cookies

Tropical Fruit Cup with
Raspberry Sauce
Bagels with
French Herbed Cheese Spread

Elegant Dinner Parties

Zucchini-Pimento Hot Bites
Honey-Pear Waldorf Salad
on Bed of Lettuce
Angel Hair Pasta with
Sicilian Lentil Pasta Sauce
Party Vegetable Loaf
Chocolate Mousse Cake

Eggplant Caviar on
Whole Wheat Crackers
Millet Butternut Soup
Tofu Dinner Loaf
Broccoli with Mushrooms and
Walnuts
Razzleberry Crisp

Special Holiday Dinner

Tossed Salad
with
Blueberry Vinaigrette
Tofu Croquettes with Currant Spice Sauce
Brown and Wild Rice
Steam Broccoli
Steam Christmas Pudding with
Apple-Brandy Sauce

Appetizers, Dips and Spreads

Appetizers set the tone for the rest of the meal. They should be light and should whet the appetite rather than fill you up. Since they are the "first act" of the meal, I like them to be a positive indication of the delicious tastes that follow.

Appetizers can also be used as party foods. Dips, spreads and delectable "munchies" are all that are needed to cater a party.

I try to keep the fat content as low as possible in the spreads by using only lowfat and nonfat dairy products. I have added fiber by using lots of fruits, vegetables and legumes. As accompaniments to dips and spreads, choose cut-up fresh fruits and vegetables and whole grain crackers that are high in fiber and low in fat.

For lunches or light dinners, try our spreads as sandwich fillings. Add a tossed salad and a bowl of soup and you have a quick, nutritious meal. Also, remember that dips packed in small containers, along with some fruits or vegetables, make a deliciously different lunchbox treat.

There are lots of other recipes in this book that make good appetizers. All of my salads, for example, can be used in this way and many of my entrees and fruits will also work.

Following is a list of just a few of our recipes ***(see index for page number)*** *that are easily adaptable to becoming appetizers or party foods:*

- Tahini Dressing – Use as a dip for fresh vegetables.
- Tofu Russian dressing – Use as a dip for fresh vegetables.
- Mexican Salad in a Burrito – Pile them on a platter.
- Counterfeit (Carrot) Tuna Salad – Serve with crackers.
- Great Northern Mock Tuna Salad – Serve with crackers.
- Antipasto-Stuffed Hoagies – Slice and arrange on a platter.
- California Layered Loaf – Cut into wedges
- Yellow Submarine – Slice and serve hot.
- Grilled Cheese and Apple Special – Cut into quarters and pile on a platter.
- Zucchini Mock Crab Cakes – Serve on crackers with ketchup or cocktail sauce.
- Mexican Pizza – Cut into wedges and arrange on a platter.
- Taco Fries – Serve with salsa as a dip.
- Fruit-to-Go – Serve with small bowls and toothpicks.

Let's party!

Zucchini Pimento Hot Bites

One of my favorite appetizers, this can also be spooned onto English muffins and served as a delicious brunch dish. Also look for light English muffins with a generous amount of added fiber.

Makes 6 servings

1 cup finely shredded zucchini, unpeeled
¼ cup plain nonfat yogurt
¼ cup reduced-calorie mayonnaise
2 tablespoons grated Parmesan cheese
2 tablespoons very finely chopped onions
1 2-ounce jar chopped pimentos, drained
2 tablespoons sunflower seeds
1/8 teaspoon garlic powder
24 slices party rye bread (¼ ounce slices)

Preheat oven to 400°.

Have a large, ungreased baking sheet ready.

Spread zucchini, in a thin layer, on several layers of paper towels. Top with several more towels, press down, and let drain while mixing other ingredients.

In a small bowl, combine remaining ingredients, *except* bread. Mix well.

Stir in drained zucchini, mixing well.

Spoon mixture onto bread, using a rounded teaspoonful on each slice. Spread almost to the edges of the bread. Place bread on baking sheet.

Bake 10 to 12 minutes, until bread is lightly toasted and topping is hot.

Serve hot.

Each serving provides: 132 Calories, 5 g Fat, 5 mg Cholesterol, 18 g Carbohydrate, 253 mg Sodium, 1 g Fiber, 5 g Protein

Tomato Party Puffs

Friends suggested this appetizer, and they just love it. I've also made it using a few asparagus tips in place of each tomato slice. Yum!

Makes 4 servings

16 slices party rye bread (¼ – ounce slices)
4 small tomatoes, sliced ¼ inch thick (or, cut 2 large tomatoes into quarters, then slice. The idea is to end up with tomato slices about the same size as the bread.)
2 egg whites
¼ teaspoon cream of tartar
2 tablespoons grated Parmesan cheese

Preheat oven to 400°.

Have a large, ungreased baking sheet ready.

Place bread slices on baking sheet. Place a slice of tomato on each piece of bread.

Place egg whites in a medium bowl. Beat at medium speed with an electric mixer until frothy. Add cream of tartar. Beat at high speed until egg whites are stiff.

Fold in Parmesan cheese gently, but thoroughly.

Place a heaping tablespoonful of egg white mixture on top of each tomato. Using a table knife, spread mixture, covering tomato and top of edges of bread.

Bake 10 minutes, until nicely browned.

Serve hot.

Each serving provides: 108 Calories, 1 g Fat, 2 mg Cholesterol, 19 g Carbohydrate, 240 mg Sodium, .5 g Fiber, 6 g Protein

Cheese Stuffed Snow Peas

These easy appetizers make a colorful presentation when arranged on a platter like the spokes of a wheel. For color, add cherry tomatoes between the spokes.

Makes 4 servings

- 16 snow pea pods
- ½ cup part-skim ricotta cheese
- 2 tablespoons finely chopped green onion (green part only)
- 1/8 teaspoon dill weed
- 1/16 teaspoon garlic powder

Wash pea pods, trim ends, and remove strings. Place in a steamer basket. Bring 2 quarts of water to a boil in a medium saucepan. Dip steamer basket into boiling water and remove right away. Run basket under cold water and spread pea pods on a towel to drain.

In a small bowl, combine ricotta cheese with remaining ingredients.

With a sharp knife, slit pea pods open along one side. Spoon cheese mixture into pods, using 1½ teaspoons of cheese for each one. (A cake-decorating tube can also be used.)

Place on a platter and chill several hours or overnight.

Serve cold.

Each serving provides: 48 Calories, 2 g Fat, 10 mg Cholesterol, 3 g Carbohydrate, 39 mg Sodium, 1 g Fiber, 4 g Protein

Eggplant Caviar

Not really caviar at all, this tangy dish is great spread on crackers. Be sure to chop everything very finely for the best texture.

Makes 12 servings

1 medium eggplant (about 1¼ pounds)
½ cup finely chopped onions
1 cup finely chopped tomatoes
¼ cup chopped walnuts (1 ounce)
1 tablespoon olive oil
2 teaspoons lemon juice
2 teaspoons wine vinegar
1 tablespoon dried parsley flakes
¼ teaspoon garlic powder
Salt and pepper to taste

Preheat oven to 375°.

Prick eggplant with a fork several times. Place directly on oven rack and bake 45 minutes, until tender. Cool until comfortable to handle.

Peel and finely chop eggplant. (You will have about 2 cups.) Combine in bowl with remaining ingredients, mixing well.

Chill several hours to blend flavors. Mix before serving.

Each serving provides: 41 Calories, 3 g Fat, 0 mg Cholesterol, 4 g Carbohydrate, 4 mg Sodium, 2 g Fiber, 1 g Protein

Cheese Stuffed Cucumbers

These pretty cucumber "boats" make a unique salad course, as well as a delicious appetizer.

Makes 6 servings

3 large cucumbers
1 cup lowfat cottage cheese
¼ cup finely chopped green onion (green part only)
¼ teaspoon dill weed
1/8 teaspoon garlic powder
Salt and pepper to taste

If cucumbers have been waxed, peel them. Cut each one in half, lengthwise. With a teaspoon, scoop out and discard the seeds.

Combine remaining ingredients in a small bowl. Mix well.

Chill cucumbers and cheese mixture, separately, for several hours or overnight.

To serve, blot cucumbers with a towel and fill with cheese.

Each serving provides: 48 Calories, 1 g Fat, 2 mg Cholesterol, 6 g Carbohydrate, 156 mg Sodium, .5 g Fiber, 6 g Protein

Lentil Paté

If you're a lover of chopped liver or liver paté, but don't want the cholesterol that's in liver, try this delicious spread. Your taste buds will be delighted.

Makes 10 servings

- 1 cup lentils, uncooked (7½ ounces)
- 4 cups water
- 2 teaspoons canola oil
- 1½ cups chopped onions
- ¼ teaspoon salt
- ¼ teaspoon pepper

Bring water to boil in a medium saucepan. Add lentils, cover pot, reduce heat, and simmer 40 to 45 minutes until lentils are tender. Drain.

Heat oil in a large nonstick skillet over medium heat. Add onions and cook until browned. Stir frequently and add small amounts of water, if necessary, to avoid sticking. (The secret to the flavor of this dish is to make sure the onions are nicely browned.)

In a food processor, combine lentils, cooked onions, salt and pepper. Process until smooth. Transfer to a bowl and chill several hours to blend flavors.

Serve on crackers or make a delicious sandwich on rye bread with lettuce, tomato and sliced onion.

Each serving provides: 88 Calories, 1 g Fat, 0 mg Cholesterol, 14 g Carbohydrate, 57 mg Sodium, 3 g Fiber, 6 g Protein

GOOD HEALTH ALERT:

To minimize vitamin loss due to exposure to air, cut fruits and vegetables in thick slices or chunks, if at all. Ideally, slicing should be done close to serving time.

Festive Cheese Log

I've added the protein and fiber of beans, the tang of pepperoncini and the festive color of tomatoes to this unique cheese log. Spread it on crackers for an appetizer or on a toasted English muffin for a delicious lunch.

Makes 10 servings

1 1-pound can Great Northern beans, rinsed and drained. (This will yield 10 ounces of beans.)
4 ounces shredded lowfat Cheddar cheese (1 cup)
¼ cup part-skim ricotta cheese
1/8 teaspoon garlic powder
¼ cup finely chopped pepperoncini (salad peppers)
½ cup finely chopped plum tomatoes, drained well
2 tablespoons wheat germ
1 teaspoon dried parsley flakes

Place beans in a large bowl and mash with a fork or a potato masher. Add Cheddar cheese and ricotta cheese and mash until well blended.

Sprinkle garlic powder over bean mixture. Mix well. Add pepperoncini and tomatoes, mixing well. Shape mixture into a log about 2 inches in diameter and about 6 inches long.

Combine wheat germ and parsley and spread on a plate or a sheet of waxed paper. Roll log in mixture. Cover and chill overnight.

Each serving provides: 82 Calories, 3 g Fat, 10 mg Cholesterol, 7 g Carbohydrate, 172 mg Sodium, 4 g Fiber, 6 g Protein

Tortilla Cheese Triangles

I like to serve these crispy appetizers hot along with a bowl of our favorite salsa for dipping.

Makes 4 servings

4 corn tortillas
2 ounces shredded lowfat Cheddar cheese

Preheat broiler.

Place tortillas on an ungreased baking sheet. Sprinkle evenly with cheese.

Broil 3 to 4 minutes or until cheese is melted and edges of tortillas are crispy.

While still hot, cut each tortilla into 6 triangles. (Kitchen shears work great.)

Serve hot, either plain or on a platter alongside a bowl of salsa for dipping.

Each serving provides: 112 Calories, 4 g Fat, 10 mg Cholesterol, 13 g Carbohydrate, 153 mg Sodium, 1 g Fiber, 6 g Protein

Hot Pizza Dip

This delicious dip is served hot and tastes just like the real thing.

Makes 8 servings

Filling:

1 cup part-skim ricotta cheese
1 cup shredded part-skim mozzarella cheese (4 ounces)
½ teaspoon dried oregano
¼ teaspoon dried basil
1/8 teaspoon garlic powder

Topping:

½ cup salt-free (or regular) tomato sauce
¼ teaspoon dried oregano
¼ teaspoon dried basil
3 tablespoons finely chopped onions
3 tablespoons finely chopped green pepper

Preheat oven to 375°.
Have a 9-inch pie pan ready.

Prepare filling:
In a medium bowl, combine ricotta cheese, mozzarella cheese and spices. Mix well. Spread mixture even in pie pan, smoothing the top with the back of a spoon.

Prepare topping:
In a small bowl, combine tomato sauce, oregano and basil. Mix well. Spread evenly over cheese. Sprinkle onions and green pepper evenly over sauce.

Bake, uncovered, 25 minutes.

Serve hot as a dip or spread for crackers, pita breads, bagels or French bread.

Each serving provides: 86 Calories, 5 g Fat, 18 mg Cholesterol, 4 g Carbohydrate, 108 mg Sodium, 1 g Fiber, 7 g Protein

GOOD HEALTH ALERT:
While dark green, leafy vegetables can provide much needed calcium to your diet, don't count on spinach. Spinach also has a lot of oxalate, which binds with calcium, making it unavailable to the body.

Guacamole Dip

Lots of cookbooks have recipes for this wonderful Mexican dip. Many of the recipes have oil and many have sour cream. Mine just has flavor! For vegetable dippers or for spreading on crackers, this one can't be beat.

Makes 12 servings

2 medium, ripe avocados, peeled, pit removed
2 teaspoons lemon juice
2 tablespoons very finely chopped onion
½ cup finely chopped tomato
½ teaspoon garlic powder
¼ teaspoon chili powder
Salt and pepper to taste

Place avocados in a large bowl and mash with a fork until smooth. Add remaining ingredients, mixing well.

Serve right away or chill for later serving.

Note: Avocados will discolor after preparing so it is best to serve the dip as soon as possible. I prefer to chill the avocados first and prepare the dip just before serving time.

Each serving provides: 57 Calories, 5 g Fat, 0 mg Cholesterol, 3 g Carbohydrate, 5 mg Sodium, 1 g Fiber, 1 g Protein

Cranberry Orange Dip

This is a perfect dip for holiday entertaining. You can place it in a small bowl, in the center of a platter of fresh fruit or pass it around the table as a sauce for fruit salad. (I also make it when it isn't a holiday.)

Makes 8 servings

3/4 cup plain nonfat yogurt or plain Greek yogurt
½ cup canned whole-berry cranberry sauce
½ cup mandarin oranges packed in own juice (drain juice)
½ teaspoon vanilla extract
1/8 teaspoon orange extract

In a small bowl, combine all ingredients, mixing well.

Chill several hours to blend flavors.

Each serving provides: 39 Calories, 0 g Fat, 0 mg Cholesterol, 8 g Carbohydrate, 21 mg Sodium, 1 g Fiber, 1 g Protein

Mexicali Bean Dip

Wonderfully spicy, this dip is great for veggies. I've also heated it and spooned it over a baked potato. Yum!

Makes 10 servings

1 1-pound can kidney beans, rinsed and drained. (This will yield 10 ounces of beans.)
3/4 cup plain nonfat yogurt or plain Greek yogurt
¼ cup chopped onions
1 teaspoon chili powder
¼ teaspoon garlic powder
¼ teaspoon ground cumin

In a blender container, combine all ingredients. Blend until smooth. Chill several hours to blend flavors.

Each serving provides: 45 Calories, 0 g Fat, 0 mg Cholesterol, 7 g Carbohydrate, 74 mg Sodium, 3 g Fiber, 3 g Protein

Tofu Spinach Dip

It seems that everyone makes a spinach dip these days. Well, this is my version. I've replaced the usual sour cream with tofu for a delicious high-protein imposter.

Makes 12 servings

9 ounces soft tofu
1 tablespoon lemon juice
¼ cup reduced-calorie mayonnaise
1 cup water
1 10-ounce package frozen chopped spinach, thawed, drained well
1 4-serving package dried vegetable soup mix
¼ teaspoon garlic powder
¼ cup chopped green onions (green part only)

In a blender container, combine tofu, lemon juice, mayonnaise and water. Blend until smooth. Spoon into a medium bowl. Add remaining ingredients, mixing well. Chill overnight to blend flavors. Serve cold with vegetable dippers.

Each serving provides: 43 Calories, 2 g Fat, 2 mg Cholesterol, 4 g Carbohydrate, 330 mg Sodium, 2 g Fiber, 2 g Protein

Honey Sweet Pineapple Dip

This delicious dip is perfect for dipping fresh fruits or as a topping for your favorite fruit desserts.

Makes 12 servings

1 cup lowfat cottage cheese
1 cup canned crushed pineapple (unsweetened), drained
1 tablespoon honey
½ teaspoon vanilla extract
1/8 teaspoon coconut extract
1/16 teaspoon lemon extract

In a blender, combine all ingredients. Blend until smooth. Chill several hours to blend flavors.

Each serving provides: 32 Calories, 0 g Fat, 1 mg Cholesterol, 5 g Carbohydrate, 77 mg Sodium, Less than 1 g Fiber, 2 g Protein

Nut Butter

Tired of peanut butter? Try this! It's wonderful! (Thanks, Jon, for the great idea.)

Makes 32 servings

1½ cups chopped pecans
1½ cups cashew pieces (unsalted)
1½ cups sliced almonds

Combine nuts in a food processor. Using a steel blade, process until mixture is the consistency of peanut butter. Spoon into a jar and keep refrigerated.

Each serving provides: 97 Calories, 9 g Fat, 0 mg Cholesterol, 4 g Carbohydrate, 2 mg Sodium, 2 g Fiber, 2 g Protein

GOOD HEALTH ALERT:
"Good health is not something we can buy. However, it can be an extremely valuable savings account."—Anne Wilson Schaef

Orange Fig Spread

This easy spread tastes so-o-o-o good on toast or crackers, and it really complements peanut butter.

Makes 15 servings

12 large dried figs, coarsely chopped*
¼ cup plus 2 tablespoons frozen orange juice concentrate, thawed
½ cup water

In a blender container, combine figs, orange juice concentrate and half of the water. Blend until figs are finely chopped, adding a little more of the water, if necessary, for blending. Place fig mixture in a small saucepan and add remaining water. Cook over medium heat, stirring frequently, until mixture boils. Reduce heat to low and cook 20 minutes, until thick. Stir frequently while cooking and add small amounts of water if spread is too thick.

Cool slightly, then spoon into a jar and chill.

*An easy way to chop figs is to snip them with kitchen shears.

Each serving provides: 59 Calories, 0 g Fat, 0 mg Cholesterol, 15 g Carbohydrate, 2 mg Sodium, 1 g Fiber, 1 g Protein

Pine Apricot Spread

Tart n' tangy, this spread is great on bread or crackers and even doubles as a topping for ice milk.

Makes 6 servings

3/4 cup chopped dried apricots (16 apricot halves)
1 cup pineapple juice (unsweetened)
2 tablespoons firmly packed brown sugar
1/16 teaspoon ground cinnamon

In a blender container, combine all ingredients. Blend until apricots are finely chopped. Pour mixture into a small saucepan. Bring to a boil over medium heat, stirring occasionally. Reduce heat to low and cook 20 minutes, stirring frequently.

Serve warm or spoon into a small bowl or jar and chill.

Each serving provides: 61 Calories, 0 g Fat, 0 mg Cholesterol, 15 g Carbohydrate, 3 mg Sodium, 1 g Fiber, 1 g Protein

Orange Peanut Butter Spread

This super spread is not only great on bread, crackers or rice cakes, but it is also wonderful spread on slices of fresh apple.

Makes 4 servings

¼ cup smooth or crunchy peanut butter
2 tablespoons frozen orange juice concentrate, thawed
1/8 teaspoon ground cinnamon

In a small bowl, combine all ingredients, mixing well. Serve right away or chill for later servings.

Each serving provides: 114 Calories, 8 g Fat, 0 mg Cholesterol, 6 g Carbohydrate, 63 mg Sodium, 2 g Fiber, 4 g Protein

Honey Apple Spread

This sweet spread tastes just like apple pie. Try it on toast or crackers, in a sandwich with peanut butter, or over cottage cheese. It's delicious hot or cold.

Makes 8 servings

4 small Golden Delicious apples, peeled, coarsely shredded
2 tablespoons honey
¼ teaspoon ground cinnamon
1/8 teaspoon ground nutmeg

Combine all ingredients in a small saucepan. Cook over medium heat 5 minutes, stirring occasionally.

Reduce heat to low and cook 45 minutes or until mixture is thick and apples are translucent. Stir frequently while cooking, especially toward the end of cooking time, to prevent sticking.

Serve hot, or chill and serve cold.

Each serving provides: 45 Calories, 0 g Fat, 0 mg Cholesterol, 12 g Carbohydrate, 0 mg Sodium, 1 g Fiber, 0 g Protein

GOOD HEALTH ALERT:
Mind your mother and live longer by eating your vegetables and fruits.

Crunchy Tropical Peanut Butter Spread

This heavenly sandwich spread takes just a few minutes to make and your enjoyment is guaranteed! If you prefer, smooth peanut butter can be used. Whichever you buy, choose a brand without added sugar or fat.

Makes 2 servings

2 tablespoons crunchy peanut butter
½ medium, ripe banana, mashed
1/16 teaspoon ground cinnamon
1/16 teaspoon coconut extract

In a small bowl, combine all ingredients, mixing well. Spread on bread, crackers or rice cakes.

Use within 2 days and stir before serving. Keep refrigerated.

Each serving provides: 127 Calories, 8 g Fat, 0 mg Cholesterol, 10 g Carbohydrate, 63 mg Sodium, 2 g Fiber, 4 g Protein

French Herbed Cheese Spread

If you love the expensive, imported herbed cheese spreads, this one's for you. It's a hit every time.

Makes 6 servings

3/4 cup part-skim ricotta cheese
2 tablespoons dried chives
1/8 teaspoon garlic powder
¼ teaspoon dried basil
Pepper to taste
1 tablespoon dried parsley
2 teaspoons grated Parmesan cheese
¼ teaspoon dried marjoram

In a small bowl, combine all ingredients, mixing well.

Chill several hours or overnight to blend flavors.

Spread on crackers or bread.

Each serving provides: 46 Calories, 3 g Fat, 10 mg Cholesterol, 2 g Carbohydrate, 49 mg Sodium, Less than 1 g Fiber, 4 g Protein

GOOD HEALTH ALERT:
About 7% - or 15 million American adults – consider themselves to be vegetarians.

Pineapple Pepper Cheese Spread

Dotted with color and delicious as well, this easy spread will make a hit at your next party. It's also a nutritious after-school snack or a delicious toast-topper.

Makes 16 servings

1 cup part-skim ricotta cheese
1 cup canned crushed pineapple (unsweetened), drained well
¼ cup finely chopped sweet red pepper
2 tablespoons finely chopped green onion (green part only)

In a medium bowl, combine all ingredients, mixing well.
Chill several hours over overnight to blend flavors.
Serve with crackers.

Each serving provides: 31 Calories, 1 g Fat, 5 mg Cholesterol, 3 g Carbohydrate, 19 mg Sodium Less than 1 g Fiber, 2 g Protein

Currant Walnut Spread

This is a deliciously sweet spread that's great on crackers or toast. In place of currants, you can also try raisins or any dried fruit, cut into small pieces.

Makes 8 servings

1 cup part-skim ricotta cheese
2 teaspoons firmly packed brown sugar
2 teaspoons grated fresh orange peel
2 tablespoons chopped walnuts (½ ounce)
¼ cup currants

In a small bowl, combine ricotta cheese, brown sugar, and orange peel. Mix well.
Add walnuts and currants. Mix until well blended.
Chill several hours. Serve cold as a spread for crackers or toast.

Each serving provides: 71 Calories, 4 g Fat, 10 mg Cholesterol, 6 g Carbohydrate, 39 mg Sodium, 2 g Fiber, 4 g Protein

Caraway Spread

This smooth spread can really liven up a plain cracker or a toasted bagel.

Makes 8 servings

1 cup part-skim ricotta cheese
1½ teaspoons caraway seeds
½ teaspoon onion powder
1/8 teaspoon pepper
Salt to taste

In a small bowl, combine all ingredients, mixing well.
Chill several hours or overnight to blend flavors.
Serve cold as a spread for crackers, rice cakes or toast.

Each serving provides: 44 Calories, 2 g Fat, 10 mg Cholesterol, 2 g Carbohydrate, 39 mg Sodium Less than 1 g Fiber, 4 g Protein

Vegetarian Paté

Your guests will exclaim how good this special paté tastes (better than chopped liver) and provided by my good friend, Rhoda. You'll be asked to make it again and again.

Makes 14 servings

2 tablespoons canola or sunflower oil
1 large sweet onion - diced
1 can LeSuer Sweet Green Peas – drained – these are the best
3/4 cup pecans – chopped
1 egg – hard boiled – chopped

Sauté diced onion in canola oil until golden brown and combine all ingredients in food processor for 30 to 40 seconds.

Salt and pepper to taste. Serve with any cracker and cold sliced tomatoes chilled.

Each serving provides: 85 Calories, 10 g Fat, 0 mg Cholesterol, 2 g Carbohydrate, 45 mg Sodium, 2 g Fiber, 2 g Protein

GOOD HEALTH ALERT:

Lactose (milk sugar) and Vitamin D help the body absorb calcium, making dairy products a special food group for obtaining this often deficient nutrient.

Breakfast Ideas

Yes, this is the most important meal of the day. It's the meal that fuels our bodies and gets us off to a good start. Nutritionally speaking, carbohydrates are our bodies' main source of fuel. A breakfast that supplies you with the necessary carbohydrates should consist mainly of fruits, vegetables and grains. To many people, breakfast means having the same boring cold cereal and fruit day after day after day. Now, there's nothing wrong with cold cereal and fruit, provided you choose a whole grain cereal without lots of added sugar and fat, and top it with fresh fruit, rather than sweetened, canned fruit.

Now, let's be creative. How about topping your cereal with fruit juice instead of milk? Or, try leftover grains for breakfast. Cooked rice, mixed with raisins and cinnamon and topped with nonfat yogurt becomes "Breakfast Rice Pudding." Oatmeal, topped with sliced bananas and a spoonful of strawberry jam becomes a "Breakfast Banana Split." Don't overlook vegetables for breakfast. Baked potatoes and baked sweet potatoes make nutritious, filling breakfast foods.

In this section I have given you some delicious, healthy alternatives for breakfast. I have kept the fat and cholesterol contents low by using egg whites in place of whole eggs, and lowfat dairy products. I have added lots of fiber to breakfast by using whole grains and fruits. I have even included some dishes that can be prepared the night before so that breakfast will be ready when you are. Use of whole eggs have been studied and the favorable results say they are okay to use in recipes. Egg whites and egg substitutes are available in liquified form, so your options are many.

Throughout this book there are recipes for lots of other dishes that make great breakfasts. Everything in my "Fruits" chapter, for example, works for breakfast. Just add a whole grain in the form of cereal, bread or muffin and you have a nutritious meal. All of the breads and muffins will also work well, as will many of my appetizers, dips, and spreads. Here are some other ideas – **see index for page numbers:**

- Cranberry Crunch Salad – Top with nonfat yogurt and sprinkle with a granola-type cereal.
- Grilled Cheese and Apple Special – An unusual sweet sandwich.
- Crunchy Tropical Peanut Butter Spread – Spread on whole wheat toast.
- Cranberry Orange Dip – Spoon over hot or cold cereal.
- Pineapple Pepper Cheese Spread – Spread on an English muffin or whole wheat toast.
- Kasha and Apple Bake – Good hot or cold.
- Raggedy Rice Patties – Serve hot spread with jam.

Sausage Imposters

Serve these unique links with our Scrambled Tofu Spanish Omelet–next page – for a zero cholesterol look alike breakfast. Or, cook them with sliced onions and green peppers for a delicious Italian dinner.

Makes 4 servings

- 1 1-pound can kidney beans, rinsed and drained (this will yield 10 ounces of beans)
- 1 cup cooked brown rice
- 2 tablespoons ketchup
- ¼ teaspoon ground sage
- 1/8 teaspoon dried thyme
- 1/8 teaspoon ground savory
- 1/8 teaspoon garlic powder
- ¼ teaspoon salt
- ¼ teaspoon pepper
- ¼ teaspoon fennel seeds, crushed slightly (Roll between 2 layers of waxed paper with a rolling pin.)

Place beans, rice and ketchup in a large bowl. Sprinkle evenly with spices.

Mash well with a fork or potato masher, making sure that spices are evenly distributed. (Rice will be lumpy.) Chill mixture several hours or overnight to blend flavors.

Divide chilled mixture into 12 portions. Roll each portion into a log—like a sausage link—approximately 2½ inches long.

Preheat a large nonstick skillet or griddle over medium heat. Oil it lightly or spray with a nonstick cooking spray. Cook sausages until browned on all sides, turning frequently to brown evenly. Oil or spray pan again if necessary.

Serve hot.

Each serving provides: 148 Calories, 1 g Fat, 0 mg Cholesterol, 27 g Carbohydrate, 374 mg Sodium, 2 g Fiber, 7 g Protein

GOOD HEALTH ALERT:
Get a good night's sleep. Rest heals the body and has been shown to lessen the risk of heart trouble and psychological problems.

Scrambled Tofu Spanish Omelet

Here's a delicious, cholesterol-free substitute for a favorite egg dish. The use of turmeric, a delicately flavored spice, also adds a yellow color.

Makes 4 servings

2 teaspoons canola oil
1 cup chopped onions
1 cup chopped green pepper
1 pound medium or firm tofu, sliced, drained well between towels
¼ teaspoon garlic powder
¼ teaspoon turmeric
1/8 teaspoon pepper
Salt to taste

Sauce:
1 8-ounce can salt-free (or regular) tomato sauce
¼ teaspoon dried basil
¼ teaspoon dried oregano
1/8 teaspoon garlic powder

Heat oil in a large nonstick skillet over medium heat. Add onions and green pepper. Cook, stirring frequently, until onions are lightly browned, about 15 minutes.

While onions are browning, place tofu in a large bowl and mash with a fork. Add spices and mix well.

Combine all sauce ingredients in a small saucepan and heat until hot and bubbly.

Add tofu mixture to vegetables in skillet. Cook, stirring frequently, until heated thoroughly.

To serve, divide tofu mixture onto 4 serving plates. Top with sauce.

Each serving provides: 148 Calories, 8 g Fat, 0 mg Cholesterol, 11 g Carbohydrate, 22 mg Sodium, 2 g Fiber, 11 g Protein

GOOD HEALTH ALERT:

If you know a smoker who won't quit because of the fear of weight gain, pass on this news. Smokers usually do gain weight during the first year or two after quitting, but a Canadian study found that afterwards most female ex-smokers (but fewer men) lose all or most of the extra pounds. It also found that two years after quitting, the women were actually less likely to be obese than were smokers. As a means of staying thin, smoking is a poor bargain.

Tofu and Cheese Blintzes

I've lightened up my favorite blintz recipe. Using packaged egg roll wrappers, which are found in the produce section of most large grocery stores, really eliminates the fuss.

Makes 4 servings

6 ounces medium tofu, sliced and drained well between towels
1 cup part-skim ricotta cheese
2 egg whites
2 teaspoons vanilla extract
¼ teaspoon ground cinnamon
1 tablespoon firmly packed brown sugar
1 tablespoon all-purpose flour
1 12- or 16-ounce package egg roll wrappers. (You will need 8 wrappers. Unused wrappers can be frozen for later use, or make a double batch of blintzes and freeze the leftovers.)

Place drained tofu in a large bowl. Mash with a fork. Add remaining ingredients, *except* egg roll wrappers. Mix well.

Place 3 tablespoons of tofu mixture in the center of each wrapper. Fold the top corner over mixture. Then fold in both side corners. Finally, fold the bottom corner up and around the blintz, wetting it slightly so it will seal.

Preheat a large nonstick skillet or griddle over medium-low heat. Oil it lightly or spray with a nonstick cooking spray.

Place blintzes in skillet and cook until lightly browned on both sides, turning several times.

Serve hot, topped with your favorite jam or fruit sauce.

Each serving provides: 312 Calories, 8 g Fat, 20 mg Cholesterol, 41 g Carbohydrate, 124 mg Sodium, 2 g Fiber, 19 g Protein

GOOD HEALTH ALERT:
Laugh and cry! Having a good sob is reputed to be good for you. So is laughter, which has been shown to help heal bodies, as well as broken hearts. Laughter also boosts the immune system and helps the body shake off allergic reactions.

Blueberry Cornmeal Pancakes

Cornmeal provides a delicious way to add both protein and fiber to a hearty breakfast. The blueberries are an added bonus.

Makes 4 servings

- 1 cup yellow cornmeal (6 ounces)
- ¼ cup plus 2 tablespoons whole wheat flour
- 2 teaspoons baking powder
- 1 tablespoon sugar
- 2 egg whites
- 1 cup skim milk
- 1 tablespoon plus 1 teaspoon canola oil
- 1 teaspoon vanilla extract
- 1 cup fresh or frozen blueberries (if using frozen berries, there's no need to thaw).

In a large bowl, combine cornmeal, flour, baking powder and sugar. Mix well.

In a small bowl, combine egg whites, milk, oil and vanilla. Beat with a fork or wire whisk until blended. Add to cornmeal mixture, mixing until all ingredients are moistened. Stir in blueberries.

Preheat a nonstick griddle or skillet over medium heat. Oil it lightly or spray with a nonstick cooking spray. Drop batter onto griddle, using ¼ cup for each pancake. Turn pancakes once, when edges are dry and bottoms are lightly browned.

Cook until golden brown on both sides. (Makes twelve 4-inch pancakes.)

Serve hot, drizzled with maple syrup.

Each serving provides: 301 Calories, 6 g Fat, 1 mg Cholesterol, 53 g Carbohydrate, 277 mg Sodium, 1 g Fiber, 9 g Protein

GOOD HEALTH ALERT:
Most people who choose meatless meals do so for the health benefits. Those abstaining from meat tend to have lower blood cholesterol levels, lower blood pressure and healthier weights than the typical American.

Gingerbread Raisin Pancakes

What a breakfast treat! Just a drizzle with maple syrup and dig in!

Makes 4 servings

1 cup whole wheat flour
½ cup all-purpose flour
1 teaspoon baking powder
1 teaspoon baking soda
1 teaspoon ground cinnamon
1 teaspoon ground ginger
1/8 teaspoon ground cloves
¼ cup raisins
2 egg whites
1¼ cups skim milk
¼ cup molasses
2 tablespoons plus 2 teaspoons sunflower oil
1 teaspoon vanilla extract

In a large bowl, combine both flours, baking powder, baking soda and spices. Mix well. Add raisins.

In another bowl, combine remaining ingredients. Beat with a fork or wire whisk until blended. Add to dry mixture, mixing just until all ingredients are moistened. (Don't worry about lumps.)

Preheat a nonstick griddle or skillet over medium heat. Oil it lightly or spray with a nonstick cooking spray. Drop batter onto griddle, using ¼ cup for each pancake. Turn pancakes once, when edges are dry and bottoms are lightly browned.

Cook until golden brown on both sides. (Makes twelve 4-inch pancakes.)

Each serving provides: 362 Calories, 10 g Fat, 2 mg Cholesterol, 59 g Carbohydrate, 386 mg Sodium, 1 g Fiber, 10 g Protein

GOOD HEALTH ALERT:
Beta carotene is just one of about 50 carotenes that the body can convert to Vitamin A. Several carotenes also have antioxidant properties, making fruits and vegetables – the home of the complete carotene family – a nutritional bonanza.

Whole Wheat Pancakes or Waffles

One basic mix makes light and luscious pancakes or hot and crispy waffles. I like to serve them both topped with a combination of frozen (thawed) strawberries and blueberries.

Makes 4 servings

1 cup whole wheat flour
½ cup all-purpose flour
2 teaspoons baking powder
1 tablespoon sugar
3 egg whites
2/3 cup nonfat dry milk
1½ cups water
1 tablespoon plus 1 teaspoon sunflower oil
1 teaspoon vanilla extract

In a large bowl, sift together both types of flour, baking powder and sugar.

In a small bowl, combine remaining ingredients. Beat with a fork or wire whisk until blended. Add to dry mixture, mixing just until all ingredients are moistened.

For pancakes:

Preheat a nonstick griddle or skillet over medium heat. Oil it lightly or spray with a nonstick cooking spray. Drop batter onto griddle, using ¼ cup for each pancake. Turn pancakes once, when edges are dry and bottoms are lightly browned. Cook until golden brown on both sides. (Makes twelve 4-inch pancakes)

For waffles:

Preheat an oiled waffle iron according to manufacturer's directions. Pour batter into center of hot iron, using 1 cup for each waffle. Close iron and cook until done, again following manufacturer's directions. (Makes 12 waffle sections.)

Each serving provides: 269 Calories, 5 g Fat, 2 mg Cholesterol, 44 g Carbohydrate, 319 mg Sodium, 1 g Fiber, 12 g Protein

Tropical Oat Bran Pancakes

High in fiber and loaded with fruit, these pancakes are delicious.

Makes 4 servings

2/3 cup oat bran (3 ounces)
½ cup whole wheat flour
¼ cup all-purpose flour
1 tablespoon sugar
1 teaspoon baking powder
½ teaspoon baking soda
1 teaspoon ground cinnamon
1 cup skim milk
1 tablespoon lemon juice
2 teaspoons canola oil
2 egg whites
1½ teaspoons vanilla extract
1 medium, ripe banana, coarsely chopped
1 cup canned crushed pineapple (unsweetened), drained

In a large bowl, combine oat bran, both flours, sugar, baking powder, baking soda and cinnamon. Mix well.

Place milk in a small bowl. Add lemon juice and let stand 1 minute. Add oil, egg whites and vanilla. Beat with a fork or wire whisk until blended. Add to dry ingredients, along with banana and pineapple. Mix until all ingredients are moistened.

Preheat a nonstick griddle or skillet over medium heat. Oil it lightly or spray with a nonstick cooking spray. Drop batter onto griddle, using a scant ¼ cup for each pancake. Turn pancakes once, when edges are dry and bottoms are lightly browned.

Cook until golden brown on both sides. (Makes sixteen 4-inch pancakes.)

Serve hot, drizzled with maple syrup.

Each serving provides: 268 Calories, 5 g Fat, 1 mg Cholesterol, 55 g Carbohydrate, 272 mg Sodium, 2 g Fiber, 11 g Protein

GOOD HEALTH ALERT:

Vitamin B12 is found ONLY in foods of animal origin. Strict vegans need to obtain this essential nutrient though a vitamin supplement or fortified food.

Corny Oatmeal Breakfast Patties

You'll love my unusual combination of cornmeal and oatmeal in these make-ahead patties. Just mix 'em at night and fix 'em in the morning. They keep well in the refrigerator, so, for a small family, this is breakfast for several days.

Makes 8 servings

3½ cups water
½ cup yellow cornmeal (3 ounces)
1 cup rolled oats (3 ounces)
2 teaspoons ground cinnamon
3 tablespoons sugar
1 tablespoon vanilla extract
½ cup raisins

Lightly oil a 7 x 11-inch baking pan or spray with a nonstick cooking spray.

Bring water to a boil, combine cornmeal, oats, cinnamon and sugar, mixing well.

Add to boiling water, stirring briskly with a fork or wire whisk to prevent lumps.

Reduce heat to low and cook 15 minutes, stirring frequently. Remove from heat and stir in vanilla and raisins. Spread mixture evenly in prepared pan.

Cover and chill overnight.

To serve:

Cut chilled mixture into 8 even pieces.

Preheat a nonstick skillet or griddle over medium heat. Oil it lightly or spray with a nonstick cooking spray. Place patties in skillet and cook until crisp on both sides, turning several times.

Serve hot, drizzled with maple syrup or spread with your favorite jam.

Each serving provides: 133 Calories, 1 g Fat, 0 mg Cholesterol, 28 g Carbohydrate, 2 mg Sodium, 1 g Fiber, 3 g Protein

GOOD HEALTH ALERT:

Weigh your bagel. Many fresh-baked bagels now weigh six or seven ounces and pack 500 calories or more. Plain bagels, like any plain bread, have 70 to 80 calories per ounce.

Pina Colada French Toast

This is French toast with a flair. You'll love it.

Makes 2 servings

1/3 cup pineapple juice
¼ teaspoon coconut extract
1 egg white
2 slices whole wheat bread (1-ounce slices)
2 teaspoons reduced-calorie butter
1 teaspoon shredded coconut (unsweetened)

Sauce:
1/3 cup pineapple juice
1 teaspoon cornstarch
1 teaspoon sugar
1/16 teaspoon coconut extract

In a small bowl, combine 1/3 cup pineapple juice, ¼ teaspoon coconut extract and egg white. Beat with a fork or wire whisk until blended. Place bread slices in a shallow pan and pour egg white mixture over bread. Turn bread so that both sides soak up mixture.

Melt 1 teaspoon of the butter in a preheated nonstick skillet or griddle.

Sprinkle half of the coconut in the pan and add the bread. Sprinkle the bread with the remaining coconut and dot with remaining butter. Cook until toast is lightly browned on both sides, turning several times.

While toast is cooking, prepare sauce:

In a small saucepan, combine pineapple juice, cornstarch and sugar, mixing well to dissolve cornstarch. Cook over medium heat, stirring constantly, until mixture comes to a boil. Boil 1 minute, stirring. Remove from heat, stir in coconut extract and cover.

To serve, place a slice of toast on each of 2 plates. Spoon sauce over toast.

Each serving provides: 155 Calories, 4 g Fat, 1 mg Cholesterol, 27 g Carbohydrate, 254 mg Sodium, 1 g Fiber, 5 g Protein

GOOD HEALTH ALERT:

The concept of combining protein-containing foods at the same meal to ensure an appropriate mix of amino acids has been disproved. Protein foods eaten throughout the day can be efficiently used by the body.

Eggless French Toast

I tried this on a whim and it turned out to be quite good! You can add other extracts if you like, or sprinkle with cinnamon. Drizzle with either maple syrup or any of the delicious toppings in our Sauces and Toppings chapter.

Makes 2 servings

- ½ cup skim milk
- 1 teaspoon vanilla
- 2 slices whole wheat bread (1-ounce slices)
- 1 tablespoon cornstarch
- 2 teaspoons butter

In a small bowl, combine milk, cornstarch and vanilla. Stir until cornstarch is dissolved. Place bread slices in a shallow pan and pour milk mixture over bread.

Melt 1 teaspoon of the butter in a preheated nonstick skillet or griddle over medium heat. Place bread in skillet and brown lightly. Turn, add remaining butter, and brown the other side.

Serve hot.

Each serving provides: 130 Calories, 3 g Fat, 2 mg Cholesterol, 20 g Carbohydrate, 258 mg Sodium, 1 g Fiber, 5 g Protein

Just Peachy French Toast

You can make these delicious French toast sandwiches with any flavor jam. Peach just happens to be my favorite. *Makes 2 servings*

- 1 egg white
- 1 teaspoon vanilla extract
- 4 slices thin-sliced whole wheat bread (½-ounce slices)
- 1 tablespoon plus 1 teaspoon reduced-sugar jam, any flavor (8 calories per teaspoon), or fruit-only jam
- ¼ cup skim milk
- 2 teaspoons butter

In a small bowl, combine egg white, milk and vanilla. Mix well with a fork or wire whisk. Pour into a shallow pan.

Make 2 sandwiches from the bread and jam, putting 2 teaspoons of jam inside each sandwich. Dip sandwiches in milk mixture, coating both sides.

Melt 1 teaspoon of the butter in a preheated nonstick skillet or griddle over medium heat. Place sandwiches in skillet and brown lightly. Turn, add remaining butter, and brown the other sides.

Serve hot.

Each serving provides: 128 Calories, 3 g Fat, 1 mg Cholesterol, 19 g Carbohydrate, 269 mg Sodium, 1 g Fiber, 6 g Protein

Peaches n' Cream Casserole

It's elegant enough for a Sunday brunch and provides a different way to enjoy your breakfast oatmeal. It can be enjoyed as is or topped with skim milk or maple syrup.

Makes 6 servings

1½ cups rolled oats (4½ ounces)
1½ cups thinly sliced peaches, peeled (Canned peaches, packed in juice, may be used.)
¼ cup sugar
2 teaspoons vanilla extract
3 cups skim milk
2 egg whites
¼ teaspoon almond extract

Preheat oven to 350°.

Lightly oil an 8-inch square baking pan or spray with a nonstick cooking spray.

In a large bowl, combine oats, peaches, and sugar. In another bowl, combine remaining ingredients. Beat with a fork or wire whisk until blended. Add to oat mixture, mixing well.

Place mixture in prepared pan.

Bake, uncovered, 50 minutes.

Serve hot. (Leftovers are good cold or can be reheated in an oven or microwave.)

Each serving provides: 186 Calories, 2 g Fat, 2 mg Cholesterol, 34 g Carbohydrate, 83 mg Sodium, 1 g Fiber, 9 g Protein

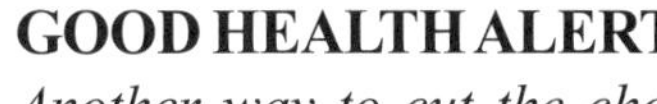

GOOD HEALTH ALERT:

Another way to cut the cholesterol you get from eggs: substitute two whites for every whole egg. Omelets can be made with whites, nonfat dry milk, and skim milk, and so can some soufflés, cakes and muffins. You can also substitute two whites plus one whole egg for two eggs.

Swiss Apple Fruit and Nut Muesli

This popular European breakfast is so easy to make and so delicious. My version combines apples with the oats, but you can vary the fruit and try your own combinations.

Makes 6 servings

1 cup rolled oats (3 ounces)
¼ cup plus 2 tablespoons wheat germ (1½ ounces)
½ teaspoon ground cinnamon
1/8 teaspoon ground nutmeg
1 tablespoon firmly packed brown sugar
1½ cups skim milk
½ cup apple juice
1 small, sweet apple, unpeeled, coarsely shredded
½ cup plus 1 tablespoon chopped mixed dried fruit (3 ounces)
¼ cup chopped walnuts (1 ounce)
1½ teaspoons vanilla extract

In a medium bowl, combine oats, wheat germ, cinnamon, nutmeg and brown sugar. Mix well.

Add remaining ingredients. Mix well. Smooth the top and press mixture down lightly with the back of a spoon.

Cover and chill overnight.

Serve cold.

Each serving provides: 201 Calories, 5 g Fat, 1 mg Cholesterol, 34 g Carbohydrate, 37 mg Sodium, 3 g Fiber, 7 g Protein

Six Grain Crockpot Breakfast

I've combined the taste, texture and nutritional benefits of six grains in this real rib-stickin' breakfast. Throw it together at night and enjoy a wonderful hot breakfast in the morning. My selection of grains is only a suggestion – any grains will work. Just use 1 cup of grain to 3 cups of water.

Makes 6 servings

2½ tablespoons bulgur, uncooked (1 ounce)
2½ tablespoons brown rice, uncooked (1 ounce)
2 tablespoons barley, uncooked (3/4 ounce)
2 tablespoons millet, uncooked (3/4 ounce)
2 tablespoons cornmeal (3/4 ounce)
¼ cup rolled oats (3/4 ounce)

3/4 cup plus 2 tablespoons chopped dried mixed fruit (4½ ounces)
1½ teaspoons ground cinnamon
3 cups water
1 tablespoon vanilla extract

Combine grains, dried fruit and cinnamon in a crockpot. Mix well. Stir in water and vanilla. Cover and cook 6 to 8 hours on low setting.

Stir before serving and add more water if desired.

Serve hot, topped with brown sugar or drizzled with maple syrup.

Each serving provides: 147 Calories, 1 g Fat, 0 mg Cholesterol, 32 g Carbohydrate, 6 mg Sodium, 4 g Fiber, 3 g Protein

Fruit n' Rice Breakfast

What a wonderful use for leftover rice. I like this unusual breakfast treat so much that I always make extra rice so that I have plenty for the morning.

Makes 4 servings

2 cups cooked brown rice
2 small, sweet apples, unpeeled, coarsely shredded
2 tablespoons raisins
6 dried apricot halves, chopped (An easy way to chop dried fruit is to snip it with kitchen shears.)
2 tablespoons brown sugar
1 teaspoon vanilla extract
3/4 teaspoon ground cinnamon
1/8 teaspoon ground nutmeg

In a medium bowl, combine all ingredients, mixing well.

Chill overnight.

Serve plain or topped with skim milk or yogurt. If you prefer a hot breakfast, this cereal can be quickly heated in a microwave.

Each serving provides: 196 Calories, 1 g Fat, 0 mg Cholesterol, 45 g Carbohydrate, 8 mg Sodium, 3 g Fiber, 3 g Protein

Couscous Porridge

Grains make a hearty, high-carbohydrate breakfast. If you like, you can add any type of fruit to this easy porridge.

Makes 4 servings

2 cups hot cooked couscous (Cook according to package directions.)
2/3 cup nonfat dry milk
2 tablespoons pure maple syrup or honey
1 teaspoon vanilla extract
ground cinnamon to taste

Stir dry milk, maple syrup and vanilla into cooked couscous.

Divide mixture evenly into 4 serving bowls and sprinkle generously with cinnamon.

Serve right away.

Each serving provides: 170 Calories, 0 g Fat, 2 mg Cholesterol, 33 g Carbohydrate, 68 mg Sodium, 1 g Fiber, 7 g Protein

Soups

Nothing can equal the flavor and warmth of a steamy bowl of homemade soup. Soups are so versatile. They can be used as meal starters or, as I often serve them, as a complete meal. Most of my soups contain beans or lentils, vegetables and grains, and by themselves are hearty and filling enough to make a meal. Just add a salad and a slice of whole grain bread and your meal is complete.

Your base for most of the soups is either tomatoes or vegetable broth mix. You can find vegetable broth mix in most health food stores or you can make your own. **(See next page.)** It consists of a combination of soup-flavored spices and can be mixed together and kept in a jar on your spice shelf.

To lower the fat content of these soups, I use only a minimal amount of oil and make my cream-style soups with skim milk instead of cream.

To add fiber to my soups, I use lots of whole grains and vegetables. Any cooked grain or vegetable left over from yesterday can easily be added to today's soup, and you'll be delighted with the interesting new soup varieties you'll discover.

Legumes are another healthy addition to soup, adding protein, vitamins and fiber. I've used all types of legumes in my recipes, including kidney beans, black beans, and lentils. Don't forget cooked pasta, a delicious, high-carbohydrate addition to soup. It's a great way to use leftovers and can help turn a bowl of soup into a filling meal.

To keep the sodium content low, I use salt-free tomato products whenever possible, and in most of my recipes, I recommend using salt "to taste." This way, you can add salt according to your own taste and dietary needs. I think you'll find that using tasty spice combinations eliminates the need for a lot of salt.

Most soups tend to taste better on the second day; so, whenever possible, I cook my soups a day ahead. They are so much thicker and richer when reheated. Most soups freeze well too, so don't be afraid to make a big potful, even if your family is small.

Vegetable Broth Mix

You can mix this easy spice combo in a jar and keep it on hand for those recipes that call for broth mix. (Or look for vegetable broth mix in jars or packets in most health food stores and select supermarkets.)

Makes about ¼ cup

- 1 tablespoon onion powder
- 1 tablespoon dried parsley flakes
- 1½ teaspoons salt
- ½ teaspoon dried marjoram
- ¼ teaspoon pepper
- ¼ teaspoon ground sage
- 1 tablespoon celery salt
- 1½ teaspoons garlic powder
- ½ teaspoon ground savory
- ½ teaspoon dried thyme
- ¼ teaspoon turmeric

Combine all ingredients and mix well. Mix again before using. (Dried vegetable flakes can also be added for a real flavor bonus.)

Each serving provides: 4 Calories, 0 g Fat, 0 mg Cholesterol, 1 g Carbohydrate, 634 mg Sodium, 0 g Fiber, 0 g Protein

Chunky Lentil Soup

Chunks of onions, celery and green pepper add to the wonderful taste and texture of this hearty soup.

Makes 8 servings

- 1 tablespoon plus 1 teaspoon olive oil
- 1 cup chopped celery
- 2 cloves garlic, finely chopped
- 1 teaspoon dried basil
- 1 cup lentils, uncooked (7½ ounces)
- 1 bay leaf
- ½ teaspoon dried rosemary, crumbled
- 1 cup chopped onions
- 1 cup chopped green pepper
- 2 1 pound cans tomatoes, undrained, chopped
- 3½ cups water
- 1 teaspoon dried oregano
- Salt and pepper to taste

Heat oil in a large saucepan over medium heat. Add onions, celery, green pepper and garlic. Cook 10 minutes, stirring frequently. Add remaining ingredients and bring mixture to a boil. Reduce heat to low, cover and cook 45 minutes, until lentils are tender. Remove and discard bay leaf before serving.

Each serving provides: 147 Calories, 3 g Fat, 0 mg Cholesterol, 23 g Carbohydrate, 202 mg Sodium, 2 g Fiber,, 9 g Protein

Creamy Cauliflower Soup

The subtle blend of basil and tarragon gives this creamy soup a truly elegant flavor.

Makes 6 servings

1 tablespoon canola oil
4 cups chopped cauliflower (¼ to ½ inch pieces)
1 cup chopped onions
1 cup chopped celery
2½ cups water
2 teaspoons instant vegetable broth mix (See previous broth mix recipe)
1 small bay leaf
¼ teaspoon salt
1/8 teaspoon pepper
1/8 teaspoon dried basil
1/8 teaspoon dried tarragon
1½ cups evaporated skim milk

Heat oil in a large saucepan over medium heat. Add cauliflower, onions and celery. Cook 15 minutes, stirring frequently. Add small amounts of water, a little at a time, if necessary, to keep vegetables from sticking. (This is in addition to the water called for.)

Add 2½ cups water and remaining ingredients, *except* milk. Bring mixture to a boil, cover, reduce heat to low, and simmer 20 minutes or until vegetables are very tender. Remove and discard bay leaf.

Place about 2/3 of the vegetables in a blender container. Blend until smooth, adding a little of the soup liquid if necessary. Return blended mixture to saucepan.

Add milk and heat thoroughly. (Do not boil.)

Each serving provides: 100 Calories, 3 g Fat, 3 mg Cholesterol, 14 g Carbohydrate, 403 mg Sodium, 2 g Fiber, 7 g Protein

Black and White Bean Soup

If you love thick soups, this one's for you. It's hearty and rich and full of flavor.

Makes 8 servings

8 ounces dried black beans, uncooked (1 heaping cup)
8 ounces dried Great Northern beans, uncooked (1 heaping cup)
2 tablespoons plus 2 teaspoons olive oil
4 cloves garlic, finely chopped
1 cup chopped leeks (white part only)
1 cup chopped carrots
1 cup chopped celery
1½ teaspoons dried oregano
1/16 teaspoon ground cloves
1 cup chopped onions
7 cups water
½ teaspoon dried thyme
1 bay leaf

Soak beans, using one of the following methods:

Overnight method – Place beans into 2 separate bowls and add enough water to cover beans by 3 inches. Soak overnight. Drain.

Quick soak – Place beans in 2 separate pots and add enough water to cover beans by 3 inches. Bring to a boil over medium heat. Boil 2 minutes. Remove from heat, cover and let stand 1 hour. Drain.

Heat oil in a large saucepan over medium heat. Add garlic, leeks, carrots, onions and celery. Cook 5 minutes, stirring frequently.

Add remaining ingredients and bring to a boil. Cover, reduce heat to low and simmer 1-½ hours. Remove and discard bay leaf. Remove 3 cups of beans from soup and place in a blender container. Blend until smooth. Stir into soup.

Each serving provides: 259 Calories, 5 g Fat, 0 mg Cholesterol, 41 g Carbohydrate, 27 mg Sodium, 2 g Fiber, 13 g Protein

Millet Butternut Soup

As warm and soothing as a soup can be, this one combines the sweetness of butternut squash with a perfect blend of spices. Look for vegetable broth mix and millet in your favorite health food store.

Makes 8 servings

2 teaspoons canola oil
2 cups chopped onions
½ teaspoon dried thyme
1 bay leaf
3 cloves garlic, coarsely chopped
5 cups water
¼ teaspoon dried tarragon
Salt and pepper to taste
½ cup millet, uncooked (3 ounces)
4 cups butternut squash, peeled, cut into ½-inch cubes

4 teaspoons instant vegetable broth mix (See previous broth mix recipe)

Heat oil in a large saucepan over medium heat. Add garlic and onions.

Cook 5 minutes, stirring frequently. Add small amounts of water, if necessary, to prevent sticking.

Add remaining ingredients, *except* millet. Bring to a boil. Add millet, cover, reduce heat to low and simmer 40 minutes or until squash is tender.

Remove and discard bay leaf before serving.

Each serving provides: 100 Calories, 2 g Fat, 0 mg Cholesterol, 20 g Carbohydrate, 321 mg Sodium, 2 g Fiber, 2 g Protein

Convenience Vegetable Soup

This soup is aptly named because every ingredient comes from either a package or a jar, so there's no chopping. Just dump everything in the pot and amaze your family and friends with a truly delectable soup.

Makes 10 servings

1 tablespoon minced onion flakes
½ teaspoon dried thyme
¼ teaspoon garlic powder
1 bay leaf
1½ teaspoons dried basil
5 cups water
1 10-ounce package frozen cut green beans
1 10-ounce package frozen peas and carrots
1 10-ounce package frozen lima beans
1 10-ounce package frozen corn
1 10-ounce package frozen chopped spinach
2 1-pound cans tomatoes
1 1-pound can kidney beans, rinsed and drained. (This will yield 10-ounces of beans.)
1 8-ounce can salt-free (or regular) tomato sauce
1 cup (4½ ounces) orzo, or any type of very small pasta.
Salt and pepper to taste

In a large soup pot, combine all ingredients, *except* pasta. Bring to a boil over medium heat, stirring occasionally. Use a spoon to break up large clumps of frozen vegetables and also to cut up the tomatoes. Cover, reduce heat to medium-low and simmer 45 minutes or until vegetables are tender.

Add pasta, cover and cook 10 to 15 more minutes, until pasta is tender. Remove and discard bay leaf before serving.

Each serving provides: 194 Calories, 1 g Fat, 0 mg Cholesterol, 39 g Carbohydrate, 407 mg Sodium, 3 g Fiber, 10 g Protein

Cabbage and Potato Soup

This sweet and sour soup just begs to be served with a piece of dark, crusty rye bread. As delicious as this soup is, it's even better the next day.

Makes 8 servings

4 cups coarsely shredded cabbage
2 medium potatoes (12 ounces total), unpeeled, cut into ½ inch pieces
1 cup chopped onions
3 cups water
2 1-pound cans tomatoes, undrained, chopped
3 tablespoons lemon juice
2 tablespoons plus 2 teaspoons sugar
¼ teaspoon dried thyme
Salt and pepper to taste

In a large soup pot, combine cabbage, potatoes and onions. Add 2 cups of the water, cover and cook on medium heat 15 minutes.

Add remaining ingredients. Bring to a boil, cover, reduce heat to low and simmer 45 minutes to 1 hour, until potatoes and cabbage are tender.

Each serving provides: 87 Calories, 0 g Fat, 0 mg Cholesterol, 20 g Carbohydrate, 196 mg Sodium, 2 g Fiber, 3 g Protein

Barley Mushroom Soup

This is really a comfort food. For the stock I use instant vegetable broth mix, which is available in most large grocery stores and in health food stores.

Makes 8 servings

2 teaspoons canola oil
½ cup chopped carrots
½ cup chopped celery leaves
5 cups water
½ cup chopped onions
½ cup thinly sliced celery
3 cups sliced mushrooms
½ cup barley, uncooked (4 ounces)
4 teaspoons instant vegetable broth mix (See previous broth mix recipe)
1/8 teaspoon garlic powder
Salt and pepper to taste

Heat oil in a large soup pot over medium heat. Add vegetables. Cook 5 minutes, stirring frequently.

Add remaining ingredients and bring to a boil. Cover, reduce heat to low, and simmer 1 hour.

Each serving provides: 78 Calories, 2 g Fat, 0 mg Cholesterol, 14 g Carbohydrate, 330 mg Sodium, 1 g Fiber, 3 g Protein

Ratatouille Soup

I've taken all the flavor and spice of one of my favorite vegetable dishes, added a tomato broth and pasta, and turned it into a thick and hearty soup.

Makes 8 servings

1 tablespoon plus 1 teaspoon canola oil
1 cup chopped onions
1 cup chopped green pepper
2 cloves garlic, chopped
3 cups eggplant, peeled, cut into ¼ inch cubes
2 1-pound cans tomatoes, undrained, chopped
3 cups zucchini, unpeeled, cut in half lengthwise, then sliced ¼ inch thick
4 cups water
1 bay leaf
1¼ teaspoons dried basil
1¼ teaspoons dried oregano
1/8 teaspoon pepper
2/3 cup (3 ounces) orzo, or any type of very small pasta
Salt to taste

Heat oil in a large soup pot over medium heat. Add onions, green pepper and garlic. Cook until tender, about 5 minutes.

Add eggplant. Cook 5 minutes, stirring frequently and adding small amounts of water, if necessary, to prevent sticking.

Add remaining ingredients, *except* orzo. Bring mixture to a boil, then reduce heat to low, cover and cook 45 minutes.

Add orzo and cook, covered, 10 minutes.

Remove and discard bay leaf before serving.

Each serving provides: 110 Calories, 3 g Fat, 0 mg Cholesterol, 19 g Carbohydrate, 189 mg Sodium, 2 g Fiber, 4 g Protein

GOOD HEALTH ALERT:
If a health claim sounds too good to be true, it probably is.

Vichyssoise

This traditional soup can be served hot or cold. The choice is yours. Either way, you won't believe that lowfat ingredients can produce a soup so rich and creamy. If you haven't tried leeks, look for them in the produce section of your grocery store. A member of the onion family, they look like large green onions and have a delicate, sweet flavor.

Makes 4 servings

2 teaspoons olive oil
½ cup thinly sliced leeks, white part only
(wash leeks thoroughly as they are often quite sandy.)
½ cup chopped onions
2 medium potatoes (12 ounces total), peeled, sliced lengthwise into eighths, and then into thin slices
4 cups water
4 teaspoons vegetable broth mix (See previous broth mix recipe)
2/3 cup nonfat dry milk
Salt and pepper to taste

Heat oil in a large saucepan over medium heat. Add leeks and onions. Cook 3 to 5 minutes, until tender.

Add potatoes, water and broth mix. Bring to a boil, then reduce heat to low, cover and simmer 30 minutes or until potatoes are tender.

Scoop out about half of the potato and leek mixture with a spoon and place it in a blender container. Add about ½ cup of the liquid and the dry milk.

Blend until smooth. Pour back into saucepan.

Heat until soup is hot, adding salt and pepper to taste. Do not boil.

Each serving provides: 130 Calories, 2 g Fat, 2 mg Cholesterol, 22 g Carbohydrate, 703 mg Sodium, 2 g Fiber, 6 g Protein

Miso Soup

If you haven't tried miso, it's worth an adventurous trip to the health food store. Miso is a thick paste that's made from soybeans. It may be new to many Americans, but the Japanese use it daily in soups and spreads to promote good health and to aid digestion. Choose a medium to dark miso for a rich, full-bodied flavor. For a thicker soup, add cooked noodles or brown rice.

Makes 6 servings

1 tablespoon canola oil
2 cloves garlic, finely chopped

½ cup onions, sliced lengthwise into thin slices
½ cup very thinly sliced carrots
1 cup sliced mushrooms
¼ cup miso
4¼ cups water

Heat oil in a medium saucepan over medium heat.

Add garlic, onions, carrots and mushrooms.

Cook, stirring frequently, 5 to 10 minutes, until vegetables are tender.

Gradually stir ¼ cup of the water into the miso in a small bowl, mixing until smooth. Add to saucepan, along with remaining water.

Cook until hot.

Each serving provides: 57 Calories, 3 g Fat, 0 mg Cholesterol, 6 g Carbohydrate, 422 mg Sodium, Less than 1 g Fiber, 2 g Protein

Kasha Tomato Soup

If you like the toasty flavor of kasha (buckwheat groats), you'll love this chunky soup. Add other vegetables, if you like, for variation.

Makes 8 servings

1 tablespoon plus 1 teaspoon canola oil
2 cups thinly sliced onions
1 cup thinly sliced carrots
1 cup chopped celery
2 bay leaves
2 1-pound cans tomatoes, chopped, undrained
Salt and pepper to taste
4½ cups water
½ cup kasha, uncooked (3 oz.)

Heat oil in a large saucepan over medium heat. Add onions, carrots and celery. Cook, stirring frequently, 10 minutes. Add small amounts of water, if necessary, to prevent sticking. Add remaining ingredients, *except* kasha. Bring mixture to a boil, cover, reduce heat to low and simmer 40 minutes.

Stir in kasha, cover and cook 20 more minutes. Remove and discard bay leaves before serving.

Each serving provides: 102 Calories, 3 g Fat, 0 mg Cholesterol, 18 g Carbohydrate, 205 mg Sodium, 3 g Fiber, 3 g Protein

Russian Beet Borscht

There's absolutely no fat added to this delicious soup. The traditional way to serve borscht is with a dollop of sour cream, so, if you like it that way, simply substitute nonfat or plain Greek yogurt (even better)! It's also great plain.

Makes 6 servings

3 cups coarsely shredded, peeled beets (Wearing rubber gloves during this process will prevent your hands from staining.)
1 cup coarsely shredded carrots
1 cup finely chopped onions
2 cups finely shredded cabbage
4 cups water
¼ teaspoon salt
1/8 teaspoon pepper
½ teaspoon paprika
1 tablespoon lemon juice

Combine all ingredients, *except* lemon juice, in a large saucepan. Bring to a boil over medium heat. Reduce heat to low, cover and simmer 30 minutes. Stir in lemon juice and serve.

Each serving provides: 54 Calories, 0 g Fat, 0 mg Cholesterol, 12 g Carbohydrate, 151 mg Sodium, 2 g Fiber, 2 g Protein

GOOD HEALTH ALERT:
When dining out, always ask for food exactly the way you want it – don't hesitate to send it back.

Salads and Salad Dressings

Salads are becoming increasingly popular these days. With the growing popularity of the salad bar, it is relatively easy to grab a salad on the run" or to take one home when you don't have time to cut vegetables. Just be careful – not all salads are low in calories and high in nutrition. If salads are loaded with creamy dressings or covered with nuts or coconut, they may have more fat and calories than a large, gooey dessert.

To keep our salads low in fat, I use nonfat yogurt or the plain Greek yogurt in place of sour cream, and I have greatly decreased the amount of oil in these dressings. I make up for the missing oil by adding water or fruit juice. The oils that I use are monounsaturated oils such as canola oil or olive oil. In my recipes that use mayonnaise, I specify reduced-calorie mayonnaise, which has been whipped with water to give it half the amount of calories and fat as regular mayonnaise.

In my fruit salads, I use either fresh fruit, unsweetened frozen fruit or canned fruit packed in fruit juice or water. If nuts are called for, I use a very small amount. In some recipes, I substitute the wonderful crunch of water chestnuts for the nuts.

Be creative with your salads. A good guideline to follow when making a tossed salad is to include a vegetable of every color. For example, red cabbage, green snow pea pods, yellow squash and white turnips are just a few unusual ingredients that will add vitamins, fiber and crunch to an otherwise boring bowl of lettuce.

Add leftovers to your salads and create brand new recipes. Leftover cooked grains and legumes, as well as yesterday's tofu or pasta, can add lots of flavor, variety and nutrition to a salad.

Be sure to check these chapters on *Appetizers, Dips* and *Spreads*, *Fruits*, and *Sandwiches and Burgers* for dishes that can be easily adapted to salads. Here are just a few suggestions – **see index for page numbers**:

- Mexicali Bean Dip – Makes a great salad dressing.
- Tofu Spinach Dip – Makes a great salad dressing.
- Honey Sweet Pineapple Dip – Delicious on fruit salads.
- Eggless "Egg" Salad – Mound it on a tossed salad.
- Counterfeit (Carrot) Tuna Salad – Pile it on lettuce leaves.

Szechuan Noodle Salad

This tangy, cold noodle salad is one of our tried and true favorite Oriental specialties. I serve it as a side dish with dinner or with a tossed salad for a delicious and filling lunch.

Makes 4 servings

3 cups cooked thin noodles or spaghetti (I prefer the thin whole wheat noodles found in health food stores, specialty stores or supermarkets.)
¼ cup thinly sliced green onions (green part only)
2 teaspoons toasted sesame seeds*
1/3 cup pineapple juice
2 tablespoons vinegar
2 tablespoons reduced-sodium (or regular) soy sauce
2 teaspoons sesame oil
2 teaspoons canola oil
1 teaspoon sugar
1/8 teaspoon ground ginger
1/8 teaspoon pepper
1/8 teaspoon garlic powder
Few drops bottled hot pepper sauce (optional)

In a large bowl, combine noodles, green onions and sesame seeds.
In a small bowl, combine remaining ingredients.
Add to noodles, mixing well.
Chill several hours or overnight, stirring several times.
Stir before serving.

***To toast sesame seeds**, place them in a single layer on a baking sheet or piece of aluminum foil in a 350-degree oven. Cook until lightly toasted, about 5 minutes.

Each serving provides: 219 Calories, 6 g Fat, 0 mg Cholesterol, 35 g Carbohydrate, 302 mg Sodium, 2 g Fiber, 6 g Protein

GOOD HEALTH ALERT:
To enhance your body's ability to absorb the iron in food, combine iron rich foods with foods filled with Vitamin C.

Pepper Corn Salad

This tangy salad is as pretty as it is delicious. Serve it all year round and use it to jazz up your next cookout. *Makes 4 servings*

1 1-pound can corn, drained
1/3 cup finely chopped onions
1/3 cup finely chopped green pepper
¼ cup wine vinegar
1/3 cup finely chopped sweet red pepper
1 tablespoon plus 1 teaspoon canola oil
1 tablespoon plus 1 teaspoon sugar
Salt and pepper to taste

In a medium bowl, combine all ingredients, mixing well.
Chill several hours to blend flavors.
Mix well before serving.

Each serving provides: 123 Calories, 5 g Fat, 0 mg Cholesterol, 19 g Carbohydrate, 3 mg Sodium, 1 g Fiber, 2 g Protein

Fiesta Macaroni Salad

This salad is colorful and delicious and makes a perfect addition to any party or picnic. For added nutrition, look for whole wheat elbow macaroni in your grocery store or health food store. *Makes 8 servings*

4 cups cooked elbow macaroni
¼ cup finely chopped sweet red pepper
2 tablespoons finely chopped onion
½ teaspoon dry mustard
¼ cup finely chopped green pepper
½ cup finely chopped celery
½ cup reduced-calorie mayonnaise
½ teaspoon dill weed
2 tablespoons sweet pickle relish (There is a sweet pickle relish sweetened with Splenda – for those who use artificial sweeteners.)
Salt to taste

In a large bowl, combine macaroni, green and red pepper, celery and onion. In a small bowl, combine remaining ingredients. Add to macaroni, mixing well. Chill several hours to blend flavors. Stir before serving.

Each serving provides: 149 Calories, 5 g Fat, 5 mg Cholesterol, 23 g Carbohydrate, 116 mg Sodium, 1 g Fiber, 4 g Protein

Pennsylvania Dutch Cucumber Salad

I enjoyed this salad in many Pennsylvania restaurants before I finally came up with my own lowfat version. I like to serve it atop a bed of lettuce or as a tasty addition to a tossed salad. *Makes 8 servings*

3 cups very thinly sliced cucumber, peeled (2 medium cucumbers)
1 cup very thinly sliced onions, separated into rings
3/4 cup plain nonfat yogurt or plain Greek yogurt
1 tablespoon dried parsley flakes
½ teaspoon dill weed
1 teaspoon sugar
¼ teaspoon garlic powder
¼ teaspoon salt
1/8 teaspoon pepper

Place cucumbers and onions in a large bowl. In a small bowl, combine remaining ingredients. Add to cucumbers, mixing well. Chill several hours or overnight to blend flavors. Stir before serving.

Each serving provides: 29 Calories, 0 g Fat. 0 mg Cholesterol, 5 g Carbohydrate, 88 mg Sodium, 1 g Fiber, 2 g Protein

Sweet and Tangy Cole Slaw

This is a delicious, fat-free, sweet and sour version of an American favorite. It's slightly sweet with a pleasant bite. *Makes 8 servings*

4 cups finely shredded cabbage
½ cup finely chopped green pepper
½ teaspoon salt
2 tablespoons sugar
¼ cup water
¼ cup finely chopped onion
½ teaspoon celery seed
¼ teaspoon pepper
¼ cup vinegar

In a large bowl, combine cabbage, onion, and green pepper. Sprinkle with celery seed, salt, pepper and sugar and mix well. Add vinegar and water. Mix well, cover and chill overnight. Toss well before serving.

Each serving provides: 25 Calories, 0 g Fat, 0 mg Cholesterol, 6 g Carbohydrate, 144 mg Sodium, 1 g Fiber, 1 g Protein

Pineapple Slaw

Tired of the same old cole slaw? Try this delicious version. It's sparked with crushed pineapple, green pepper and a bit of Dijon mustard. As with most slaws, it tastes best when made a day ahead. *Makes 8 servings*

- 4 cups finely shredded cabbage
- ¼ cup very finely chopped green pepper
- 1 teaspoon Dijon mustard
- ½ cup finely shredded carrots
- 1 tablespoon wine vinegar
- 1 tablespoon sugar
- 1 cup canned crushed pineapple (unsweetened), undrained
- 2 tablespoons plus 2 teaspoons reduced-calorie mayonnaise
- Salt and pepper to taste

In a large bowl, combine cabbage, carrots, green pepper and pineapple. In a small bowl, combine remaining ingredients. Add to cabbage mixture, mixing well.

Chill several hours or overnight. Mix before serving.

Each serving provides: 51 Calories, 1 g Fat, 2 mg Cholesterol, 10 g Carbohydrate, 55 mg Sodium, 2 g Fiber, 1 g Protein

Piquant Garbanzo Salad

Piquant is just my fancy way of saying tart and tangy. I like to serve this delicious salad on a bed of lettuce, alongside a scoop of lowfat cottage cheese. It makes a great lunch.

Makes 4 servings

- 1 1-pound can garbanzo beans, rinsed and drained (This will yield 10 ounces of beans.)
- ¼ cup finely chopped onions
- 1 tablespoon plus 1 teaspoon canola oil
- 1/8 teaspoon garlic powder
- 1/8 teaspoon pepper
- 3 tablespoons wine vinegar
- 2 tablespoons water
- 1 teaspoon sugar
- Salt to taste

Place garbanzo beans in a medium bowl. Add onions and mix well. In a small bowl, combine remaining ingredients. Add to beans, mixing well. Chill several hours or overnight to blend flavors. Mix several times while chilling.

Stir before serving.

Each serving provides: 136 Calories, 7 g Fat, 0 mg Cholesterol, 15 g Carbohydrate, 142 mg Sodium, 3 g Fiber, 5 g Protein

Lentil Salad Italiano

Add a tossed salad and a chunk of crusty whole grain bread and you'll have a delicious, nutritious lunch.
Makes 6 servings

1 cup lentils, uncooked (7½ ounces)
1 bay leaf
3 tablespoons wine vinegar
½ cup coarsely shredded carrots
1 4-ounce jar chopped pimentos, drained
3 cups water
2 tablespoons canola oil
½ cup finely chopped onions
1 teaspoon dried basil
¼ teaspoon garlic powder
Salt and pepper to taste

Place lentils, water and bay leaf in a medium saucepan. Bring to a boil over medium heat, then reduce heat to low, cover and simmer 25 minutes until lentils are just slightly tender. Drain lentils and discard bay leaf. In a large bowl, combine lentils with remaining ingredients, mixing well. Chill several hours or overnight to blend flavors. Stir before serving.

Each serving provides: 176 Calories, 5 g Fat, 0 mg Cholesterol, 24 g Carbohydrate, 13 mg Sodium, 2 g Fiber, 10 g Protein

Chili Bean Salad

Lovers of spicy food will adore this tangy salad. Serve it over a bed of lettuce, add a piece of corn bread, and you have an easy lunch with a Mexican flair.
Makes 4 servings

1 1-pound can kidney beans, rinsed and drained (This will yield 10 ounces of beans.)
½ cup finely chopped green pepper
1 teaspoon chili powder
¼ teaspoon ground cumin
½ cup finely chopped onions
¼ teaspoon garlic powder
¼ teaspoon dried oregano
¼ cup plain nonfat yogurt or plain Greek yogurt
Salt to taste

In a large bowl, combine kidney beans, onions and green peppers. Mix well.

In a small bowl, combine yogurt and spices. Add to bean mixture, mixing until well blended. Chill several hours to blend flavors. Stir before serving.

Each serving provides: 104 Calories, 1 g Fat,0 mg Cholesterol, 17 g Carbohydrate, 165 mg Sodium, 3 g Fiber, 7 g Protein

Italian Tomato and Pasta Salad

Chunks of tomatoes and lots of Italian spices make this a real winner. It serves 8 as a side dish or 4 as a tasty main meal. *Makes 8 servings*

4 cups cooked macaroni, any shape (Whole wheat is recommended.)
2 1-pound cans tomatoes, drained, chopped into 1 inch chunks (Reserve liquid.)
1 tablespoon plus 1 teaspoon canola oil
¼ teaspoon garlic powder
2 tablespoons grated Parmesan cheese
2 tablespoons wine vinegar
1 teaspoon dried basil
1 teaspoon dried oregano
Salt and pepper to taste

In a large bowl, combine all ingredients, mixing well. Add small amounts of tomato liquid until pasta is evenly moistened. Chill several hours to blend flavors.

Mix well before serving.

Each serving provides: 149 Calories, 3 g Fat, 1 mg Cholesterol, 25 g Carbohydrate, 210 mg Sodium, 2 g Fiber, 5 g Protein

Chunky Tomato Salad

For the best salad, I like to use fresh summer tomatoes that are ripe, yet still fairly firm. Add some spices and you'll just love the results.

Makes 4 servings

2 cups fresh tomatoes, cut into ½ nch chunks
1 cup sliced mushrooms
¼ cup thinly sliced green onions (green part only)
1 tablespoon canola oil
1 tablespoon vinegar
1 tablespoon water
1 teaspoon dried basil
1/8 teaspoon dried oregano
1/8 teaspoon garlic powder
½ teaspoon sugar
Salt and pepper to taste

In a medium bowl, combine tomatoes, mushrooms and green onions. In a small bowl, combine remaining ingredients. Add to tomato mixture. Toss gently, until spices are evenly distributed. Chill several hours or overnight.

Each serving provides: 57 Calories, 4 g Fat, 0 mg Cholesterol, 6 g Carbohydrate, 8 mg Sodium, 1 g Fiber, 1 g Protein

Cauliflower Confetti Salad

If you love crunchy salads, this colorful one is for you. Serve it by itself or use it to top your favorite greens. *Makes 4 servings*

1 cup cauliflower, cut into very small flowerets
½ cup thinly sliced radishes
½ cup coarsely shredded carrots
1 tablespoon canola oil
1 tablespoon wine vinegar
1 tablespoon water
1 teaspoon Dijon mustard
2 teaspoons dried chives
1 teaspoon sugar
1/16 teaspoon garlic powder

In a medium bowl, combine cauliflower, radishes and carrots. In a small bowl, combine remaining ingredients. Add to cauliflower mixture, mixing well. Chill overnight. To serve, mix well, then divide evenly onto 4 salad plates or into bowls lined with a bed of lettuce.

Each serving provides: 51 Calories, 4 g Fat, 0 mg Cholesterol, 5 g Carbohydrate, 50 mg Sodium, 1 g Fiber, 1 g Protein

Carrot and Rice Salad

A nice way to serve this colorful salad is on a bed of lettuce, garnished with tomato wedges. It makes a tasty dinner accompaniment or a filling lunch.
Makes 4 servings

2 cups cooked brown rice
1 cup finely shredded carrots
¼ cup finely chopped green pepper
2 tablespoons finely chopped onions
2 tablespoons lemon juice
1 tablespoon wine vinegar
2 teaspoons water
2 teaspoons sugar
1 teaspoon Dijon mustard
1 tablespoon plus 1 teaspoon canola oil
Salt and pepper to taste

In a large bowl, combine rice, carrots, green pepper and onions. Toss to combine. In a small bowl, stir together remaining ingredients. Add to rice mixture. Mix well. Chill several hours or overnight.

Each serving provides: 175 Calories, 6 g Fat, 0 mg Cholesterol, 29 g Carbohydrate, 55 mg Sodium, 2 g Fiber, 3 g Protein

Oriental Carrot Salad

Sesame oil gives this salad an unusual and delicious flavor. Makes 4 servings

2 cups shredded carrots
¼ cup finely minced green pepper
2 teaspoons sesame oil
2 teaspoons canola oil
1 tablespoon plus 1 teaspoon lemon juice
1 tablespoon reduced-sodium (or regular) soy sauce
1/8 teaspoon ground ginger
1 teaspoon sugar
1 tablespoon toasted sesame seeds*
Dash garlic powder

In a medium bowl, combine carrots and green pepper. In a small bowl, combine remaining ingredients. Add to carrots, mixing well. Chill several hours to blend flavors.

***To toast sesame seeds**, place them in a single layer on a baking sheet or piece of aluminum foil in a 350 degree oven. Cook until lightly toasted, about 5 minutes.

Each serving provides: 86 Calories, 6 g Fat, 0 mg Cholesterol, 8 g Carbohydrate, 171 mg Sodium, 1 g Fiber, 1 g Protein

French Potato Salad

You'll love the sharp bite from the dry mustard in our delicious version of an American favorite. Makes 8 servings

4 medium potatoes (1½ pounds total), peeled, cut into quarters
3/4 cup chopped celery
¼ cup thinly sliced green onions (green part only)
2 tablespoons reduced-calorie French dressing (25 calories or less per tablespoon)
¼ cup reduced-calorie mayonnaise
3/4 teaspoon dry mustard
½ teaspoon celery seed
½ teaspoon dried oregano
1 teaspoon dried parsley flakes
Salt to taste

Place potatoes in a medium saucepan. Cover with water and bring to a boil over medium heat. Cover pot and cook until potatoes are tender, about 15 minutes. Drain and set potatoes aside to cool. When potatoes are cool enough to handle, cut into 1-inch chunks. Place in a large bowl and add celery and onions.

In a small bowl, mix remaining ingredients together. Add to potatoes, mixing well. Chill several hours to blend flavors.

Each serving provides: 81 Calories, 3 g Fat, 2 mg Cholesterol, 13 g Carbohydrate, 92 mg Sodium, 1 g Fiber, 2 g Protein

Carrot and Broccoli Medallions

Tired of throwing away broccoli stems after paying for them by the pound? Well, finally, here's a delicious use for them. (The inside of the stem will delight your taste buds!)

Makes 6 servings

2 cups carrots, sliced crosswise into ¼ inch slices
2 cups broccoli stems, sliced crosswise into ¼ inch slices
(Peel stems and trim off tough knobs.)
2 tablespoons canola oil
¼ cup water
1/8 teaspoon pepper
¼ teaspoon dried basil
2 tablespoons vinegar
¼ teaspoon salt
1 teaspoon dried oregano
1/8 teaspoon garlic powder

Place carrots and broccoli in a medium saucepan. Combine remaining ingredients and pour over vegetables.

Bring to a boil over medium heat, stirring occasionally. Reduce heat to low, cover and simmer 10 minutes, until vegetables are tender-crisp.

Pour into a bowl and chill several hours or overnight. Stir before serving.

Each serving provides: 66 Calories, 5 g Fat, 0 mg Cholesterol, 6 g Carbohydrate, 111 mg Sodium, 1 g Fiber, 1 g Protein

Mediterranean Bread Salad

I had to come up with a use for leftover bread when I made the fabulous California Layered Loaf (in Sandwiches and Burgers section). This is my tasty answer. Served on a bed of lettuce, it's a really economical side dish.

Makes 6 servings

3 cups leftover whole wheat or rye bread, cubed (6 ounces)
1-½ cups chopped tomatoes, in ½-inch pieces
1 cup chopped cucumber, in ½-inch pieces (Peel cucumbers if they have been waxed and discard seeds if they are very large.)
½ cup chopped red onion
2 tablespoons olive oil
3 tablespoons water
1/8 teaspoon salt
¼ teaspoon dried dill weed
3 tablespoons lemon juice
2 teaspoons dried parsley flakes
¼ teaspoon pepper

Preheat oven to 350 degrees.

Spread bread cubes on a baking sheet and bake until dry, about 10 minutes. Set aside to cool.

In a large bowl, combine remaining ingredients. Mix well.

Add bread cubes. Toss until well mixed.

Chill several hours or overnight, mixing several times.

Stir before serving.

Each serving provides: 127 Calories, 6 g Fat, 0 mg Cholesterol, 17 g Carbohydrate, 232 mg Sodium, 1 g Fiber, 3 g Protein

Mexican Salad in a Burrito

This is really a fun way to eat a salad. Kids (and adults) will love it. My favorite way to serve it is with salsa from a jar or my delicious Guacamole Dip (found in "Appetizers, Dips and Spreads").

Makes 2 servings

- 2 flour tortillas
- 1 cup shredded lettuce
- ½ cup chopped tomatoes
- ¼ cup chopped onions
- 10 small, pitted black olives, sliced (3 tablespoons)
- 2 ounces shredded lowfat Cheddar cheese (or ½ cup)
- 1 teaspoon chili powder

Preheat oven to 350°.

Wrap tortillas tightly in aluminum foil and heat 10 minutes.

While tortillas are heating, combine lettuce, tomatoes, onions, olives, and Cheddar cheese in a medium bowl.

Sprinkle with chili powder and toss until evenly distributed.

Divide vegetable mixture evenly onto warm tortillas.

Add salsa or guacamole, if desired, and wrap tortilla around filling.

Serve right away.

Each serving provides: 243 Calories, 7 g Fat, 20 mg Cholesterol, 31 g Carbohydrate, 539 mg Sodium, 1 g Fiber, 13 g Protein

GOOD HEALTH ALERT:
When making airline reservations, request a lowfat meal.

Millie's Everything Salad

This chunky salad contains lots of flavors, colors and textures. Add any other vegetables you like – the more, the merrier! And, don't be put off by the long list of ingredients. Everything just gets thrown together.

Makes 8 servings

¼ cup chopped onions
¼ cup chopped green pepper
¼ cup chopped sweet red pepper
1½ cups chopped tomatoes
20 small stuffed green olives, sliced (1/3 cup)
20 small pitted black olives, sliced (1/3 cup)
1 cup sliced mushrooms
½ cup thinly sliced carrots
1 cup zucchini, unpeeled, cut into ½ inch chunks
1 cup yellow summer squash, unpeeled, cut into ½ inch chunks
1 cup cucumber, cut in half lengthwise, then into 1/8 inch slices (Peel cucumber if it has a wax coating.)
2 tablespoons dried parsley flakes
½ teaspoon dried dill weed
¼ teaspoon garlic powder
¼ cup plus 2 tablespoons reduced-calorie Italian dressing (16 calories or less per tablespoon)

In a large bowl, combine all ingredients. Mix well.

Cover and chill overnight. Mix several times while chilling.

Serve either by itself, on a bed of lettuce or, atop a scoop of lowfat cottage cheese.

Each serving provides: 40 Calories, 2 g Fat, 0 mg Cholesterol, 6 g Carbohydrate, 348 mg Sodium, 2 g Fiber, 1 g Protein

Cranberry Crunch Salad

Cranberries add a wonderful zing to this unusual version of one of my favorite salads. Be sure to freeze plenty of cranberries in the fall so you can enjoy them all year long.

Makes 4 servings

1 cup cranberries
1 small, sweet apple, unpeeled, finely chopped

- ½ cup finely chopped celery
- 2 tablespoons chopped walnuts (½ ounce)
- 2 tablespoons sugar
- 2 tablespoons plus 2 teaspoons reduced-calorie mayonnaise
- ¼ teaspoon orange extract or use canned mandarin orange sections in their own juice (drain liquid).

Place cranberries in a blender container and blend for just a few seconds, until cranberries are finely chopped, but not pureed. Place in a medium bowl. Add apple, celery and walnuts, mixing well.

In a small bowl, combine remaining ingredients. Add to cranberry mixture, mixing well. Chill.

Each serving provides: 107 Calories, 5 g Fat, 3 mg Cholesterol, 16 g Carbohydrate, 68 mg Sodium, 2 g Fiber, 1 g Protein

Honey Pear Waldorf Salad

Serve my interesting version of this traditional salad on a bed of lettuce for a delicious appetizer or salad. It also makes a great snack.

Makes 4 servings

- 2 small, ripe pears, unpeeled, cut into ½ inch pieces
- 1 cup seedless green grapes, cut in half (about 24 grapes)
- ½ cup chopped celery
- 2 tablespoons chopped walnuts (½ ounce)
- 3/4 cup plain nonfat yogurt or plain Greek yogurt
- 1 tablespoon plus 1 teaspoon reduced-calorie mayonnaise
- 2 tablespoons honey
- 1 teaspoon lemon juice
- ½ teaspoon vanilla extract

In a medium bowl, toss together pears, grapes, celery and walnuts.

In a small bowl, combine remaining ingredients. Add to pear mixture, mixing well. Chill several hours or overnight.

Mix before serving.

Each serving provides: 162 Calories, 4 g Fat, 2 mg Cholesterol, 30 g Carbohydrate, 74 mg Sodium, 2 g Fiber, 4 g Protein

Corn Relish

Serve this tangy salad as an accompaniment to any meal, as a topper for cottage cheese or as a delicious addition to a tossed salad.

Makes 8 servings

- 1 tablespoon cornstarch
- ¼ cup cider vinegar
- ½ teaspoon mustard seed
- ½ teaspoon turmeric
- 1 1-pound can corn, drained
- ¼ cup finely chopped celery
- ¼ cup finely chopped sweet red pepper
- 1/3 cup water
- 3 tablespoons sugar
- ½ teaspoon celery seed
- 1/16 teaspoon pepper
- ¼ cup finely chopped onions
- ¼ cup finely chopped green pepper

In a small saucepan, combine cornstarch and water. Mix until cornstarch is dissolved. Add vinegar, sugar and spices.

Add corn and remaining ingredients. Bring mixture to a boil over medium heat, stirring frequently. Boil 3 minutes, stirring.

Pour into a bowl and chill overnight.

Stir before serving.

Each serving provides: 57 Calories, 0 g Fat, 0 mg Cholesterol, 13 g Carbohydrate, 4 mg Sodium, 2 g Fiber, 1 g Protein

Zucchini Relish

What a wonderful way to add zing to a sandwich – your own homemade relish! Try it on a cheese sandwich, on any of our meatless burgers or on tofu hot dogs, which can be found in any health food store or supermarket that offers a healthy selection.

Makes 16 servings

- 2 cups finely chopped zucchini, unpeeled (1/8-inch pieces)
- ½ cup finely chopped onions
- ½ cup finely chopped green pepper
- 2 teaspoons salt
- ½ cup cider vinegar
- 3 tablespoons sugar
- ½ teaspoon celery seed
- ¼ teaspoon turmeric
- 1/16 teaspoon ground nutmeg
- 1/8 teaspoon pepper

In a large bowl, combine zucchini, onions, green pepper and salt. Mix and let stand 2 to 3 hours. Then drain, rinse with cold water, and drain again.

In a small saucepan combine remaining ingredients. Add zucchini mixture.

Bring to a boil over medium heat, stirring occasionally. Reduce heat to low and simmer 20 minutes.

Cool slightly, then spoon into a jar and chill overnight.

This relish will keep for several weeks in the refrigerator.

Each serving provides: 15 Calories, 0 g Fat, 0 mg Cholesterol, 4 g Carbohydrate, 276 mg Sodium, 1 g Fiber, 0 g Protein

Bread and Butter Pickles

These easy pickles are slightly tangy and slightly sweet. They're a perfect accompaniment for any meal or a great lunchbox treat.

Makes 16 servings

- 4 cups sliced cucumbers, ¼ inch thick (Peel cucumbers if they have a wax coating.)
- 2 tablespoons salt
- 1 cup water
- 1 cup vinegar
- ½ cup sugar
- 1 teaspoon celery seed
- 1 teaspoon mustard seed
- 1 teaspoon ground turmeric
- ½ teaspoon dry mustard

Place cucumber slices in a large bowl. Add salt and enough water to cover cucumbers. (This is in addition to the water called for in the recipe.)

Soak cucumbers for 1 hour, then drain, discarding soaking water.

In a small saucepan, combine the 1 cup of water with the remaining ingredients. Bring to a boil. Pour hot liquid over cucumbers.

Cover and chill several days, stirring occasionally.

Each serving provides: 32 Calories, 0 g Fat, 0 mg Cholesterol, 8 g Carbohydrate, 207 mg Sodium, Less than 1 g Fiber, 0 g Protein

GOOD HEALTH ALERT:
About 70% of the world's people eat a semi-vegetarian, lowfat diet.

Pickled Beets and Onions

I have a friend's mom to thank for sharing her old family recipe. I love these beets as a side dish or as a spicy addition to a tossed salad.

Makes 8 servings

1 1-pound can sliced beets, drained
½ cup thinly sliced onions
¼ cup cider vinegar
3/4 cup water
3 tablespoons sugar
1 tablespoon whole mixed pickling spices*

Layer *half* of the beets in a shallow 1-quart bowl or casserole.
Top with the onions, then the remaining beets.
In a small saucepan, combine remaining ingredients.
Bring to a boil over medium heat. Pour over beets.
Cover and refrigerate for 2 days.

*This ready-mixed spice is found in most grocery stores.

Each serving provides: 34 Calories, 0 g Fat, 0 mg Cholesterol, 9 g Carbohydrate, 87 mg Sodium, 1 g Fiber, 0 g Protein

Lemon Vinaigrette

Tart and tangy, this lemony dressing adds a real pick-me-up to an ordinary tossed salad.

Makes 6 servings

2 tablespoons lemon juice (Bottled lemon juice will work, but fresh tastes better.)
2 tablespoons wine vinegar
¼ cup water
1/8 teaspoon garlic powder
¼ cup canola oil
1 teaspoon Dijon mustard
1/8 teaspoon *each* salt and pepper

In a small bowl or jar, combine all ingredients, mixing well.
Chill several hours to blend flavors.
Stir before serving.

Each serving provides: 84 Calories, 9 g Fat, 0 mg Cholesterol, 1 g Carbohydrate, 72 mg Sodium, 0 g Fiber, 0 g Protein

Oriental Sesame Dressing

Add a different twist to your tossed salad by adding this Oriental dressing and topping with a sprinkling of toasted sesame seeds. Sesame oil is available in most large grocery stores. It has a wonderful flavor, but go easy – a little goes a long way.

Makes 8 servings

¼ cup wine vinegar
1 tablespoon sesame oil
1/3 cup water
1/8 teaspoon ground ginger
3 tablespoons canola oil
1 tablespoon sherry
1/8 teaspoon garlic powder
1 teaspoon sugar
1 tablespoon reduced-sodium (or regular) soy sauce

In a small bowl or jar, combine all ingredients, mixing well.
Chill several hours to blend flavors.
Stir before serving.

Each serving provides: 68 Calories, 7 g Fat, 0 mg Cholesterol, 1 g Carbohydrate, 76 mg Sodium, 0 g Fiber, 0 g Protein

Cranberry Vinaigrette

This quick dressing is mellow, smooth, and fruity. You can add a sprinkling of herbs if you like or enjoy it as is.

Makes 8 servings

2/3 cup cranberry juice cocktail
2 tablespoons wine vinegar
3 tablespoons canola oil

In a small bowl or jar, combine all ingredients. Mix and chill.
Stir before serving.

Each serving provides: 58 Calories, 5 g Fat, 0 mg Cholesterol, 3 g Carbohydrate, 1 mg Sodium , 0 g Fiber, 0 g Protein

GOOD HEALTH ALERT:
Copy your kitty: Learn to do stretching exercises when you wake up. It boosts circulation and digestion and eases back pain.

Blueberry Vinaigrette

Both sweet and tart at the same time, this is a very special dressing. Your family and guests will love it, and it makes a great holiday or housewarming gift.

Makes 8 servings

1 cup fresh or frozen blueberries
(If using frozen berries, thaw partially before using.)
1/3 cup wine vinegar
1 tablespoon sugar
¼ cup plus 2 tablespoons water
1 teaspoon dried basil
2 tablespoons plus 2 teaspoons canola oil
1/8 teaspoon garlic powder
1/8 teaspoon pepper
Salt to taste

In a blender container, combine blueberries, vinegar and sugar. Blend until smooth. Pour mixture through a strainer into a bowl or jar and discard skins and seeds.

Add remaining ingredients to blueberry mixture, mixing well. Chill several hours to blend flavors.

Mix well before serving.

Each serving provides: 58 Calories, 5 g Fat, 0 mg Cholesterol, 5 g Carbohydrate, 3 mg Sodium, 0 g Fiber, 0 g Protein

Tofu Russian Dressing

I use tofu in place of mayonnaise in this thick, rich, high-protein dressing. It doubles as a very tasty sandwich spread. (Take any of our meatless burgers, top with this delicious dressing, add lettuce and tomato, and you have a terrific fast-food look-alike.)

Makes 16 servings

6 ounces soft tofu
¼ cup wine vinegar
½ cup water
¼ teaspoon garlic powder
½ cup ketchup
¼ cup canola oil
2 tablespoons minced onion flakes
2 tablespoons sweet pickle relish

In a blender container, combine all ingredients, *except* relish. Blend until smooth. Stir in relish. Chill several hours to blend flavors. Mix well before serving.

Each serving provides: 50 Calories, 4 g Fat, 0 mg Cholesterol, 3 g Carbohydrate, 105 mg Sodium, 1 g Fiber, 1 g Protein

Tahini Dressing

Tahini is to sesame seeds what peanut butter is to peanuts. It's available in most health food stores and is well worth the trip. This dressing is not only great on salads, but it makes a tasty dip and a delicious spread for cheese sandwiches or veggie burgers.

Makes 8 servings

½ cup Tahini
½ cup water
1 tablespoon lemon juice
1/8 teaspoon garlic powder
2 teaspoons dried chives
1 tablespoon reduced-sodium (or regular) soy sauce

Place Tahini in a small bowl. Gradually add water, stirring until blended. Add remaining ingredients, mixing well. Chill.

Each serving provides: 91 Calories, 8 g Fat, 0 mg Cholesterol, 4 g Carbohydrate, 93 mg Sodium, 1 g Fiber, 3 g Protein

Miso Dressing

Miso is a thick paste made from fermented soybeans. The Japanese attribute much of their good health to this tasty condiment. You will find it in most health food stores and specialty sections of the supermarket.

Makes 12 servings

¼ cup miso (I prefer the rich, full-bodied flavor of the medium-to dark colored miso.)
¼ cup canola oil
¼ cup wine vinegar
½ cup water
2 teaspoons honey
2 teaspoons dried oregano
¼ teaspoon garlic powder
1/8 teaspoon pepper

In a blender container, combine all ingredients. Blend until smooth. Chill several hours to blend flavors. Mix well before serving.

Each serving provides: 57 Calories, 5 g Fat, 0 mg Cholesterol, 3 g Carbohydrate, 210 mg Sodium, Less than 1 g Fiber, 1 g Protein

Sandwiches and Burgers

In a society that is really in love with fast food, those of us who want healthy foods for ourselves and our families are sometimes at a loss. What can we make that is quick and easy and, at the same time, nutritious? What kind of sandwiches can we pack for picnics? What about backyard get-togethers when everyone else is eating high-fat sandwiches and hamburgers?

This chapter is devoted to showing you that you can prepare sandwiches and burgers that are both easy and nutritious. I have several burgers that are made from wholesome grains and legumes. They can all be served on buns and topped with your favorite "fixin's." My grilled cheese sandwiches are made with lowfat cheeses and, for healthy variations, I have added fruits and vegetables to these traditional favorites. I even have several "take-along" sandwiches that are chock full of delicious fruits and vegetables.

Of course, you aren't limited just to this section. There are lots of delicious dishes in my other chapters that make great sandwichs. Don't overlook leftovers. Last night's dinner might make a colossal sandwich.

Be sure to check the chapter called "Appetizers, Dips and Spreads." All of my spreads can be used for sandwiches. The "Entrée" chapter also has some delicious meals that can easily become sandwich fare. Here are a few specific ideas to guide you. These recipes are found throughout the book and also make great sandwiches – see index for page #:

- Tofu Dinner Load – Delicious hot or cold.
- Barbecue Tofu – Delicious hot or cold.
- Lentil-Nut Load – Delicious hot or cold.
- Piquant Garbanzo Salad – Pile it in a pita bread.
- Beans in Sherry Cream Sauce – Serve it, hot, on a toasted English muffin.
- Toasted Kasha Patties – Serve hot like a burger
- Swiss Spinach Casserole – Spread it, hot, on toast.
- Scrambled Tofu Spanish "Omelet" – Pile it in a pita bread.

Oat Burgers Parmigiana

This is my version of an Italian favorite made healthy. Serve it alongside rice or pasta, or on a bun. It's great!

Makes 6 servings

1 tablespoon plus 1 teaspoon canola oil
1½ cups finely chopped onions
2 cloves garlic, finely chopped
2 cups rolled oats (6 ounces)
¼ cup plus 2 tablespoons wheat germ (1½ ounces)
¼ cup plus 2 tablespoons whole wheat flour
1½ teaspoons dried oregano
1 teaspoon dried basil
Salt and pepper to taste
1-2/3 cups water
6 ounces shredded part-skim mozzarella cheese (1½ cups)
1 15½ ounce jar meatless spaghetti sauce
(70 calories or less per ½ cup serving)

Heat oil in a large nonstick skillet over medium heat.

Add onions and garlic. Cook, stirring frequently, until onions start to brown, about 10 minutes.

Preheat oven to 350°.

Lightly oil a baking sheet or spray with a nonstick cooking spray.

In a large bowl, combine oats, wheat germ, flour and spices. Mix well.

Add water and cooked onions. Mix until well combined.

Make 6 patties by pressing mixture into a ½ cup measuring cup and inverting onto prepared pan. Flatten burgers slightly to 3½ inches in diameter.

Bake 25 minutes.

Divide cheese evenly and place on burgers. Return them to the oven for 5 minutes. While burgers are baking, heat sauce.

To serve, place a burger on each serving plate and top with 1/3 cup of hot sauce.

Each serving provides: 321 Calories, 11 g Fat, 16 mg Cholesterol, 40 g Carbohydrate, 523 mg Sodium , 5 g Fiber, 17 g Protein

GOOD HEALTH ALERT:
Keep healthy snacks in the car to ward off hunger stops for fast food.

Marvelous Meatless Mushroom Cheeseburgers

These wonderful burgers can also be made without the cheese, but I really love the combined flavor of cheese and mushrooms. Serve on a burger bun or on a pita with your favorite burger fixin's.

Makes 4 servings

- ¼ cup plus 2 tablespoons whole wheat flour
- ¼ cup plus 2 tablespoons wheat germ (1½ ounces)
- ½ teaspoon baking powder
- 1/8 teaspoon salt
- 1/8 teaspoon pepper
- 1/8 teaspoon dried oregano
- 1/8 teaspoon dried basil
- 1/8 teaspoon garlic powder
- 4 egg whites
- ¼ cup very finely chopped onions
- 2 cups chopped mushrooms (about ¼ inch pieces)
- 4 ounces sliced lowfat Cheddar, Mozzarella, Swiss or American cheese

In a medium bowl, combine flour, wheat germ, baking powder and spices. Mix well.

In another bowl, combine egg whites, onions and mushrooms. Add to dry mixture, mixing until all ingredients are moistened.

Shape mixture into four 3½ inch burgers, wetting your hands slightly to prevent sticking.

Preheat a large nonstick skillet or griddle over medium heat. Oil it lightly or spray with a nonstick cooking spray.

Place burgers on preheated skillet. Cook until nicely browned on both sides, turning burgers several times.

When burgers are ready, top with cheese and heat just until cheese starts to melt.

Each serving provides: 199 Calories, 7 g Fat, 20 mg Cholesterol, 17 g Carbohydrate, 380 mg Sodium, 5 g Fiber, 17 g Protein

GOOD HEALTH ALERT:
Hit the stairwell for exercise during your lunch break.

Beany Burgers

Try these moist burgers on a bun with your favorite burger fixin's for a cholesterol-free fast food dinner you can make quickly at home.

Makes 8 servings

- 1 1-pound can kidney beans, rinsed and drained (This will yield 10 ounces of beans.)
- 2 cups cooked brown rice
- 2 tablespoons ketchup
- ½ teaspoon garlic powder
- 1 teaspoon dried oregano
- 1/8 teaspoon dried thyme
- ¼ teaspoon ground sage
- Salt and pepper to taste
- ¼ cup very finely chopped onions

In a large bowl, combine beans, rice, ketchup and spices. Mash with a fork or a potato masher until beans are mashed well. (Rice will be lumpy.)

Add chopped onions and mix well.

Divide mixture evenly and form into 8 burgers, ½ to 3/4-inch thick. Wet your hands slightly to avoid sticking.

Lightly oil a nonstick griddle or skillet, or spray with a nonstick cooking spray.

Preheat over medium heat. Place burgers on griddle and cook until browned on both sides, turning burgers several times.

Serve hot with lettuce, tomato, relish, ketchup or your favorite burger toppings.

Each serving provides: 103 Calories, 1 g Fat, 20 mg Cholesterol, 19 g Carbohydrate, 121 mg Sodium, 6 g Fiber, 4 g Protein

GOOD HEALTH ALERT:
Don't skip breakfast. Breakfast skippers tend to gain weight. A balanced breakfast includes fresh fruit or fruit juice, a high-fiber breakfast cereal, lowfat milk or yogurt, whole wheat toast and a boiled egg.

Lentil Grain Burgers

Now, here's the absolute best way to enjoy these burgers – serve them on a pita bread and top with lettuce, tomato, alfalfa sprouts and my Tahini Dressing. There's none better!

Makes 12 servings

½ cup brown rice, uncooked (3 ounces)
½ cup barley, uncooked (3 ounces)
½ cup dried lentils, uncooked (3-3/4 ounces)
4-3/4 cups water
½ cup coarsely shredded carrots
½ cup finely chopped onions
½ cup finely chopped celery
1 teaspoon dried oregano
½ teaspoon cayenne pepper
1¼ teaspoons garlic powder
½ teaspoon paprika
3/4 teaspoon salt

In a large, heavy saucepan, combine all ingredients. Bring to a boil over medium heat. Reduce heat to low and simmer, uncovered, 50 minutes, or until all of the liquid has cooked out and the mixture is sticky. Stir occasionally while cooking, and stir frequently toward the end of cooking time.

Place mixture in refrigerator and chill thoroughly. (Overnight is best.)

To prepare burgers:

Preheat a nonstick skillet or griddle over medium heat. Wetting your hands slightly, shape mixture into burgers, using ½ cup of mixture for each burger.

Cook until burgers are nicely browned on both sides, turning carefully.

Serve as suggested above.

Each serving provides: 88 Calories, 0 g Fat, 0 mg Cholesterol, 17 g Carbohydrate, 146 mg Sodium, 6 g Fiber, 4 g Protein

Falafel

Traditionally, in the Middle East, these tasty balls are deep fried, then served in a pita bread and topped with lettuce, tomatoes, and a Tahini sauce. Mine are baked instead, and I like to add alfalfa sprouts and top with my Tahini Dressing.

Makes 4 servings

1 1-pound can chickpeas, rinsed and drained (This will yield 10 ounces of chick peas.)
¼ teaspoon garlic powder
½ teaspoon ground cumin
1/8 teaspoon salt
1/16 teaspoon pepper
1 egg white
1 tablespoon plus 1 teaspoon olive oil
3 tablespoons wheat germ (3/4 ounce)
Tahini Dressing (see index for page #)

Preheat oven to 375°.

Lightly oil a shallow baking pan or spray with a nonstick cooking spray.

Place chick peas in a large bowl. Mash well with a fork or potato masher.

Sprinkle evenly with garlic powder, cumin, salt, and pepper. Mix well.

Add egg white and oil. Mix well.

Divide mixture evenly and shape into sixteen 1-inch balls. Place wheat germ in a small bowl. Roll balls in wheat germ and place in prepared pan.

Bake 20 minutes.

For each serving, place 4 falafel balls in a 1-ounce pita bread. Add lettuce, tomato, alfalfa sprouts and Tahini Dressing. (Or serve them on a plate and pass the dressing.)

Each serving provides: 152 Calories, 7 g Fat, 0 mg Cholesterol, 16 g Carbohydrate, 223 mg Sodium, 5 g Fiber, 7 g Protein

Eggless Egg Salad

One of the beauties of tofu is that it takes on the flavor of whatever you add to it, as in this recipe where it masquerades as egg salad. Serve on toast with lettuce and tomato and even you won't know the difference.

Makes 4 servings

1 pound medium or firm tofu, sliced and drained well between towels
1 tablespoon very finely chopped onion
2 tablespoons finely chopped celery
1 tablespoon plus 1 teaspoon reduced-calorie mayonnaise
1 tablespoon sweet pickle relish
1 teaspoon vinegar
1 teaspoon prepared yellow mustard
1½ teaspoons sugar
½ teaspoon turmeric
1/8 teaspoon dried dill weed
2 teaspoons dried parsley flakes
Salt and pepper to taste

Place drained tofu in a large bowl and crumble with a fork. Stir in onion and celery. In a small bowl, combine remaining ingredients, mixing well. Add to tofu mixture. Mix well.

Chill several hours to blend flavors.

Each serving provides: 115 Calories, 7 g Fat, 2 mg Cholesterol, 6 g Carbohydrate, 82 mg Sodium, 3 g Fiber, 9 g Protein

Counterfeit (Carrot) Tuna Salad

You won't believe how much this salad tastes like tuna salad. I love it on toast with lettuce and tomato or stuffed in a whole wheat pita.

Makes 4 servings

2 cups finely shredded carrots
½ small onion, grated (about 1 tablespoon)
½ cup finely chopped celery
2 tablespoons sweet pickle relish
1 tablespoon lemon juice
¼ cup reduced-calorie mayonnaise
Salt and pepper to taste

In a medium bowl, combine carrots, onion, celery and relish.
In a small bowl, combine remaining ingredients.
Add to carrot mixture, mixing well.
Chill several hours, or overnight, to blend flavors.

Each serving provides: 79 Calories, 4 g Fat, 5 mg Cholesterol, 10 g Carbohydrate, 169 mg Sodium, 2 g Fiber, 1 g Protein

Great Northern Mock Tuna Salad

This high-fiber salad is another delicious tuna taste-alike. Try it in a sandwich or piled on a toasted bagel, such as the thinly sliced in different varieties.

Makes 4 servings

1 1-pound can Great Northern beans, rinsed and drained (This will yield 10 ounces of beans.)
2 tablespoons finely chopped onion
2 tablespoons sweet pickle relish
1/3 cup finely chopped celery
1 tablespoon plus 1 teaspoon reduced-calorie mayonnaise
Dash garlic powder
Salt and pepper to taste

Place beans in a medium bowl and mash with a fork.
Add remaining ingredients and mix well.
Chill several hours to blend flavors.

Each serving provides: 99 Calories, 2 g Fat, 2 mg Cholesterol, 15 g Carbohydrate, 298 mg Sodium, 4 g Fiber, 5 g Protein

GOOD HEALTH ALERT:

Pure water – don't have soft drinks or energy drinks while you're exercising. Stay properly hydrated by drinking enough water during your workout (just don't overdo things, as drinking too much water can also be dangerous).

Zucchini Mock Crab Cakes

You won't believe how much these vegetable patties taste like the real thing. I like to serve them Chesapeake Bay style – on crackers, spread with ketchup or tartar sauce.

Makes 4 servings

4 slices whole wheat bread (1-ounce slices), crumbled
1 teaspoon baking powder
1 teaspoon seafood seasoning (such as Old Bay®)
1 tablespoon plus 1 teaspoon reduced-calorie mayonnaise
2 egg whites
2 cups finely shredded zucchini, unpeeled (Pack tightly in cup to measure.)

In a large bowl, combine all ingredients, *except* zucchini. Mix well.

Place zucchini in a large strainer. Press out as much liquid as possible.

Add zucchini to bread mixture. Mix with a fork for several minutes, until mixture is well combined and holds together.

Preheat a nonstick griddle or skillet over medium heat. Oil it lightly or spray with a nonstick cooking spray.

Divide zucchini mixture evenly into 8 portions and shape each portion into a patty.

Place on prepared griddle and cook, turning several times, until patties are lightly browned on both sides.

Serve hot. (Leftovers are good hot or cold.)

Each serving provides: 102 Calories, 3 g Fat, 2 mg Cholesterol, 16 g Carbohydrate, 522 mg Sodium, 1 g Fiber, 5 g Protein

Toasted Hawaiian Cheese Sandwich

I broil these toasted cheese sandwiches to avoid using butter or margarine. If you prefer to use the conventional method, you can assemble the sandwiches and grill them on a nonstick skillet with a tiny bit of butter.

Makes 2 servings

4 slices thin-sliced whole wheat bread (½ ounce slices)
2 ounces lowfat Cheddar or American cheese, sliced or shredded
¼ cup canned pineapple tidbits (unsweetened), drained
2 tablespoons finely chopped green pepper
2 tablespoons finely chopped tomato

Place 2 slices of bread on a broiler pan or baking sheet. Place 1 ounce of cheese on each slice. In a small bowl, combine pineapple, green pepper and tomato. Divide evenly and arrange on top of cheese.

Place under a preheated broiler and broil until cheese starts to melt.

Top with remaining bread and return to broiler. Broil just until top slices of bread are toasted.

Each serving provides: 182 Calories, 6 g Fat, 21 mg Cholesterol, 20 g Carbohydrate, 382 mg Sodium, 2 g Fiber, 11 g Protein

Antipasto-Stuffed Hoagies

Sliced and arranged on a platter, these sandwiches make a gorgeous appetizer, or just munch them whole. Either way, you're in for a real treat.

Makes 6 servings

12 ounces French bread (approximately 2½ inches in diameter)
¼ cup finely chopped onions
1 cup finely chopped tomatoes
10 small pitted black olives, sliced (3 tablespoons)
10 small stuffed green olives, slices (3 tablespoons)
¼ cup finely shredded carrots
¼ cup finely chopped green pepper
1 tablespoon dried parsley flakes
1/16 teaspoon garlic powder
1/16 teaspoon pepper
2 tablespoons reduced-calorie Italian dressing (16 calories or less per tablespoon)
3 ounces shredded lowfat Cheddar cheese (3/4 cup)

Cut bread, crosswise, into 4-inch sections. With a long, sharp knife, cut out the inside of each section, leaving a ½-inch shell. Crumble the insides of the bread into a large bowl.

Add remaining ingredients. Mix well. Pat mixture down firmly in bowl, cover and chill at least 1 hour. (Meanwhile, wrap bread or place in a plastic bag to retain freshness.)

Stir vegetable mixture, then using a teaspoon, stuff mixture tightly into rolls.

Wrap each roll and chill several hours or overnight.

To serve, slice each roll, crosswise, into 1-inch slices, or eat them whole as hoagies.

Each serving provides: 232 Calories, 5 g Fat, 12 mg Cholesterol, 35 g Carbohydrate, 642 mg Sodium, 2 g Fiber, 10 g Protein

Yellow Submarine

This wonderful vegetable-packed sandwich was actually invented one day when hearing the song by the same name. Dinner that night became a yellow challenge. Add a bowl of soup and you have a perfect Sunday dinner.

Makes 8 servings

- 1 tablespoon plus 1 teaspoon canola oil
- 2 cups thinly sliced onions, separated into rings
- 3 cups thinly sliced yellow summer squash
- 3 cups thinly sliced sweet yellow peppers (Sweet red pepper will work, but then we'd have to change the name of the recipe!)
- 3 cups sliced mushrooms
- ½ teaspoon garlic powder
- 1 teaspoon dried oregano
- ¼ teaspoon pepper
- 1 1-pound loaf Italian bread, unsliced
- 8 ounces thinly sliced lowfat Cheddar cheese

Heat oil in a large nonstick skillet over medium-high heat.

Add vegetables.

Sprinkle with spices. Cook, stirring frequently, until vegetables are tender-crisp, about 5 minutes.

Cut bread in half lengthwise and open to make a sandwich. (Do not cut all the way through.)

Pile vegetables in bread and top with cheese. Close sandwich and secure with toothpicks.

Serve right away.

Each serving provides: 307 Calories, 8 g Fat, 21 mg Cholesterol, 41 g Carbohydrate, 536 mg Sodium, 2 g Fiber, 15 g Protein

California Layered Loaf

I've hollowed out a round rye bread and filled it with layers of vegetables, cheese and fruit. I've even designed a recipe that uses the leftover bread – see index for Mediterranean Bread Salad. *Makes 8 servings*

- 1 1-pound round rye bread, preferably sourdough rye
- 2 tablespoons reduced-calorie mayonnaise
- 1 tablespoon spicy brown mustard
- 1 cup romaine lettuce, torn into bite-size pieces
- 2 medium tomatoes, thinly sliced
- 1 small avocado, peeled and thinly sliced (8 ounces)
- 1 small red onion, thinly sliced
- 10 stuffed green olives, sliced (3 tablespoons)
- 4 ounces thinly sliced lowfat Cheddar or Swiss cheese
- ½ cup thinly sliced cucumber (Peel cucumber if waxed.)
- ¼ cup finely chopped green pepper
- 1 8-ounce can mandarin orange sections (unsweetened), drained well

Carefully slice off top 1/3 of bread. Scoop out inside of bread and lid, leaving a ½ – to 1-inch shell.

In a small bowl or custard cup, combine mayonnaise and mustard.

Spread evenly on inside of bread and lid.

Inside the bread, layer *half* of the lettuce, *half* of the tomato and *half* of the avocado. Top with the onion and olives. Then add *half* of the cheese, topped with the cucumber and the green pepper. Next layer the remaining avocado, topped with the orange sections. Top with remaining cheese, remaining tomato and remaining lettuce.

Replace lid and secure edges with toothpicks. Wrap bread tightly and chill several hours. Place something heavy on bread to compress layers. (A plate topped with three 1-pound cans works well.)

Remove toothpicks and cut bread into wedges to serve.

Each serving provides: 185 Calories, 8 g Fat, 12 mg Cholesterol, 22 g Carbohydrate, 380 mg Sodium, 3 g Fiber, 8 g Protein

Bean and Cheese Wrap-Ups

This is one of my favorite hot lunches – cheese and beans in pita breads. I think you'll love it, too.

Makes 4 servings

2/3 cup cooked kidney beans (4 ounces)
¼ cup finely chopped onions
1 cup finely chopped tomato
4 ounces shredded part-skim mozzarella cheese (1 cup)
10 small black olives, chopped (3 tablespoons)
1 tablespoon plus 1 teaspoon reduced-calorie Italian dressing (16 calories or less per tablespoon)
4 1-ounce pita breads

Preheat oven to 400°.
In a large bowl, combine all ingredients, *except* pita breads. Mix well.
Split open one end of each pita. Divide filling evenly and spoon into open end.
Wrap each sandwich tightly in a piece of aluminum foil.
Bake 15 to 20 minutes.
Serve hot.

Each serving provides: 216 Calories, 6 g Fat, 16 mg Cholesterol, 29 g Carbohydrate, 443mg Sodium, 3 g Fiber, 13 g Protein

Italian Tofu Pitas

This is one of our favorite Saturday meals when all the older kids and grandkids are visiting at my house. The sandwich filling is the same one I use for Tofu-Spinach Lasagna (see index for page #). Just add a tossed salad and that's all you need.

Makes 6 servings

1 pound soft or medium tofu
1 10-ounce package frozen, chopped spinach, thawed and drained
1 teaspoon dried oregano
½ teaspoon dried basil
1/8 teaspoon garlic powder
6 1-ounce pita breads
3/4 cup meatless spaghetti sauce or marinara sauce (70 calories or less per ½-cup serving)

Preheat oven to 375°.
Drain tofu slightly, but do not squeeze out the water.

Place in a blender container and blend until smooth.

Spoon into a bowl and add spinach and spices. Mix well.

Split open one end of each pita. Divide filling evenly and spoon into open end (about 1/3 cup filling in each pita). Spoon 2-½ tablespoons of sauce into each pita.

Wrap each sandwich in a piece of aluminum foil.

Bake 20 to 25 minutes.

Serve hot.

Each serving provides: 159 Calories, 3 g Fat, 0 mg Cholesterol, 26 g Carbohydrate, 387 mg Sodium, 2 g Fiber, 8 g Protein

California Pizza

Try this delicious vegetable-topped tortilla for an easy and unusual open-faced sandwich.

Makes 2 servings

2 teaspoons canola oil
½ cup chopped onions
½ cup chopped green pepper
2 flour tortillas
¼ teaspoon dried oregano
1/8 teaspoon garlic powder
1 medium tomato, sliced
2 ounces shredded part-skim mozzarella cheese

Preheat oven to 400°.

Have a baking sheet ready.

Heat oil in a small nonstick skillet over medium heat. Add onions and green pepper. Cook 5 minutes, or until tender, stirring frequently.

Place tortillas on baking sheet.

Spread onions and peppers evenly over tortillas. Sprinkle with oregano and garlic powder. Arrange tomato slices over onion mixture. Top with cheese.

Bake 12 minutes, or until tomatoes are hot and cheese is melted.

Each serving provides: 259 Calories, 10 g Fat. 16 mg Cholesterol, 32 g Carbohydrate, 348 mg Sodium, 2 g Fiber, 11 g Protein

Grilled Cheese and Apple Special

This is really the ultimate grilled cheese sandwich. It tastes like the favorite European dessert of cheese and fruit.

Makes 2 servings

2 ounces shredded part-skim mozzarella cheese
½ small Granny Smith apple, unpeeled, coarsely shredded
1/16 teaspoon ground cinnamon
1/16 teaspoon ground nutmeg
2 teaspoons butter
4 slices whole wheat bread (1-ounce slices)

In a small bowl, combine cheese, apple and spices. Mix well, tossing to distribute spices evenly.

Spread ½ teaspoon of the butter on one side of each slice of bread.

Divide apple mixture evenly onto the dry sides of 2 slices of the bread. Top with remaining bread, making sure the sides of bread with butter are facing out.

Preheat a nonstick skillet or griddle over medium heat. Place sandwiches on griddle and press top slices of bread down firmly with a spatula. Cook until toasted on both sides, turning sandwiches several times.

Each serving provides: 243 Calories, 9 g Fat, 18 mg Cholesterol, 31 g Carbohydrate, 538 mg Sodium, 1 g Fiber, 12 g Protein

Entrees

For convenience of reference, I have divided this chapter into four parts: Legumes, Pasta and Pasta Sauces, Tofu, and a miscellaneous section I call Etcetera. There is a brief discussion of each type of entrée at the beginning of each section.

My main objective in creating meatless entrées is to produce meals that are filling, nutritious, low in fat and, of course, tasty. For some reason, many people think that meatless meals will be sparse and meager and consist mainly of carrots and celery. Not so! Actually, quite the opposite is true. Meatless meals can be quite filling and satisfying.

Researchers tell us that high-fat foods may be at least partially responsible for many modern-day diseases. My meals are based on lowfat ingredients – beans, pasta, tofu, vegetables, fruits and grains. Researchers tell us that we need more fiber in our diets. Again, my meals have the answer. Legumes and grains, fruits and vegetables are all valuable sources of fiber. Medical experts also tell us to reduce the amount of cholesterol in our diets. Since cholesterol is only found in foods that are of animal origin, there is absolutely no cholesterol found in legumes, grains, pasta, fruits or vegetables. Since the cholesterol in eggs is found only in the yolk, my recipes use only egg whites. The only source of cholesterol in my recipes is in the dairy products, and I recommend using only the lowfat and nonfat varieties, keeping the fat and the cholesterol to a minimum. The healthy use of whole eggs has gone around and is strewn with different conclusions. Moderation in using whole eggs is always a safe rule of thumb.

If you are concerned about not getting enough protein, you needn't worry. Meals based on a variety of legumes, whole grains, tofu, fruits and vegetables will supply you with all of the protein needed.

For other entrée ideas, be sure to check the chapters, Appetizers, Dips and Spreads, Soups, Salads and Salad Dressings, Sandwiches and Burgers, Starchy Vegetables, and Grains. Here are just a few suggestions for some of my other recipes that make great entrées – see index for page number.

- Lentil Pâté – Spread on crackers or bread, add soup and a salad.
- Black and White Bean Soup – Add a tossed salad and a slice of whole grain bread.
- Piquant Garbanzo Salad – Pile it on a bed of lettuce, add a tossed salad and a slice of whole grain bread.
- Oat Burgers Parmigiana – Serve with or without a bun.

Legumes

I know them as beans: they are the fruits or seeds from pod-bearing plants. Among the most commonly used types of legumes are kidney beans, pinto beans, navy beans, Great Northern beans, chickpeas or garbanzo beans, black beans, split peas, and lentils. The nutritional advantage of these power-packed little morsels is that they contain high levels of complex carbohydrates and fiber, along with iron, B vitamins and minerals. They are low in fat and contain no cholesterol. In addition, they are very inexpensive.

Most legumes are available in grocery stores in either a dry form that needs to be cooked, or already cooked and packed in cans, ready to use. (In my recipes that call for canned beans, I refer to 1-pound cans. However, can sizes do vary and, as long as they are close to 1-pound, the recipes will not be affected.) If you prefer to cook your own beans, please check Cooking Legumes on the following page. While you are cooking, be sure to prepare extra for the freezer. If you prefer to use canned beans, be aware that they usually contain added salt. I recommend that you rinse and drain them before using. It's easy to be creative with beans. Just check the other sections and you will see how I add them to soups, appetizers, dips and spreads, salads, pasta and pasta sauces, and even breads and muffins.

Cooking Legumes

To cook legumes, use 2 to 3 cups of water for each cup of beans. Bring the pot of water and beans to a boil, reduce heat, cover and simmer for the amount of time specified, or until beans are tender.

Except for split peas and lentils, which need no soaking, legumes can be soaked to reduce the cooking time.

Overnight soaking method – Place beans in a bowl and add enough water to cover beans by 3 inches. Soak overnight, drain and cook as directed.

Quick soaking method – Place beans in a pot and add enough water to cover beans by 3 inches. Bring to a boil over medium heat. Boil 2 minutes. Remove from heat, cover and let stand 2 hours. Drain and cook as directed.

One cup of dried beans will yield about 3 cups of cooked beans. If you are replacing canned beans in a recipe, use 2 cups of cooked beans in place of one 1-pound can.

The following cooking times are for soaked beans, except for split peas and lentils. Cooking time may vary with the size, quality and freshness of the beans.

Legume	Cooking Time
Black beans	1½ to 2 hours
Black-eyes beans	30 to 45 minutes
Garbanzo beans	2 to 3 hours
Great Northern beans	1 to 1½ hours
Kidney beans	1½ to 2 hours
Lentils	30 to 45 minutes
Lima beans	1 to 1½ hours
Navy beans	1½ to 2 hours
Pinto beans	1½ to 2 hours
Soy beans	2 to 3 hours
Split peas	30 to 45 minutes

Lentil Nut Loaf

My wonderful meatless meatloaf not only makes a delicious hot dinner, but the leftovers make great sandwiches.

Makes 6 servings

- 4 cups water
- 1 cup lentils, uncooked (7½ ounces)
- ½ cup very finely chopped onions
- ½ cup very finely chopped celery
- ¼ cup plus 2 tablespoons finely chopped walnuts (1½ ounces)
- 5 slices whole wheat bread, crumbled (1-ounce slices)
- 2 egg whites
- 1 8-ounce can salt-free (or regular) tomato sauce
- ½ teaspoon garlic powder
- ½ teaspoon ground sage
- ¼ teaspoon salt
- ¼ teaspoon pepper

Bring water to a boil in a medium saucepan. Add lentils, cover and cook on low heat 45 minutes. Drain.

Preheat oven to 350º.

Lightly oil a 4 x 8-inch loaf pan or spray with a nonstick cooking spray.

In a large bowl, combine cooked lentils with remaining ingredients. Mix well. Place mixture in prepared pan and press down firmly with the back of a spoon.

Bake, uncovered, 45 minutes.

Let stand 10 minutes, then invert onto a serving plate. Cut into slices to serve.

Each serving provides: 249 Calories, 6 g Fat, 0 mg Cholesterol, 37 g Carbohydrate, 280 mg Sodium, 8 g Fiber, 15 g Protein

Mexican Lentil Casserole

This casserole is an easy, delicious and nutritious way to prepare lentils. If there is any left over, you can make another meal by wrapping it in tortillas for a quick burrito dinner. *Makes 6 servings*

- ½ cup chopped onions
- ½ cup chopped celery
- 1 cup lentils, uncooked (7½ oz.)
- 1 6-ounce can tomato paste
- ½ teaspoon chili powder
- ½ cup chopped green pepper
- 4 cups water
- 1½ cups cooked brown rice
- 1 1¼ ounce packet taco seasoning mix

In a medium saucepan, combine onions, green pepper, celery and water. Bring to a boil over medium heat. Stir in lentils, cover pot, reduce heat to low, and simmer 40 minutes.

Preheat oven to 375°.

Lightly oil a 1-3/4-quart casserole or spray with a nonstick cooking spray.

Remove saucepan from heat and stir in remaining ingredients, mixing well. Spoon into prepared casserole.

Bake, uncovered, 25 minutes.

Let stand 5 minutes before serving.

Each serving provides: 228 Calories, 1 g Fat, 0 mg Cholesterol, 43 g Carbohydrate, 605 mg Sodium, 6 g Fiber, 14 g Protein

Sweet and Tangy Butter Beans

All I can say is, "You'll love this dish!" It tastes even better if made a day ahead and reheated. *Makes 6 servings*

2 tablespoons canola oil
1 cup chopped onions
1 cup chopped sweet red pepper
(Green pepper will work, but the red ones add a much sweeter flavor.)
1 clove garlic, finely chopped
1 8-ounce can salt-free (or regular) tomato sauce
1/3 cup apple juice
1 tablespoon brown sugar
1 tablespoon vinegar
1 teaspoon prepared yellow mustard
2 1-pound cans butter beans, rinsed and drained (This will yield 1-¼ pounds, or 20 ounces, of beans.)
1½ teaspoons cornstarch
2 tablespoons water

Preheat oven to 350°.

Lightly oil a 1½ quart baking dish or spray with a nonstick cooking spray.

Heat oil in a large nonstick skillet over medium heat. Add onions, red pepper, and garlic. Cook until onions are tender and start to brown, about 10 minutes. Remove from heat.

Add remaining ingredients, dissolving cornstarch in the 2 tablespoons of water before adding. Mix well. Transfer to prepared baking dish.

Bake, uncovered, 1 hour.

Each serving provides: 181 Calories, 6 g Fat, 0 mg Cholesterol, 26 g Carbohydrate, 299 mg Sodium, 4 g Fiber, 7 g Protein

Chickenless ala King

Chickpeas in a sherry cream sauce make this a tasty family dinner. Serve it over pasta, rice or toast for a meal they'll love.

Makes 6 servings

1 tablespoon olive oil
1 cup chopped onions
1 cup chopped green pepper
1 cup sliced mushrooms
3 cups skim milk
¼ cup plus 2 tablespoons all-purpose flour
¼ teaspoon salt
¼ teaspoon pepper
½ teaspoon garlic powder
½ teaspoon paprika
1 teaspoon dried parsley flakes
1 1-pound can chickpeas, rinsed and drained (This will yield 10 ounces of chick peas.)
1 cup frozen green peas
1 tablespoon sherry

Heat oil in a large nonstick skillet over medium heat. Add onions, green pepper, and mushrooms. Cook until tender, about 10 minutes.

While vegetables are cooking, combine milk, flour and spices in a blender container. Blend until smooth. Add to skillet along with chick peas and green peas. Cook, stirring, until mixture thickens and starts to boil. Boil 2 to 3 minutes, stirring.

Remove skillet from heat and stir in sherry.

Serve hot over rice, noodles, toast or biscuits.

Each serving provides: 189 Calories, 4 g Fat, 2 mg Cholesterol, 28 g Carbohydrate, 276 mg Sodium, 5 g Fiber, 10 g Protein

Chickpeas Italiano

This is another one of my "in a hurry dinners" and besides being quick, it's also delicious and nutritious. I serve it over noodles or rice and have even used the leftovers to make stuffed, baked, green peppers.

Makes 4 servings

1 tablespoon plus 1 teaspoon olive oil
1½ cups chopped onions, in large chunks
1½ cups chopped green pepper, in large chunks
2 cloves garlic, finely chopped
1 1-pound can chickpeas, rinsed and drained (This will yield 10 ounces of peas.)

1 1-pound can tomatoes, undrained, chopped
1 8-ounce can salt-free (or regular) tomato sauce
½ teaspoon dried oregano
½ teaspoon dried basil

Heat oil in a large nonstick skillet over medium heat. Add onions, green pepper and garlic. Cook until onions are lightly browned, 10 to 15 minutes.

Add remaining ingredients, mixing well. Cover, reduce heat to low, and cook 20 minutes.

Spoon over noodles or rice.

Each serving provides: 202 Calories, 7 g Fat, 0 mg Cholesterol, 29 g Carbohydrate, 340 mg Sodium, 5 g Fiber, 7 g Protein

Curried Chickpea Casserole

If you like Indian food, you'll love the wonderful blend of textures and spices in this easy casserole.

Makes 6 servings

1 tablespoon canola oil
2 cloves garlic, finely chopped
1½ cups cooked brown rice
1½ cups chopped onions
1 bay leaf
1½ cups canned cream-style corn
1 1-pound can chickpeas, rinsed and drained (This will yield 10 ounces of chickpeas.)
2 teaspoons curry powder
½ teaspoon ground cumin
½ teaspoon turmeric
¼ cup water

Preheat oven to 375°.

Lightly oil a 1½-quart baking dish or spray with a nonstick cooking spray.

Heat oil in a large nonstick skillet over medium heat. Add onions, garlic and bay leaf. Cook, stirring frequently, until onions are browned, about 15 minutes. Remove from heat and discard bay leaf.

Add remaining ingredients. Mix well. Spoon into prepared baking dish.

Bake, covered, 30 minutes.

Each serving provides: 197 Calories, 5 g Fat, 0 mg Cholesterol, 35 g Carbohydrate, 280 mg Sodium, 5 g Fiber, 6 g Protein

Barbecue Chickpeas

This is truly a last-minute, throw-together dish. With only four ingredients, it can be ready in no time. Serve it over noodles, rice or any other cooked grain, add a vegetable, and dinner is complete.

Makes 6 servings

2 1-pound cans chickpeas, rinsed and drained (This will yield 20 ounces, or 1¼ pounds, of chickpeas.)
1 15½ ounce jar meatless spaghetti sauce (70 calories or less per ½ cup serving.)
1/3 cup molasses
¼ cup very finely chopped onions

Preheat oven to 350°.

Lightly oil a 1-3/4-quart casserole or spray with a nonstick cooking spray.

In a large bowl, combine all ingredients. Mix well. Place in prepared casserole.

Bake, covered, 1¼ hours.

Each serving provides: 201 Calories, 4 g Fat, 0 mg Cholesterol, 35 g Carbohydrate, 592 mg Sodium, 5 g Fiber, 8 g Protein

New Orleans Red Beans and Rice

I first tasted this wonderfully spiced dish while visiting relatives in New Orleans. I've loved it ever since.

Makes 6 servings

1 cup kidney beans (7½ ounces)
6 cups water
1 1-pound can tomatoes, chopped, undrained
4 cloves garlic, finely chopped
2 cups chopped onions
1 cup chopped green pepper
1 cup chopped celery
1 bay leaf
2 teaspoons dried basil
3/4 teaspoon dried thyme
¼ teaspoon pepper
Salt to taste
Few drops bottled hot sauce (optional)
3 cups cooked brown rice

Soak beans:

Place beans and 4 cups of the water in a large saucepan. Bring to a boil over medium heat. Boil 2 minutes. Remove from heat, cover, and let stand 1 to 2 hours.

To cook beans:

Drain beans and return to saucepan. Add remaining ingredients, ***except*** rice, along with remaining 2 cups of water. Bring to a boil over medium heat. Reduce heat to low cover and cook 1½ hours, until beans are tender.

Remove and discard bay leaf.

To serve, place ½ cup of cooked rice on each of six serving plates. Divide bean mixture evenly and spoon over rice.

Each serving provides: 272 Calories, 2 g Fat, 0 mg Cholesterol, 54 g Carbohydrate, 157 mg Sodium, 5 g Fiber, 13 g Protein

Black Bean Casserole Olé

Picture a thick cornmeal spoon pudding. Now picture that spoon pudding chock full of black beans, chilies, tomatoes, corn and spices. Now try it. You'll love it.

Makes 6 servings

1 tablespoon olive oil
1 cup chopped onions
3/4 cup plus 2 tablespoons yellow cornmeal (4½ ounces)
2 teaspoons chili powder
1¼ cups skim milk
1 1-pound can black beans, rinsed and drained
(This will yield 10 ounces of beans.)
1 1-pound can whole kernel corn, drained
1 1-pound can stewed tomatoes
1 4-ounce can chopped green chilies (mild or hot), drained
¼ cup shredded lowfat Cheddar cheese (1 ounce)

Preheat oven to 350°.

Lightly oil an 8-inch square baking pan or spray with a nonstick cooking spray. In a large bowl, combine all ingredients, ***except*** Cheddar cheese. Mix well. Place in prepared pan. Sprinkle with Cheddar cheese.

Bake, uncovered, 45 minutes.

Each serving provides: 253 Calories, 5 g Fat, 4 mg Cholesterol, 44 g Carbohydrate, 516 mg Sodium, 4 g Fiber, 11 g Protein

Mom's Best Baked Beans

Here's Mom's secret – soak the beans and her wonderful blend of spices overnight. They take a while to prepare, but the flavor is not to be believed! (Navy beans are available in almost all grocery stores.)

Makes 6 servings

8 ounces dried navy beans, uncooked (1 heaping cup)
1 cup chopped onions
1 clove garlic, finely chopped
2 cups water
¼ cup brown sugar
2 tablespoons molasses
1 tablespoon vinegar
1 small bay leaf
½ teaspoon dry mustard
1/8 teaspoon pepper
1/8 teaspoon ground cinnamon
1/8 teaspoon ground nutmeg
1/16 teaspoon ground allspice
1 8-ounce can salt-free (or regular) tomato sauce

Rinse and drain beans. Place in a large bowl with remaining ingredients, ***except*** tomato sauce. Mix well, cover, and place in the refrigerator for 24 hours.

To cook:

Transfer bean mixture to a large oven-proof pot. Add tomato sauce. Bring to a boil over medium heat. Reduce heat to low, cover, and simmer 45 minutes.

Preheat oven to 300°.

Place pot in oven. Bake 4 hours, covered. Check beans after 3 hours and, if necessary, add a little more water so that beans are covered. Remove and discard bay leaf before serving.

Each serving provides: 203 Calories, 1 g Fat, 0 mg Cholesterol, 41 g Carbohydrate, 18 mg Sodium, 4 g Fiber, 9 g Protein

GOOD HEALTH ALERT:

Folic acid should be taken regularly by all pregnant moms and people with a low immunity to disease. Folic acid prevents spina bifida in unborn babies and can play a role in cancer prevention. It is found in green leafy vegetables, liver, fruit, and bran.

Almost Hungarian Goulash

I've replaced the meat with beans in this hearty dish. It's chock full of onions and mushrooms in a sauce you'll love. Serve it over noodles, add a green vegetable, and your meal is complete.

Makes 6 servings

1 teaspoon canola oil
2 cloves garlic, minced
1 cup chopped onions
3 cups sliced mushrooms
2 cups tomato juice
2 1-pound cans kidney beans, rinsed and drained
(This will yield 20 ounces, or 1¼ pounds, of beans.)
1 tablespoon lemon juice
1 teaspoon sugar
1 teaspoon paprika
1/16 teaspoon ground cloves
3 tablespoons all-purpose flour
¼ cup water
Salt and pepper to taste

Heat oil in a medium saucepan over medium heat. Add garlic and cook several minutes, until lightly browned.

Add onions, mushrooms, and ½ cup of the tomato juice. Cover and cook 10 minutes, stirring several times.

Add remaining ingredients, ***except*** flour and water. Reduce heat to low, cover and cook 15 minutes.

In a small bowl, stir water into flour, mixing until smooth. Add to saucepan. Cook 5 minutes, stirring frequently.

Serve hot over noodles.

Each serving provides: 170 Calories, 2 g Fat, 0 mg Cholesterol, 29 g Carbohydrate, 492 mg Sodium, 4 g Fiber, 10 g Protein

GOOD HEALTH ALERT:

Set short term health goals and reward yourself when you reach them.

Savory Bean Casserole

A truly savory blend of spices makes this casserole a delicious event. Add a tossed salad and a green vegetable and you have a meal fit for royalty.

Makes 4 servings

2 teaspoons canola oil
1 cup chopped onions
½ teaspoon dried basil
¼ teaspoon dried thyme
1 bay leaf
3 cloves garlic, finely chopped
1 cup chopped carrots, in ¼ inch pieces
½ teaspoon dried rosemary, crumbled
¼ teaspoon ground sage
¼ teaspoon salt
1/8 teaspoon pepper
2 medium potatoes, unpeeled, cut into ½ inch cubes
1 1-pound can butter beans *or* Great Northern beans, rinsed and drained (This will yield 10 ounces of beans.)
2 tablespoons all-purpose flour
1½ cups water

Preheat oven to 375°.

Lightly oil a 1-3/4-quart casserole or spray with a nonstick cooking spray.

Heat oil in a large nonstick skillet over medium heat. Add garlic, onions, carrots and spices. Cook 10 minutes, stirring frequently. Remove from heat. Remove and discard bay leaf.

Add potatoes and beans, mixing well.

Place flour in a small bowl. Add a few tablespoons of the water, stirring to make a thick paste. Gradually add remaining water, stirring until smooth. Stir into skillet, mixing well.

Spoon mixture into prepared casserole. Bake, covered, 45 minutes, stirring once halfway through cooking time.

Each serving provides: 199 Calories, 3 g Fat, 0 mg Cholesterol, 36 g Carbohydrate, 360 mg Sodium, 6 g Fiber, 8 g Protein

Beans in Sherry Cream Sauce

Two kinds of cheese, laced with sherry, make this a very special dish.

Makes 4 servings

2 tablespoons plus 2 teaspoons reduced-calorie mayonnaise
2 tablespoons finely chopped onions
1 teaspoon Dijon mustard
1 tablespoon sherry
2 ounces shredded part-skim mozzarella cheese (½ cup)

2 ounces shredded lowfat Cheddar cheese (½ cup)
1 1-pound can Great Northern beans, rinsed and drained
(This will yield 10 ounces of beans.)

Preheat oven to 375°.

Lightly oil a 1 quart baking dish or spray with a nonstick cooking spray.

In a large bowl combine mayonnaise, onions, mustard and sherry. Mix well. Stir in both types of cheese.

Add beans, mixing well. Spoon into prepared pan.

Bake, uncovered, 20 minutes.

Each serving provides: 188 Calories, 8 g Fat, 22 mg Cholesterol, 14 g Carbohydrate, 466 mg Sodium, 4 g Fiber, 12 g Protein

Black Eyed Peas and Barley

Cooked with milk, this easy bean casserole has a mellow and delicately spiced flavor.

Makes 6 servings

2 1-pound cans black-eyed peas, rinsed and drained (This will yield 20 ounces, or 1-¼ pounds, of beans.)
1 cup chopped onions
½ cup chopped celery
1/3 cup barley, uncooked (2-¼ ounces)
1 cup nonfat dry milk
1-¼ cups water
1 bay leaf
1/8 teaspoon salt
¼ teaspoon pepper
¼ teaspoon dried thyme
¼ teaspoon dried rosemary
¼ teaspoon garlic powder

Preheat oven to 350°.

Lightly oil a 1-3/4-quart casserole or spray with a nonstick cooking spray.

In a large bowl, combine all ingredients, mixing well. Place in prepared casserole.

Cover tightly and bake 1-¼ hours, or until barley is tender. Stir once, halfway through cooking time.

Remove and discard bay leaf before serving.

Each serving provides: 207 Calories, 1 g Fat, 2 mg Cholesterol, 37 g Carbohydrate, 572 mg Sodium, 4 g Fiber, 13 g Protein

Mediterranean Bean Bake

These deliciously herbed beans taste great over brown rice or any other cooked grain. The leftovers can be stuffed into pita breads and heated for a tasty hot lunch.

Makes 6 servings

- 2 teaspoons olive oil
- 2 cloves garlic, finely chopped
- 1 cup chopped onions
- 2 cups sliced mushrooms
- 1 1-pound can tomatoes, chopped and drained (Reserve liquid.)
- 1 tablespoon cornstarch
- 1 teaspoon dried basil
- 1 teaspoon dried oregano
- 2 1-pound cans Great Northern beans, rinsed and drained (This will yield 20 ounces, or 1¼ pounds, of beans.)
- 10 small, pitted black olives, thinly sliced (3 tablespoons)

Heat oil in a large nonstick skillet over medium heat. Add garlic and onions. Cook 5 minutes, stirring frequently. Add mushrooms. Continue to cook, stirring frequently, 5 more minutes. Add tomatoes.

Place reserved tomato liquid in a small bowl and add cornstarch, stirring until dissolved. Add to skillet along with basil and oregano. Cook, stirring, until mixture comes to a boil. Continue to cook and stir 2 to 3 minutes.

Remove skillet from heat and add beans and olives. Mix well.

Preheat oven to 350°.

Lightly oil a 1½ quart casserole or spray with a nonstick cooking spray.

Spoon mixture into prepared pan.

Cover and bake 40 minutes.

Each serving provides: 152 Calories, 3 g Fat, 0 mg Cholesterol, 24 g Carbohydrate, 440 mg Sodium, 4 g Fiber, 8 g Protein

GOOD HEALTH ALERT:
Don't depend on the vending machines or your friends for snacks. Be prepared and bring your own.

Delhi Beans and Apples

Serve this unusual, slightly sweet, fruit and vegetable combo over brown rice for a delicious meal, Indian style.

Makes 4 servings

2 teaspoons canola oil
½ cup chopped onions
2 small Golden Delicious apples, peeled, chopped into ½ inch pieces
1 1-pound can kidney beans, rinsed and drained (This will yield 10 ounces of beans.)
1 1-pound can stewed tomatoes
2 tablespoons honey
1 teaspoon curry powder
1 tablespoon cornstarch
1 tablespoon water

Preheat oven to 350º.

Lightly oil a 1½ quart baking dish or spray with a nonstick cooking spray.

Heat oil in a large nonstick skillet over medium heat. Add onions and cook 5 minutes, stirring frequently. Add apples and continue to cook 5 more minutes, stirring frequently.

Remove skillet from heat and add remaining ingredients, dissolving cornstarch in the 1 tablespoon of water before adding. Mix well. Spoon into prepared baking dish.

Cover and bake 40 minutes.

Each serving provides: 212 Calories, 4 g Fat, 0 mg Cholesterol, 40 g Carbohydrate, 436 mg Sodium, 4 g Fiber, 8 g Protein

GOOD HEALTH ALERT:

Most people don't apply sunscreen properly and stay in the sun too long. Slather on sunscreen daily and reapply it often, especially if you've been in the water. How much? At least enough to fill a shot glass.

Middle East Casserole

The unique flavors of the Middle East abound in this unusual casserole. Served over brown rice, it makes a very flavorful entrée.

Makes 8 servings

1 tablespoon plus 1 teaspoon olive oil
3 cups chopped onions
2 cups carrots, sliced into ¼-inch slices
2 1-pound cans chickpeas, rinsed and drained
½ cup raisins
2 tablespoons wine vinegar
¼ cup honey
1 teaspoon ground cinnamon
½ teaspoon pepper
¼ teaspoon salt
3 tablespoons dried parsley flakes
2 tablespoons all-purpose flour
1-3/4 cups water

Heat oil in a large nonstick skillet over medium heat. Add onions and carrots. Cook 15 minutes, stirring frequently, until onions are translucent. Remove from heat.

Preheat oven to 350°.

Lightly oil a 2-quart casserole or spray with a nonstick cooking spray.

Place cooked onions and carrots in a large bowl. Add chickpeas, raisins, vinegar, honey and spices. Mix well.

Place flour in a small bowl. Add a few tablespoons of the water, stirring to make a thick paste. Gradually add remaining water, stirring until smooth. Stir into chickpea mixture, mixing well.

Spoon mixture into prepared casserole. Cover tightly and bake 1½ hours stirring once halfway through cooking time.

Stir before serving. Serve hot over cooked rice.

Each serving provides: 207 Calories, 4 g Fat, 0 mg Cholesterol, 38 g Carbohydrate, 221 mg Sodium, 4 g Fiber, 6 g Protein

Pasta AMD Pasta Sauces

Our mothers told us that pasta was "fattening." Now we find out that it wasn't the pasta that was the culprit. It was the way it was prepared. Buttery sauces and cream sauces can add a lot of calories, fat and cholcsterol to an otherwise healthy food.

Health experts tell us that pasta is high in carbohydrates, which is our body's main source of fuel. So, my goal in this section was to create pasta dishes that take advantage of this nutritious quality without adding unnecessary fat. I use lots of high-fiber vegetables and legumes in the pasta dishes. Where dairy products are used, I chose the nonfat or lowfat varieties. In addition, I offer the recommendation that you try whole wheat pasta for an even higher nutritional value.

For other pasta recipes, be sure to check the following section, "Tofu," and the chapter "Salads and Salad Dressings."

Greek Macaroni Bake

Modeled after the wonderful, cinnamon-laced Greek specialty, Pastitsio, my version uses beans in place of the meat. Known lovingly in my home as Greek Lasagna, it's sure to please them all.

Makes 6 servings

3 cups cooked elbow macaroni

Sauce:

1 tablespoon olive oil
1 cup chopped onions
½ teaspoon dried oregano
1/8 teaspoon ground cinnamon
1/16 teaspoon ground nutmeg
1/8 teaspoon pepper
1 1-pound can kidney beans, rinsed and drained
(This will yield 10 ounces of beans.)
2 8-ounce cans salt-free (or regular) tomato sauce
Salt to taste

Topping:

1 cup plain nonfat yogurt or plain Greek yogurt
3 egg whites
2 tablespoons grated Parmesan cheese

Preheat oven to 375°.

Lightly oil a 6 x 10-inch baking pan or spray with a nonstick cooking spray.

Heat oil in a large nonstick skillet over medium heat. Add onions. Cook until tender, about 5 minutes. Remove from heat.

Add beans to skillet. Mash beans coarsely, using a fork. Add remaining sauce ingredients. Mix well.

Spread ½ of the macaroni in bottom of prepared pan. Spread ½ of the sauce evenly over macaroni.

Then top with remaining macaroni and then remaining sauce.

Prepare topping:

In a small bowl, combine all topping ingredients. Beat with a fork or wire whisk until well blended. Spoon evenly over casserole.

Bake, uncovered, 45 minutes.

If a browner topping is desired, place finished casserole under the broiler for a few minutes. Let stand 5 minutes before serving.

Each serving provides: 248 Calories, 4 g Fat, 2 mg Cholesterol, 40 g Carbohydrate, 203 mg Sodium, 4 g Fiber, 13 g Protein

Stuffed Shells

These jumbo pasta shells are stuffed with a delicious cheese filling that's flecked with spices and bits of vegetables. All you need is a salad to make your Italian meal complete. *Makes 6 servings*

6 ounces jumbo pasta shells, uncooked (Most shells come in 12-ounce boxes. Cook half and save the rest for another time.)
1 15-ounce container part-skim ricotta cheese (1-3/4 cups)
4 ounces shredded part-skim mozzarella cheese (1 cup)
3/4 ounce grated Parmesan cheese (3 tablespoons)
½ cup finely shredded carrots
½ cup finely shredded zucchini, unpeeled, drained well
1 teaspoon dried parsley flakes
½ teaspoon dried oregano
1/8 teaspoon garlic powder
1/8 teaspoon pepper
1 15½ ounce jar meatless spaghetti sauce (70 calories or less per ½ cup serving.)

Cook pasta shells according to package directions. Drain. To keep cooked shells from sticking together, place them on waxed paper in a single layer.

In a medium bowl, combine remaining ingredients, ***except*** sauce. Mix well. Fill pasta shells with cheese mixture, using about 1½ tablespoons for each shell.

Preheat oven to 350°.

Spread ½ cup of sauce in the bottom of a 6 x 10-inch baking dish. Place shells in pan, cheese side up. Spoon remaining sauce evenly over shells.

Cover tightly and bake 35 minutes.

Each serving provides: 317 Calories, 11 g Fat, 36 mg Cholesterol, 35 g Carbohydrate, 36 mg Sodium, 3 g Fiber, 20 g Protein

Marvelous Manicotti

A combination of tofu and cheese, along with crispy sautéed mushrooms and onions, really adds flair to this Italian favorite.

Makes 6 servings

1 cup finely chopped mushrooms
1 cup finely chopped onions
9 ounces medium tofu, sliced and drained well
1 cup part-skim ricotta cheese
4 ounces shredded part-skim mozzarella cheese (1 cup)
2 tablespoons grated Parmesan cheese
1 tablespoon dried parsley flakes
½ teaspoon dried basil
¼ teaspoon garlic powder
1/8 teaspoon pepper
8 ounces manicotti, uncooked
1 cup water
1 32-ounce jar meatless spaghetti sauce
(70 calories or less per half-cup serving.)

Heat a small nonstick skillet over medium heat. Add mushrooms and onions. Cook, stirring frequently, until nicely browned, about 15 minutes. (Mushrooms and onions will be crisper without using oil.)

Place tofu in a large bowl and mash with a fork. Add cheeses, spices and mushroom mixture. Mix well. Stuff into uncooked manicotti, using ¼ cup of mixture for each one.

Preheat oven to 375°.

Lightly oil a 9 x 13-inch baking pan or spray with a nonstick cooking spray.

In a large bowl, combine spaghetti sauce and water, mixing well. Spread 1 cup of sauce in the bottom of the prepared pan. Arrange filled manicotti in a single layer over sauce. Spoon remaining sauce over manicotti. Cover with foil and bake 50 minutes.

Uncover and bake 10 more minutes.

Each serving provides: 388 Calories, 11 g Fat, 25 mg Cholesterol, 51 g Carbohydrate, 979 mg Sodium, 3 g Fiber, 22 g Protein

Seashells and Mushrooms with Basil Creme Sauce

A truly delectable dish, this one will please your family and really impress your guests. Any shape of pasta will work, but the seashells are like little cups that hold the luscious sauce.

Makes 4 servings

8 ounces macaroni shells, uncooked
4 cups sliced mushrooms
2 teaspoons dried basil
¼ teaspoon garlic powder
1/8 teaspoon pepper
1 tablespoon all-purpose flour
1 cup evaporated skim milk
3/4 ounce grated Parmesan cheese (3 tablespoons)

Cook macaroni according to package directions. Drain.

While pasta is cooking, heat a large nonstick skillet over medium-high heat. Add mushrooms. Sprinkle with basil, garlic powder, and pepper. Cook 5 minutes, or until mushrooms are tender, stirring frequently.

Place flour in a small bowl. Add a few tablespoons of the milk, stirring to make a thick paste. Gradually add the remaining milk, stirring until smooth.

Add to skillet, along with Parmesan cheese.

Reduce heat to medium and cook, stirring, until the sauce thickens slightly and coats the seashells.

Each serving provides: 312 Calories, 3 g Fat, 7 mg Cholesterol, 55 g Carbohydrate, 179 mg Sodium, 3 g Fiber, 16 g Protein

GOOD HEALTH ALERT:

Keep bacteria out of your food. Wash your hands before starting to prepare any meal. Between steps, wash all equipment that comes in contact with food – especially raw meats – including the cutting board, countertop and can opener blade. Don't let cooked or refrigerated foods sit around at room temperature. Reheat foods to at least 165° F. to be sure that any harmful microorganisms are destroyed. Thaw frozen foods in the refrigerator, in cold running water or in a microwave oven.

Tofu Spinach Lasagna

No one will believe that the cheesy, herbed filling is really tofu. You don't even cook the noodles first!

Makes 6 servings

1 8-ounce package regular or whole wheat lasagna noodles
1 32-ounce jar meatless spaghetti sauce (70 calories or less per half-cup serving.)
1½ cups water

Filling:
1 pound soft or medium tofu
1 10-ounce package frozen, chopped spinach, thawed and drained well
1 teaspoon dried oregano
½ teaspoon dried basil
1/8 teaspoon garlic powder

In a large bowl, combine sauce and water. Set aside.

Drain tofu slightly, but do not squeeze out the water. Place in a blender container and blend until smooth. Spoon into a bowl and add remaining filling ingredients, mixing well.

To assemble lasagna, spread 1 cup of the sauce in the bottom of a 9 x 13-inch lasagna pan. Top with 1/3 of the noodles, then ½ cup of the sauce. Next, spoon ½ of the tofu mixture over the noodles and top with another ½ cup of the sauce.

Top with another 1/3 of the noodles. Press them down firmly onto the filling. Repeat layers, adding ½ cup sauce, remaining tofu mixture, ½ cup sauce and remaining noodles. Again, press noodles down firmly.

Spoon remaining sauce over noodles, making sure noodles are entirely covered with sauce. Preheat oven to 350°.

Bake 40 minutes, covered. Uncover and continue to bake 20 more minutes. Cut into squares to serve.

Each serving provides: 284 Calories, 5 g Fat, 0 mg Cholesterol, 49 g Carbohydrate, 844 mg Sodium, 4 g Fiber, 13 g Protein

White Lasagna with Broccoli and Mushrooms

Instead of the traditional tomato sauce, this luscious lasagna is layered with a smooth cream sauce. You'll love the pieces of broccoli and mushrooms and the delicious hint of sherry.

Makes 6 servings

1 8-ounce package regular or whole wheat lasagna noodles
2 tablespoons canola oil
2 cups sliced mushrooms
2 cups broccoli, cut into very small flowerets
¼ cup plus 1 tablespoon all-purpose flour
¼ teaspoon salt
1/8 teaspoon pepper
¼ teaspoon garlic powder
1 cup nonfat dry milk
2-3/4 cups water
1 tablespoon sherry
2 cups lowfat cottage cheese
6 ounces shredded part-skim mozzarella cheese (1½ cups)

Preheat oven to 350°.

Lightly oil a 9 x 13-inch baking pan or spray with a nonstick cooking spray.

Cook lasagna noodles in boiling water 7 to 8 minutes, until just tender. Drain.

While noodles are cooking, heat oil in a large saucepan over medium heat. Add mushrooms and broccoli. Cook 5 minutes, stirring frequently. While vegetables are cooking, combine flour, salt, pepper, and garlic powder in a small bowl. Combine dry milk and water in another bowl.

Sprinkle flour mixture over cooked vegetables in saucepan and mix well. Gradually add milk mixture, stirring constantly. Cook, stirring frequently, until mixture boils. Continue to cook, stirring constantly 5 minutes. Remove from heat and stir in sherry.

In a medium bowl, combine cottage cheese and mozzarella cheese, mixing well.

Assemble lasagna:

Spread ½ cup of the cream sauce in bottom of prepared pan. Top with 1/3 of the noodles, then 1 cup of the sauce. Next, spoon ½ of the cheese mixture over the noodles.

Top with another 1/3 of the noodles, then 1 cup of the sauce, followed by the remaining cheese.

Top with remaining noodles and then remaining sauce.

Cover and bake 45 minutes.

Let stand 10 minutes before serving.

Each serving provides: 387 Calories, 11 g Fat, 21 mg Cholesterol, 45 g Carbohydrate, 602 mg Sodium, 4 g Fiber, 27 g Protein

Mediterranean Lasagna Rolls

In my house this is a special occasion dish. That's when I invite the family. Lasagna noodles rolled around a vegetable filling look so fancy. The sauce is thick because we've added – of all things - beans!

Makes 6 servings

8 ounces lasagna noodles, uncooked

Sauce:

1 1-pound can kidney beans, rinsed and drained (This will yield 10 ounces of beans.)
2 8-ounce cans salt-free (or regular) tomato sauce
1 1-pound can tomatoes, chopped, undrained
1 teaspoon dried basil
¼ teaspoon garlic powder

Filling:

1 tablespoon olive oil
2 cloves garlic, finely chopped
2 cups eggplant, peeled, cut into ¼-inch pieces
1 cup chopped onions
1 teaspoon dried basil
1 cup part-skim ricotta cheese

To prepare sauce:

Place kidney beans in a large bowl. Mash with a fork or potato masher. Add remaining sauce ingredients and mix well. Set aside.

To prepare filling:

Heat oil in a large nonstick skillet over medium heat. Add garlic, eggplant, onions and basil. Cook, stirring frequently, 10 minutes. Remove from heat and let cool for 10 minutes. Spoon into a large bowl and add ricotta cheese. Mix well.

Cook lasagna noodles according to package directions. Drain.

Place noodles, in a single layer, on a sheet of waxed paper. (This will keep them from sticking together.)

Preheat oven to 375°.

Lightly oil a 7 x 11-inch baking pan or spray with a nonstick cooking spray.

To assemble rolls:

Spread ¼ cup of filling down the length of each piece of lasagna. Roll up lasagna tightly. With a sharp knife, cut rolls in half crosswise. Spread 1½ cups of sauce in the bottom of prepared pan. Place rolls, ruffled edge up, over sauce. Spoon remaining sauce over rolls.

Cover with foil and bake 40 minutes.

Each serving provides: 334 Calories, 7 g Fat, 13 mg Cholesterol, 52 g Carbohydrate, 293 mg Sodium, 4 g Fiber, 16 g Protein

Creamy Chili Macaroni

This creamy casserole is a pretty one too. Topped with a layer of yogurt and sprinkled with chopped olives, it's both different and delicious.

Makes 4 servings

1 tablespoon canola oil
½ cup thinly sliced green onions (green part only)
3 tablespoons all-purpose flour
1 cup skim milk
¼ cup dry white wine
2 ounces shredded lowfat Cheddar cheese (½ cup)
1 4-ounce can chopped green chilies (mild or hot), drained
2½ cups cooked elbow macaroni
3/4 cup plain nonfat yogurt or plain Greek yogurt
10 small, stuffed green olives, chopped (3 tablespoons)

Preheat oven to 375°.

Lightly oil a 1-quart baking dish or spray with a nonstick cooking spray.

Heat oil in a small saucepan over medium heat. Add onions. Cook 3 minutes, stirring. Sprinkle flour over onions and mix well. Gradually add milk, stirring constantly. Cook, stirring, until mixture boils. Continue to cook, stirring, 3 minutes.

Add wine. Cook, still stirring, 3 more minutes.

Remove saucepan from heat and stir in cheese, chilies, and macaroni. Mix well.

Place mixture in prepared baking dish. Stir yogurt until smooth and spread evenly over top of macaroni. Sprinkle with chopped olives.

Bake, uncovered, 20 minutes.

Let stand 5 minutes before serving.

Each serving provides: 285 Calories, 8 g Fat, 12 mg Cholesterol, 39 g Carbohydrate, 492 mg Sodium, 3 g Fiber, 14 g Protein

Italian Spaghetti Casserole

I accidently invented this easy casserole when trying to find a use for leftover spaghetti. Now we make it intentionally. *Makes 6 servings*

Sauce:

1 1-pound can tomatoes, chopped, undrained
1 cup chopped onions
1 cup chopped green pepper
1 6-ounce can tomato paste
1 teaspoon dried oregano
1 teaspoon dried basil
¼ teaspoon garlic powder

Filling:

1 cup part-skim ricotta cheese
1 ounce shredded part-skim mozzarella cheese (¼ cup)

Spaghetti layer:

8 ounces thin spaghetti, broken into 2-½-inch pieces
2 tablespoons olive oil
3 egg whites
3 ounces part-skim mozzarella cheese (3/4 cup)

Pour ¼ cup of the canned tomato liquid into a small saucepan. Add onions and green pepper and bring mixture to a boil. Cover and cook 15 minutes. Stir in remaining sauce ingredients, mixing well. Cover and cook 5 minutes. Remove from heat.

To make filling, combine ricotta cheese and 1 ounce of mozzarella cheese in a small bowl. Mix well.

Cook spaghetti according to package directions. Drain. Run spaghetti under cold water to cool. Drain again. Place spaghetti in a large bowl and add oil, egg whites, and remaining mozzarella cheese. Mix well.

Preheat oven to 350°. Lightly oil an 8-inch square baking pan or spray with a nonstick cooking spray.

To assemble casserole:

Spread spaghetti mixture evenly in prepared pan. Drop cheese filling by tablespoonfuls onto spaghetti. Spread filling over spaghetti, using the back of a spoon. Spoon sauce evenly over cheese.

Baked, uncovered, 35 minutes. Let stand 5 minutes before serving.

Each serving provides: 348 Calories, 12 g Fat, 24 mg Cholesterol, 43 g Carbohydrate, 518 mg Sodium, 4 g Fiber, 18 g Protein

Party Pasta Salad

Thanks to my daughter, Jennifer, for this colorful and wonderfully delicious pasta salad. Don't wait for a party to try it.

Makes 12 servings

- 6 cups cooked macaroni (I prefer spirals, but any shape will work.)
- 1 cup broccoli, cut into tiny flowerets
- 1 cup tomato, chopped
- ½ cup chopped celery
- ½ cup finely grated carrots
- ½ cup cucumber, cut into quarters and finely sliced
- ½ cup finely chopped red cabbage
- ½ cup canned baby corn
- 15 small, stuffed green olives, sliced (about ¼ cup)
- 15 small, pitted black olives, sliced (about ¼ cup)
- 4 mild pickled salad peppers, sliced (about ¼ cup)
- ¼ cup olive oil
- ¼ cup wine vinegar
- ¼ cup water
- 1 3/4-ounce packet Italian dressing mix
- 1 teaspoon dried oregano

In a large bowl, combine all ingredients. Mix well. Chill several hours, or overnight, mixing several times.

Serve cold.

Each serving provides: 106 Calories, 6 g Fat, 0 mg Cholesterol, 23 g Carbohydrate, 345 mg Sodium, 4 g Fiber, 4 g Protein

GOOD HEALTH ALERT:

Non-dairy milks, like rice, soy and tofu, vary immensely in the amount of calcium they provide. Be sure to read the nutrition label if you rely on these foods to meet your calcium needs.

Green and White Pasta Salad

This unusual pasta salad serves 4 as an entrée or 6 to 8 as a side dish. When I serve it as a main dish, all I need to add is a tossed salad and I have a cool, refreshing meal.

Makes 4 servings

1 cup snow peas, cut into ½ inch pieces
2 cups broccoli, cut into small flowerets
8 ounces macaroni (any shape), uncooked
3/4 cup plain nonfat yogurt
¼ cup skim milk
2 teaspoons reduced-calorie mayonnaise
3/4 ounce grated Parmesan cheese (3 tablespoons)
1 teaspoon Dijon mustard
½ teaspoon dill weed
1/8 teaspoon garlic powder
1/8 teaspoon pepper
10 small pitted green olives, chopped (3 tablespoons)
¼ cup finely chopped pepperoncini (salad peppers)
½ cup chopped green onion (green part only)

Place snow peas and broccoli in a colander. Cook macaroni according to directions. Pour macaroni and cooking water into colander, over vegetables. (This will slightly cook the vegetables.) Then rinse under cold water and drain.

In a large bowl, combine remaining ingredients, mixing well. Add macaroni and vegetables. Mix well.

Chill several hours, or overnight, to blend flavors.

Each serving provides: 312 Calories, 4 g Fat, 6 mg Cholesterol, 53 g Carbohydrate, 496 mg Sodium, 3 g Fiber, 15 g Protein

GOOD HEALTH ALERT:
Starches, in addition to sugars, are linked to the formation of dental cavities. Practicing good dental hygiene – with regular brushing, flossing, and check-ups – is the key to a healthy smile.

Chinese Vegetable Pasta

Aside from being delicious, this is one of our prettiest and most colorful recipes, making it a great buffet dish. The only time-consuming part is cutting the vegetables. After that, it's a cinch.

Makes 6 servings

1 8-ounce package very thin spaghetti, or noodles

Sauce:

¼ cup plus 2 tablespoons reduced-sodium (or regular) soy sauce
2 tablespoons sherry
3/4 cup water
2 teaspoons cornstarch
1 teaspoon instant vegetable broth mix (see page)
½ teaspoon garlic powder

Vegetables:

1 teaspoon sesame oil
1 cup sliced onions
1 cup sliced sweet red pepper
1 cup sliced celery, ¼ inch thick
1 cup sliced mushrooms
½ cup carrots, cut into matchstick-size pieces
2 cups bean sprouts
½ cup sliced green onions (green and white parts)
1 cup snow pea pods, ends trimmed and strings removed

Cook spaghetti according to package directions. Drain.

In a small bowl, combine sauce ingredients, mixing to dissolve cornstarch.

Heat oil in a large nonstick skillet or wok over medium-high heat. Add onions, red pepper, celery, mushrooms and carrots. Cook 5 minutes, stirring constantly with a tossing motion. Add ¼ cup of the sauce and continue to cook and stir 5 more minutes.

Add bean sprouts, green onions, and pea pods. Cook, stirring, 3 minutes.

Stir remaining sauce and add to skillet, along with spaghetti. Cook and stir 3 minutes, until mixture is thoroughly combined and heated through.

Each serving provides: 228 Calories, 3 g Fat. 0 mg Cholesterol, 41 g Carbohydrate, 735 mg Sodium, 4 g Fiber, 9 g Protein

Thai Peanut Noodles

Ground peanuts give these noodles a wonderful texture. After enjoying this dish in Thai restaurants for years, I finally came up with my own version.

Makes 4 servings

- 8 ounces very thin spaghetti, or noodles
- ½ cup peanuts, unsalted (2 ounces)
- 3 tablespoons reduced-sodium (or regular) soy sauce
- 2 tablespoons lemon juice
- 1 tablespoon honey
- 3 tablespoons water
- 1 tablespoon plus 1 teaspoon sesame oil
- 2 cloves garlic, finely chopped
- ½ cup very thinly sliced onions (Cut onion in half lengthwise, then cut into very thin slivers.)
- 1 cup snow peas, cut into 1 inch pieces, ends trimmed and strings removed
- 3 cups fresh bean sprouts
- ¼ cup thinly sliced green onions (green part only)

Cook spaghetti according to package directions. Drain.

Place peanuts in a blender container and blend until finely chopped. Set aside.

In a small bowl, combine soy sauce, lemon juice, honey and water.

Heat oil in a large nonstick skillet over medium-high heat. Add garlic and onions. Cook, stirring 2 minutes or until onions are slightly tender. Add snow peas, bean sprouts, and ***half*** of the soy mixture. Cook 2 or 3 minutes, stirring, until bean sprouts are just barely tender.

Add remaining soy sauce mixture to skillet, along with chopped peanuts, green onions, and drained pasta. Toss well and serve.

Each serving provides: 405 Calories, 13 g Fat, 0 mg Cholesterol, 60 g Carbohydrate, 465 mg Sodium, 3 g Fiber, 15 g Protein

Lemon Pepper Pasta

Red and yellow peppers and a lemony cheese coating make this easy pasta as pretty as a picture. Add a colorful tossed salad and that's all you need for a gourmet feast.

Makes 4 servings

- 8 ounces very thin spaghetti, uncooked
- 2 teaspoons olive oil
- 1 large sweet red pepper, cut into strips 1/8 inch thick (1½ cups)
- 1 large yellow pepper, cut into strips 1/8 inch thick (1½ cups)

1 tablespoon grated fresh lemon peel
¼ teaspoon pepper
1 cup skim milk
4 ounces shredded lowfat Cheddar cheese (1 cup)

Cook pasta according to package directions. Drain.

While pasta is cooking, heat oil in a large nonstick skillet over medium-high heat.

Add peppers. Cook, stirring frequently, 5 minutes. Sprinkle with lemon peel and pepper and mix well.

Reduce heat to low. Add cooked pasta, along with milk and cheese. Toss until pasta is heated through and cheese is melted and evenly distributed. (Add a little more milk if a thinner sauce is desired.)

Serve right away.

Each serving provides: 362 Calories, 9 g Fat, 21 mg Cholesterol, 51 g Carbohydrate, 238 mg Sodium, 3 g Fiber, 18 g Protein

Pasta with Ricotta Walnut Sauce

You'll love the creamy, rich sauce and the subtle crunch of walnuts in this elegant dish. I like to serve it with steamed broccoli or asparagus and a crusty whole grain bread.

Makes 4 servings

8 ounces linguine or thin spaghetti, uncooked
½ cup part-skim ricotta cheese
3/4 cup plain nonfat yogurt or Greek plain yogurt
3/4 ounce grated Parmesan cheese (3 tablespoons)
¼ cup finely chopped walnuts (1 ounce)
3 tablespoons dried parsley flakes
1 teaspoon dried basil
¼ teaspoon garlic powder
¼ teaspoon pepper

Cook linguine according to package directions. Drain.

While pasta is cooking, combine remaining ingredients in a large bowl. Mix well.

Add drained pasta to sauce. Mix well until pasta is coated.

Serve right away.

Each serving provides: 349 Calories, 9 g Fat, 15 mg Cholesterol, 11 g Carbohydrate, 177 mg Sodium, 4 g Fiber, 17 g Protein

Linguine with Tomatoes and Cream

These noodles are coated with a creamy tomato sauce for an unusual dish that is sure to become one of your favorites.

Makes 4 servings

2 teaspoons olive oil
1 clove garlic, finely chopped
1 teaspoon dried basil
½ cup evaporated skim milk
1 cup chopped onions
1 1-pound can stewed tomatoes
1/8 teaspoon pepper
8 ounces linguine, uncooked
3/4 ounce grated Parmesan cheese (3 tablespoons)

Heat oil in a large nonstick skillet over medium heat. Add onions and garlic. Cook 5 minutes, stirring frequently.

Add stewed tomatoes, basil and pepper. Bring to a boil, then reduce heat to low and simmer 10 minutes, uncovered. Stir in milk and continue to simmer 5 more minutes.

While sauce is cooking, prepare linguine according to package directions. Drain.

Add cooked linguine to tomato mixture, along with Parmesan cheese. Toss until pasta is coated with sauce.

Serve right away.

Each serving provides: 324 Calories, 5 g Fat, 5 mg Cholesterol, 19 g Carbohydrate, 430 mg Sodium, 3 g Fiber, 14 g Protein

Italian Mushroom Noodle Bake

A layer of cheese and noodles topped with a rich mushroom sauce makes this a special dish. It's my "lazy day lasagna." Look for noodles made without egg yolks or, for added flavor and fiber, try whole wheat noodles.

Makes 8 servings

Mushroom sauce:

2 teaspoons olive oil
1 cup chopped onions
1 cup chopped green pepper
3 cloves garlic, finely chopped
6 cups sliced mushrooms
1 teaspoon dried basil
1 teaspoon dried oregano
¼ teaspoon dried thyme

¼ teaspoon dried rosemary, crumbled
Salt and pepper to taste
1 1-pound can tomatoes, undrained, chopped
1 6-ounce can tomato paste

Noodle layer:
3/4 ounce grated Parmesan cheese (3 tablespoons)
1 cup part-skim ricotta cheese
3 egg whites
4 cups cooked medium or thin noodles

Topping:
4 ounces shredded part-skim mozzarella cheese (1 cup)

Preheat oven to 350°.
Lightly oil a 9 x 13-inch baking pan or spray with a nonstick cooking spray.

Prepare sauce:
Heat oil in a large nonstick skillet over medium heat. Add onions, green pepper and garlic. Cook for 5 minutes, stirring frequently. Add mushrooms and spices. Continue to cook, stirring frequently, until mushrooms are tender, about 10 minutes.

Remove from heat and stir in tomatoes and tomato paste, mixing well.

Prepare noodle layer:
In a large bowl, combine Parmesan cheese, ricotta cheese and egg whites, mixing until blended. Add noodles. Mix well.

To assemble:
Spread noodle mixture in prepared pan, pressing gently with the back of a spoon.

Spoon mushroom sauce evenly over noodles.

Cover tightly and bake 40 minutes.

Uncover, sprinkle with mozzarella cheese, and return to oven for 5 minutes, until cheese is melted.

Remove from oven, let stand 5 minutes, then cut into squares to serve.

Each serving provides: 236 Calories, 7 g Fat, 20 mg Cholesterol, 29 g Carbohydrate, 447 mg Sodium, 4 g Fiber, 15 g Protein

Alpine Spinach and Noodles

This easy dinner casserole also doubles as a great brunch dish.

Makes 6 servings

8 ounces medium noodles, uncooked
(Choose yolkless noodles or whole wheat eggless noodles.)
2 10-ounce packages frozen, chopped spinach, thawed and drained well
2 slices whole wheat bread (1-ounce slices), crumbled
3 egg whites
3/4 ounce grated Parmesan cheese (3 tablespoons)
1 tablespoon lemon juice
2 teaspoons dried oregano
¼ teaspoon garlic powder
¼ teaspoon pepper
1 32-ounce jar meatless spaghetti sauce
(70 calories or less per ½ cup serving.)
4 ounces shredded lowfat Swiss cheese

Cook noodles according to package directions. Drain.

While noodles are cooking, place drained spinach in a large bowl. Add bread, egg whites, Parmesan cheese, lemon juice and spices. Mix well.

Preheat oven to 350°.

Lightly oil a 9 x 13 inch baking pan.

Spread cooked noodles in prepared pan. Top with ***half*** of the spaghetti sauce.

Spread spinach mixture evenly over sauce. Then cover with remaining sauce. Cover and bake 30 minutes.

Uncover, sprinkle cheese evenly over casserole and return to oven for 5 minutes or until cheese is melted.

Each serving provides: 369 Calories, 9 g Fat, 52 mg Cholesterol, 53 g Carbohydrate, 1,063 mg Sodium, 4 g Fiber, 23 g Protein

Herbed Noodles and Cheese

It's amazing what can be done with a few herbs, a little bit of cheese, and some noodles. The same sauce also works well with cooked rice in place of the noodles.

Makes 4 servings

2 teaspoons canola oil
2/3 cup lowfat cottage cheese

2 ounces shredded part-skim mozzarella cheese (1/2 cup)
1/8 teaspoon garlic powder
1/2 teaspoon dried oregano
1/2 teaspoon dried basil
1/8 teaspoon pepper
2 cups cooked medium or thin noodles (Choose yolkless noodles or whole wheat eggless noodles.)

In a small saucepan, combine all ingredients, except noodles.

Heat, stirring over medium-low heat until cheese is melted.

Place hot, cooked noodles in a serving bowl and top with cheese sauce.

Toss and serve.

Each serving provides: 159 Calories, 5 g Fat, 10 mg Cholesterol, 17 g Carbohydrate, 228 mg Sodium, 2 g Fiber, 11 g Protein

Lemon Parmesan Noodles

This quick, easy side dish adds a gourmet flair to any meal. For the best flavor, use freshly squeezed lemon juice.

Makes 4 servings

2 cups cooked medium or thin noodles
(Choose yolkless noodles or whole wheat eggless noodles.)
1 tablespoon plus 1 teaspoon canola oil
2 tablespoons lemon juice
3/4 ounce grated Parmesan cheese (3 tablespoons)

Place hot, cooked noodles in a serving bowl.

Combine oil and lemon juice and pour over noodles. Toss. Sprinkle with Parmesan cheese.

Toss and serve.

Each serving provides: 140 Calories, 6 g Fat, 4 mg Cholesterol, 16 g Carbohydrate, 109 mg Sodium, 2 g Fiber, 5 g Protein

GOOD HEALTH ALERT:
To test how much fat is in a cracker, rub it with a paper napkin. If it leaves a grease mark, there's lots of oil in it. Even if the fat in the cracker comes from highly unsaturated vegetable oil, you don't need the extra fat.

Saucy Noodles and Cheese

This layered noodle dish can be made with other vegetables in addition to the mushrooms. Try onions, green peppers, or anything you choose.

Makes 6 servings

8 ounces medium noodles, uncooked
(Choose yolkless noodles or whole wheat eggless noodles.)
1 tablespoon canola oil
3 cups sliced mushrooms
3 cloves garlic, finely chopped
2 8-ounce cans salt-free (or regular) tomato sauce
1 tablespoon cornstarch
1 teaspoon dried basil
1½ cups plain nonfat yogurt or plan Greek yogurt
½ cup part-skim ricotta cheese
½ cup thinly sliced green onions
1/8 teaspoon pepper
4 ounces shredded lowfat Cheddar cheese (1 cup)

Cook noodles according to package directions. Drain.

Heat oil in a medium saucepan over medium heat. Add mushrooms and garlic. Cook, stirring frequently, until mushrooms are tender, about 5 minutes. Add very small amounts of water, if necessary, to prevent sticking.

In a small bowl, combine tomato sauce, cornstarch, and basil, stirring to dissolve cornstarch. Add to mushrooms. Bring mixture to a boil, then reduce heat to low and simmer 5 minutes, stirring frequently. Remove sauce from heat.

Combine yogurt, ricotta cheese, green onions, and pepper in a small bowl. Mix well.

Preheat oven to 350°.

Lightly oil an 8-inch square baking pan or spray with a nonstick cooking spray. Place ***half*** of the noodles in prepared baking pan. Spread with ***half*** of the ricotta mixture, then ***half*** of the sauce, and ***half*** of the Cheddar cheese. Repeat layers, using remaining noodles, ricotta mixture, sauce, and cheese.

Bake uncovered, 30 minutes. Let stand 5 minutes before serving.

Each serving provides: 331 Calories, 9 g Fat, 57 mg Cholesterol, 43 g Carbohydrate, 229 mg Sodium, 3 g Fiber, 18 g Protein

Barbecue Franks and Noodles

What? Frankfurters in a meatless cookbook? Look closely: they're tofu franks and they're available in health food stores everywhere. They look and taste just like the originals.

Makes 6 servings

- 2 teaspoons canola oil
- 1 cup chopped onions
- 1 8-ounce can salt-free (or regular) tomato sauce
- ½ cup bottled chili sauce
- 1 tablespoon firmly packed brown sugar
- 3 tablespoons lemon juice
- ¼ teaspoon paprika
- 4 ounces medium noodles, uncooked (Choose yolkless noodles or whole wheat eggless noodles.)
- 12 ounces tofu frankfurters, sliced crosswise into ¼ inch slices

Heat oil in a small saucepan over medium heat. Add onions. Cook until tender, about 5 minutes, stirring frequently. Add small amounts of water, if necessary, to prevent sticking.

Add tomato sauce, chili sauce, brown sugar, lemon juice and paprika. Bring mixture to a boil, then reduce heat to low and simmer, uncovered, 15 minutes.

While sauce is cooking, cook noodles according to package directions. Drain.

Preheat oven to 350º.

Lightly oil an 8-inch square baking pan or spray with a nonstick cooking spray.

Spread cooked noodles in prepared pan. Spread frankfurter slices evenly over noodles. Spoon sauce evenly over frankfurters.

Cover with aluminum foil and bake 30 minutes.

Each serving provides: 297 Calories, 14 g Fat, 0 mg Cholesterol, 36 g Carbohydrate, 590 mg Sodium, 2 g Fiber, 11 g Protein

Backyard Macaroni Casserole

I've added sliced tofu frankfurters to this super-easy casserole for a quick cook-out dish or a fast meal when you're in a hurry.

Makes 8 servings

8 ounces elbow macaroni, uncooked
1 pound tofu frankfurters, sliced crosswise into ¼ inch slices
3 8-ounce cans salt-free (or regular) tomato sauce
1½ cups water
½ cup very finely chopped onions
1 teaspoon chili powder
½ teaspoon dry mustard
½ teaspoon garlic powder
½ teaspoon paprika
4 ounces shredded lowfat Cheddar cheese (1 cup)

Preheat oven to 350º.
Lightly oil a 2-quart casserole or spray with a nonstick cooking spray.
Cook macaroni according to package directions. Drain.
Place cooked macaroni in a large bowl.
Add remaining ingredients and mix well.
Spoon into prepared casserole.
Cover and bake 1 hour.

Each serving provides: 347 Calories, 16 g Fat, 10 mg Cholesterol, 38 g Carbohydrate, 391 mg Sodium, 2 g Fiber, 16 g Protein

Marinara Sauce – Best and Basic

Just as it says – this is the best and basic pasta sauce. I love it the way it is, or it can be varied by adding green peppers, mushrooms, broccoli, or any other vegetables you wish. It's great in lasagna, too. *Makes 6 servings*

1 tablespoon olive oil
3 cloves garlic, finely chopped
1 cup thinly sliced onions
1 28-ounce can Italian plum tomatoes, finely chopped, undrained
1 6-ounce can tomato paste
1 cup water
2 teaspoons dried oregano
1 teaspoon sugar
1/8 teaspoon pepper
Salt to taste

Heat oil in a large saucepan over medium heat. Add garlic and onions.

Cook 5 minutes, stirring frequently and adding small amounts of water, if necessary, to prevent sticking.

Add remaining ingredients and bring to a boil.

Reduce heat to low, cover, and simmer 30 minutes.

Serve over pasta or use in your favorite Italian recipe.

Each serving provides: 86 Calories, 3 g Fat, 0 mg Cholesterol, 14 g Carbohydrate, 440 mg Sodium, 1 g Fiber, 3 g Protein

Pasta Sauce alla Romano

I definitely recommend making this sauce a day ahead. The deliciously unusual spice combination gets even better when the flavors have a chance to marry.

Makes 6 servings

1 tablespoon olive oil
2 cups onions, cut lengthwise into slices ¼ inch thick
2 cups green pepper, sliced lengthwise into ¼ inch strips, then each strip cut in half crosswise
3 cups sliced mushrooms
3 cloves garlic, chopped
1 1-pound can tomatoes, undrained, chopped
1 6-ounce can tomato paste
1 8-ounce can salt-free (or regular) tomato sauce
½ teaspoon dried oregano
1/8 teaspoon ground sage
¼ teaspoon dried thyme
¼ teaspoon pepper
¼ teaspoon fennel seeds, slightly crushed*
Salt to taste

Heat oil in a large saucepan over medium heat. Add onions, green pepper, mushrooms and garlic. Cook, stirring frequently, until tender, about 10 minutes.

Add remaining ingredients. Bring mixture to a boil, reduce heat to low, cover and cook 20 minutes, stirring occasionally.

Serve over pasta.

*Place seeds between 2 pieces of waxed paper and crush with a rolling pin.

Each serving provides: 111 Calories, 3 g Fat, 0 mg Cholesterol, 19 g Carbohydrate, 359 mg Sodium, 2 g Fiber, 4 g Protein

Black Olive Tomato Sauce

My thanks to Jennifer for this tangy sauce that's chock full of black olives and onions. It's easy to prepare and tastes great over any type of pasta or rice.

Makes 4 servings

2 teaspoons olive oil
2 cups chopped onions
3/4 cup sliced black olives (about 27 medium olives)
1 4-ounce can mushroom pieces, drained
3 8-ounce cans salt-free (or regular) tomato sauce
1 teaspoon dried oregano
¼ teaspoon garlic powder
Salt and pepper to taste
Few drops bottled hot pepper sauce (optional)

Heat oil in a large nonstick skillet over medium heat. Add onions and cook until tender, about 15 minutes. Add small amounts of water, if necessary, to prevent sticking.

Add remaining ingredients.

Cook, stirring, until hot and bubbly.

Serve over your favorite pasta or cooked grain.

Each serving provides: 143 Calories, 6 g Fat, 0 mg Cholesterol, 21 g Carbohydrate, 373 mg Sodium, 1 g Fiber, 4 g Protein

Garden Pasta Sauce

A simple package of frozen vegetables makes this one of my favorite, and most interesting, pasta sauces. This recipe makes a lot, and you'll be glad!

Makes 9 servings

1 tablespoon olive oil
2 cups chopped onions
2 cloves garlic, finely chopped
2 1-pound cans tomatoes, chopped, undrained
2 8-ounce cans salt-free (or regular) tomato sauce
1 6-ounce can tomato paste
½ teaspoon dried oregano
½ teaspoon dried basil
¼ teaspoon dried thyme
¼ teaspoon paprika
¼ teaspoon dried rosemary, crumbled

1 teaspoon sugar
1/8 teaspoon pepper
Salt to taste
1 1-pound package frozen mixed broccoli, cauliflower and carrots (Try other vegetable combinations if you like.)

Heat oil in a large saucepan over medium heat. Add onions and garlic. Cook 5 minutes, stirring frequently.

Add remaining ingredients, mixing well. Bring mixture to a boil. Reduce heat to low, cover and simmer 30 minutes, or until vegetables are tender.

Serve over your favorite shape of pasta.

Each serving provides: 98 Calories, 2 g Fat, 0 mg Cholesterol, 18 g Carbohydrate, 340 mg Sodium, 2 g Fiber, 4 g Protein

Sicilian Spinach Sauce

Spinach makes this sauce thick and hearty. It's not only great over pasta; it can turn a baked potato into a filling meal.

Makes 6 servings

1 tablespoon olive oil
1 cup chopped onions
½ cup chopped celery
2 cloves garlic, finely chopped
½ cup coarsely shredded carrots
1 8-ounce can salt-free (or regular) tomato sauce
1 6-ounce can tomato paste
1 10-ounce package frozen, chopped spinach, thawed, undrained
½ cup water
1 tablespoon lemon juice
1 teaspoon dried oregano
½ teaspoon dried basil
¼ teaspoon dried thyme
¼ teaspoon pepper

Heat oil in a medium saucepan over medium heat. Add onions, celery, garlic, and carrots. Cook, stirring frequently, 5 to 10 minutes, or until vegetables are tender.

Add remaining ingredients, mixing well. Bring mixture to a boil. Cover, reduce heat to low, and simmer 5 minutes.

Spoon over pasta, baked potatoes, or any cooked grain.

Each serving provides: 86 Calories, 3 g Fat, 0 mg Cholesterol, 14 g Carbohydrate, 280 mg Sodium, 3 g Fiber, 3 g Protein

Quick Tomato Bean Sauce

Only you will know that the secret to this thick sauce is beans. It's a great way to add fiber to your pasta dinner. For a real quickie, in place of tomato sauce and spices, use your favorite jarred pasta sauce.

Makes 4 servings

2 8-ounce cans salt-free (or regular) tomato sauce
2/3 cup cooked kidney beans (4 ounces)
½ teaspoon sugar
½ teaspoon dried oregano
½ teaspoon dried basil
¼ teaspoon garlic powder
Salt to taste

In a blender container, combine all ingredients. Blend until smooth.

Pour mixture into a small saucepan. Heat over medium heat until hot and bubbly.

Serve over cooked pasta or rice.

Each serving provides: 80 Calories, 1 g Fat, 0 mg Cholesterol, 16 g Carbohydrate, 25 mg Sodium, 3 g Fiber, 4 g Protein

Fresh Tomato and Basil Sauce

I like to make this delicately spiced sauce in the summer when fresh, ripe tomatoes are sweet and plentiful. The addition of fresh basil definitely adds a gourmet touch.

Makes 8 servings

8 cups chopped, peeled, very ripe tomatoes (about 5 pounds)
1 tablespoon plus 1 teaspoon olive oil
1 cup chopped onions
2 cloves garlic, minced
3 tablespoons finely chopped fresh basil leaves *or* 1 tablespoon dried basil
1 tablespoon sugar
Salt and pepper to taste
1 6-ounce can tomato paste

Place chopped tomatoes in a colander or strainer for 30 minutes to drain. Press down with a spoon several times to squeeze out excess liquid.

In a medium saucepan, heat oil over medium heat. Add onions and garlic and cook until onions are tender, 5 to 10 minutes.

Add tomatoes, basil, sugar, salt and pepper to saucepan and bring to a boil.

Reduce heat to low and simmer, uncovered, 1 hour.

Stir in tomato paste and continue to cook 10 more minutes.

Serve over your favorite shape of pasta.

Each serving provides: 102 Calories, 3 g Fat, 0 mg Cholesterol, 19 g Carbohydrate, 189 mg Sodium, 1 g Fiber, 3 g Protein

Sicilian Lentil Pasta Sauce

Thick and rich with mushrooms, lentils and spices, this sauce is high in protein and fiber as well as in flavor. If you like a thick pasta sauce, this is it.

Makes 8 servings

2 teaspoons olive oil
1 cup chopped onions
2 cups sliced mushrooms
3 cloves garlic, finely chopped
1 cup lentils, uncooked (7½ ounces)
3 cups water
2 8-ounce cans salt-free (or regular) tomato sauce
1 6-ounce can tomato paste
1½ teaspoons sugar
½ cup water

Heat oil in a large saucepan over medium heat. Add onions, mushrooms and garlic. Cook until tender, about 5 minutes.

Add lentils and water. Bring to a boil, stirring occasionally. Reduce heat to low, cover and cook 40 minutes.

Add remaining ingredients and bring to a boil. Cover and cook 20 minutes, stirring occasionally. Add more water if a thinner sauce is desired.

Serve over pasta or rice.

Each serving provides: 153 Calories, 2 g Fat, 0 mg Cholesterol, 27 g Carbohydrate, 184 mg Sodium, 3 g Fiber, 10 g Protein

Creamy Cheese Sauce

No one will guess that the secret to the thick, creamy texture of this cheesy sauce is a can of beans! It has so many uses. In addition to topping pasta with it, try it on steamed vegetables or baked potatoes, or use it as a dip for vegetables or crackers. *Makes 4 servings*

- 1 1-pound can Great Northern beans, rinsed and drained (This will yield 10 ounces of beans.)
- 1 cup skim milk
- 4 ounces shredded lowfat Cheddar cheese (1 cup)
- 1 tablespoon minced onion flakes
- ½ teaspoon dry mustard
- 1/8 teaspoon garlic powder
- 1/8 teaspoon pepper
- Salt to taste

In a blender container, combine all ingredients. Blend until smooth. Pour into a small saucepan. Heat over medium-low heat, stirring, until mixture just begins to boil. Serve over pasta.

Each serving provides: 187 Calories, 6 g Fat, 21 mg Cholesterol, 17 g Carbohydrate, 440 mg Sodium, 4 g Fiber, 15 g Protein

Red Pepper Pasta Sauce

Sweet red peppers and onions make a wonderfully unique gourmet pasta sauce. It's also delicious over steamed vegetables or rice, or on a baked potato. *Makes 6 servings*

- 1 tablespoon olive oil
- 1 cup chopped onions
- 1 teaspoon dried basil
- Salt and pepper to taste
- 6 cups chopped sweet red peppers
- 2 cloves garlic, finely chopped
- 1 teaspoon dried oregano

Heat oil in a large nonstick skillet over medium heat.

Add all ingredients and cook until peppers are very tender, about 25 minutes. Stir frequently while cooking.

Spoon mixture into a blender container. Blend until smooth. Add a few teaspoons of water if necessary for blending, or more if a thinner sauce is desired.

Spoon over cooked pasta.

Each serving provides: 57 Calories, 3 g Fat, 0 mg Cholesterol, 8 g Carbohydrate, 4 mg Sodium, 1 g Fiber, 1 g Protein

Tofu

Tofu is made from soy beans in much the same way that cheese is made from milk. It actually looks a lot like cheese, and comes in the shape of white blocks. Tofu is high in protein, low in saturated fat, low in sodium and contains no cholesterol. Another advantage of tofu is its blandness, which allows it to take on the flavor of whatever it is combined with. These qualities, in addition to the fact that tofu is very inexpensive, make it an ideal entrée ingredient.

Tofu can be sliced and stir-fried, or blended and used in dips and puddings. You can even substitute a 3-ounce piece of tofu, blended until smooth, for 1 egg or for 2 egg whites, in breads, cakes and muffins.

Look for tofu in the produce section of any large grocery store, where it is usually available as either soft, medium or firm. Tofu is usually packed in water and should be kept refrigerated in a covered container. Change the water daily to keep the tofu fresh for one week.

Be sure to check for other delicious uses for tofu in the chapters Appetizers, Dips and Spreads, Breakfast Ideas, and Desserts, and in the preceding section, Pasta and Pasta Sauces.

Tofu Croquettes with Currant Spice Sauce

Pretty as a picture, these easy croquettes make a great company or holiday dish. Add your favorite potato or some steamed brown and wild rice and a green vegetable, and what a meal!

Makes 4 servings

1 tablespoon plus 1 teaspoon canola oil
½ cup chopped onions
½ cup chopped celery
2 cloves garlic, finely chopped
1 pound medium tofu, thickly sliced and drained between towels
2 egg whites
1¼ teaspoons poultry seasoning
½ teaspoon salt
1/8 teaspoon pepper
2 slices whole wheat bread (1 ounce slices), crumbled
2 teaspoons wheat germ
Paprika if desired

Currant-Spice Sauce:

½ cup water
½ cup orange juice
3 tablespoons currant jelly
1 tablespoon plus 2 teaspoon cornstarch
1/8 teaspoon ground allspice

Preheat oven to 350°.

Lightly oil a baking sheet or spray with a nonstick cooking spray.

Heat oil in a small nonstick skillet over medium heat. Add onions, celery, and garlic. Cook 10 minutes, until onions are tender and start to brown. Remove from heat.

Place tofu in a large bowl and mash with a fork. Stir in egg whites and spices. Mix well. Add onion mixture and crumbled bread, mixing well.

Divide mixture evenly and shape into 4 balls. Place on prepared baking sheet. Flatten balls slightly so that you have 4 rounded mounds.

Sprinkle croquettes with wheat germ and paprika.

Bake 35 minutes.

When croquettes are almost ready, prepare sauce:

Combine sauce ingredients in a small saucepan. Stir to dissolve cornstarch.

Cook over medium heat, stirring, until mixture comes to a boil. Continue to cook 2 more minutes, stirring.

Remove from heat.
Serve with croquettes.

For Croquettes:
Each serving provides: 186 Calories, 11 g Fat, 0 mg Cholesterol, 12 g Carbohydrate, 413 mg Sodium, 2 g Fiber, 13 g Protein

For Currant-Spice Sauce:
Each serving provides: 63 Calories, 0 g Fat, 0 mg Cholesterol, 16 g Carbohydrate, 3 mg Sodium, 0 g Fiber, 0 g Protein

Shanghai Grilled Tofu

Whether cooked under the broiler or on an outside grill, these tender, marinated tofu slices are sure to please. Serve them over rice or as a delicious sandwich filling. The leftovers even make great cold sandwiches.

Makes 4 servings

2 tablespoons canola oil
3 tablespoons reduced-sodium (or regular) soy sauce
2 tablespoons plus 2 teaspoons wine vinegar
2/3 cup water
2 teaspoons dried oregano
¼ teaspoon garlic powder
1/8 teaspoon pepper
2 teaspoons sugar
1 pound medium or firm tofu, sliced ½ inch thick

In a shallow bowl or baking pan, combine all ingredients, ***except*** tofu. Mix well.

Add tofu, cover, and marinate in the refrigerator 4 to 5 hours. Turn tofu slices several times while marinating.

Preheat broiler.

Lightly oil a shallow baking pan or spray with a nonstick cooking spray.

Remove tofu slices from marinade and place on prepared pan in a single layer.

Broil, turning several times, until desired crispness is reached. (Tofu can also be grilled on a barbecue grill.)

While tofu is cooking, heat marinade in a small saucepan. Serve with tofu.

Each serving provides: 166 Calories, 12 g Fat, 0 mg Cholesterol, 6 g Carbohydrate, 460 mg Sodium, 3 g Fiber, 10 g Protein

Marinated Tofu Kabobs

My daughter, Jennifer, gets rave reviews when she serves these delicious kabobs. Grilled or broiled and served on a bed of brown rice, they're at home at any dinner, whether casual or elegant.

Makes 4 servings

8 pearl onions, peeled
8 medium mushrooms
2 cups fresh pineapple, cut into 1-inch pieces
1 1-pound can small, whole potatoes, drained
1 cup green pepper, cut into 1-inch squares
1 pound firm tofu, cut into 1-inch cubes
8 cherry tomatoes

Marinade:

¼ cup reduced-sodium (or regular) soy sauce
¼ cup dry red wine
¼ cup water
1 teaspoon sesame oil
½ teaspoon dried oregano
¼ teaspoon garlic powder
1/8 teaspoon ground ginger

Place onions, mushrooms, pineapple, potatoes and green pepper in a large plastic bag and set bag in a large bowl. Add tofu. Set cherry tomatoes aside.

In a small bowl, combine all marinade ingredients, mixing well. Pour over ingredients in bag. Marinate in the refrigerator 4 to 5 hours, or longer, turning bag over several times.

To cook:

Thread the marinated ingredients, along with the cherry tomatoes, alternately on 4 skewers. Place on a broiler rack or outdoor grill.

Cook until edges of fruits and vegetables are crisp. Turn several times and baste with marinade while cooking.

Each serving provides: 312 Calories, 12 g Fat, 0 mg Cholesterol, 34 g Carbohydrate, 623 mg Sodium, 4 g Fiber, 22 g Protein

Barbecue Tofu

This deliciously spiced hot entrée also makes great leftover cold sandwiches.

Makes 4 servings

1 pound medium or firm tofu
1 8-ounce can salt-free (or regular) tomato sauce
2 teaspoons prepared yellow mustard
2 teaspoons vinegar
2 teaspoons reduced-sodium (or regular) soy sauce
1 tablespoon canola oil
1 tablespoon molasses
2 tablespoons grated onion
1/8 teaspoon garlic powder

Slice tofu into slices 1 inch thick. Press slices between 2 pans for 1 hour to squeeze the water out and compress the tofu. (Place slices between 2 baking sheets, top them with something heavy, such as 8 one-pound cans of food or a pile of cookbooks. Prop up one end so the water can drain into the lower end of the pan.)

While tofu is draining, combine remaining ingredients. Spoon about 1/3 of the mixture into the bottom of a 6 x 10-inch shallow baking pan that has been lightly oiled or sprayed with a nonstick cooking spray.

Preheat oven to 350°.

Place pressed tofu on sauce and top with remaining sauce.

Bake, uncovered, 1 hour.

Each serving provides: 155 Calories, 9 g Fat, 0 mg Cholesterol, 11 g Carbohydrate, 154 mg Sodium, 3 g Fiber, 10 g Protein

Broccoli Tofu Divan

This deliciously spiced hot entrée also makes great leftover cold sandwiches.

Makes 4 servings

1 10-oz package frozen broccoli spears
12 oz medium or firm tofu, cut into ½ inch cubes
3 tablespoons all-purpose flour
2 cups skim milk
2 tablespoons butter
1 oz shredded lowfat Cheddar cheese (¼ cup)
2 teaspoons prepared mustard
1 tablespoon minced onion flakes
1 tablespoon sherry
Salt and pepper to taste
3 tablespoons wheat germ (3/4 ounce)
1 tablespoon grated Parmesan cheese

Preheat oven to 375°.

Lightly oil a 9-inch pie pan or spray with a nonstick cooking spray.

Cook broccoli according to package directions. Drain well. Cut into 2 to 3 inch pieces and arrange in prepared pan.

Place tofu between towels and gently squeeze out the excess water. Place tofu on top of broccoli.

Place flour in a small bowl and add a few tablespoons of milk, stirring to form a paste. Gradually add remaining milk, stirring.

Melt butter in a small saucepan over medium heat. Add milk mixture. Cook, stirring constantly, until mixture comes to a full boil. Remove from heat and stir in Cheddar cheese, mustard, onion flakes, sherry, salt, and pepper. Spoon sauce evenly over tofu and broccoli.

Combine wheat germ and Parmesan cheese and sprinkle over top.

Bake, uncovered, 25 minutes. Let stand 5 minutes before serving.

Each serving provides: 255 Calories, 13 g Fat, 8 mg Cholesterol, 20 g Carbohydrate, 255 mg Sodium, 3 g Fiber, 18 g Protein

El Paso Tofu and Macaroni

If you're a newcomer to tofu, this is a good place to start, especially if you like spicy food.

Makes 6 servings

1	tablespoon canola oil	1 cup chopped onions
2	cloves garlic, chopped	1 4-oz can chopped green chilies, drained
1	6-ounce can tomato paste	1½ cups water
½	teaspoon dried oregano	½ teaspoon chili powder
¼	teaspoon ground cumin	3 cups cooked elbow macaroni

9 ounces medium tofu, cut into ½ inch cubes, drained well between towels
3 ounces shredded lowfat Cheddar cheese (3/4 cup)

Preheat oven to 350°.

Lightly oil an 8-inch square baking pan or spray with a nonstick cooking spray.

Heat oil in a medium-size nonstick skillet over medium heat. Add onions and garlic. Cook, stirring frequently, 5 to 10 minutes, until onions are tender. Stir in chilies, tomato paste, water, and spices. Bring mixture to a boil, stirring frequently.

Remove from heat.

Place ***half*** of the macaroni in bottom of prepared pan. Top with ***half*** of the tofu and sprinkle with ***half*** of the cheese. Spread ***half*** of the sauce over mixture.

Repeat layers using remaining macaroni, tofu, and cheese—ending with sauce spread evenly over the top.

Cover and bake 45 minutes.

Each serving provides: 236 Calories, 8 g Fat, 10 mg Cholesterol, 30 g Carbohydrate, 446 mg Sodium, 2 g Fiber, 12 g Protein

Tofu and Snow Peas

Marinated tofu with a divine blend of Oriental flavors makes this colorful dish a favorite in my house. *Makes 2 servings*

- 12 ounces medium or firm tofu, cut into 1-inch cubes
- 3 tablespoons reduced-sodium (or regular) soy sauce
- 1 tablespoon sherry
- 1 teaspoon sugar
- ½ teaspoon garlic powder
- 2 teaspoons sesame oil
- ½ pound snow pea pods (about 2 cups) (Trim ends and remove strings.)
- ¼ teaspoon ground ginger
- ¼ cup water
- 1 tablespoon cornstarch

Place tofu cubes in a plastic bag and set bag in a small bowl. Combine soy sauce, sherry, sugar, ginger, garlic powder, and water and pour into bag with tofu. Marinate in the refrigerator 4 to 5 hours, turning bag over occasionally so that all pieces of tofu absorb the marinade.

At cooking time:

Heat oil in a large nonstick skillet over medium-high heat. Remove tofu from bag, reserving marinade. Place tofu in skillet. Cook, turning tofu so that it browns lightly on all sides.

Pour marinade into small bowl and add cornstarch, stirring until dissolved.

When tofu is browned, add snow peas and marinade to skillet. Cook 1 minute, stirring constantly.

Each serving provides: 269 Calories, 13 g Fat, 0 mg Cholesterol, 21 g Carbohydrate, 918 mg Sodium, 3 g Fiber, 18 g Protein

Indonesian Tofu with Peanut Butter

These peanut butter-coated tofu slices are a real favorite of ours. Add some stir-fried vegetables and brown rice and you have a real gourmet meal with foreign intrigue.

Makes 4 servings

- 1 pound medium or firm tofu
- ¼ cup creamy-style peanut butter
- ¼ cup water
- 2 tablespoons reduced-sodium (or regular) soy sauce
- 2 teaspoons lemon juice
- 2 teaspoons honey
- ¼ teaspoon garlic powder
- ¼ teaspoon ground ginger
- 1/8 teaspoon pepper
- 1 tablespoon grated onion

Slice tofu into ½ inch slices. Drain between layers of towels. Place tofu in a single layer in a 7 x 11-inch baking pan.

In a small bowl, combine remaining ingredients. Mix with a fork or wire whisk until well blended. Spread mixture evenly over tofu. Cover and marinate in the refrigerator 5 hours or longer.

Remove tofu from refrigerator and let stand at room temperature 30 minutes.

Preheat oven to 350°.

Bake tofu, uncovered, 15 minutes. Then place under broiler and broil until nicely browned.

Each serving provides: 204 Calories, 13 g Fat, 0 mg Cholesterol, 9 g Carbohydrate, 371 mg Sodium, 4 g Fiber, 14 g Protein

Tofu Sukiyaki

A favorite in Japan, this delicious dish is usually served over rice or noodles. The important thing to remember when making it is to have everything cut and lined up before you start.

Makes 6 servings

Sauce:

½ cup water	¼ cup sherry
2 teaspoons sugar	½ teaspoon garlic powder
½ teaspoon ground ginger	¼ teaspoon pepper

1/3 cup reduced-sodium (or regular) soy sauce
1 teaspoon instant vegetable broth mix (see index for page #)

Vegetables:

12 ounces firm tofu, cut into matchstick-size pieces, drained well on towels
2 cups sliced onions
1 cup sliced celery, ¼ inch thick
1 8-ounce can bamboo shoots, drained
1 8-ounce can sliced water chestnuts, drained
1 cup sliced mushrooms
2 cups bean sprouts
1 cup thinly sliced green onions (green and white parts)
4 cups fresh spinach leaves, torn into large pieces, stem and center vein removed

Combine all sauce ingredients in a small bowl. Mix well.

Preheat a large nonstick skillet or wok over medium-high heat. Add tofu, onions, celery and ½ cup of the sauce. Cook, stirring with a tossing motion, 10 minutes, until onions and celery are tender.

Add bamboo shoots, water chestnuts, and mushrooms. Cook, stirring, 3 minutes.

Add remaining sauce, bean sprouts, green onions and spinach. Cook, stirring, 3 minutes, or until spinach is wilted and thoroughly mixed into vegetables.

Serve over cooked brown rice or noodles.

Each serving provides: 184 Calories, 5 g Fat, 0 mg Cholesterol, 21 g Carbohydrate, 698 mg Sodium, 5 g Fiber, 14 g Protein

Tofu Fajitas

Serve these juicy fajitas plain or topped with salsa.

Makes 6 servings

1 pound firm tofu, cut into matchstick-size pieces
1½ cups onion, thinly sliced
1½ cups green pepper, thinly sliced
1 4-ounce can chopped green chilies, undrained
½ cup orange juice
1 tablespoon olive oil
2 tablespoons vinegar
3 cloves garlic, finely chopped
1 teaspoon ground cumin
1 teaspoon ground coriander
1 teaspoon dried oregano
6 6-inch flour tortillas

Place tofu, onions and green pepper in a 9 x 13-inch baking pan.

In a small bowl, combine remaining ingredients, ***except*** tortillas, mixing well. Pour over tofu mixture.

Cover pan and refrigerate 4 or 5 hours, gently stirring tofu mixture occasionally.

To cook:

Wrap tortillas tightly in aluminum foil and heat in a 350° oven for 10 minutes.

Heat a large nonstick skillet over medium-high heat. Drain tofu mixture (reserving marinade) and place in skillet. Cook, stirring gently, until vegetables are slightly tender. Add marinade, a little at a time, to keep mixture from sticking. (If you prefer a juicy fajita filling, add all of the marinade.)

To serve, spoon tofu filling into the center of heated tortillas, roll, and enjoy.

Each serving provides: 238 Calories, 11 g Fat, 0 mg Cholesterol, 24 g Carbohydrate, 269 mg Sodium, 3 g Fiber, 15 g Protein

Tofu Dinner Loaf

The leftovers of this delicious loaf make great sandwich fare, especially with some ketchup and a slice of onion.

Makes 6 servings

Loaf:

- 1 pound medium tofu, sliced, drained between towels
- 1 cup cooked brown rice
- 2 egg whites
- 1 tablespoon canola oil
- ½ teaspoon ground sage
- ¼ teaspoon dried thyme
- 1/8 teaspoon pepper
- Salt to taste
- 3 tablespoons dry bread crumbs
- ¼ cup very finely chopped onions
- 1 teaspoon dried parsley flakes
- ½ teaspoon dried oregano
- ¼ teaspoon garlic powder

Sauce:

- 1 8-ounce can salt-free (or regular) tomato sauce
- ½ teaspoon dried oregano
- 1/8 teaspoon garlic powder

Preheat oven to 350º.

Lightly oil a 4 x 8-inch loaf pan or spray with cooking spray.

Place tofu in a large bowl and mash well with a fork. Add remaining loaf ingredients, mixing well.

Place mixture in prepared pan. Press in firmly with the back of a spoon. Bake 45 minutes.

While loaf is baking, combine sauce ingredients and heat in a small saucepan. Invert loaf onto a serving plate. Serve with sauce.

Each serving provides: 149 Calories, 7 g Fat, 0 mg Cholesterol, 15 g Carbohydrate, 57 mg Sodium, 3 g Fiber, 9 g Protein

GOOD HEALTH ALERT:

Not all tofu and tortillas are the same. Tofu processed with calcium sulfate and tortillas made from lime-processed corn are good sources of calcium. Be sure to read the fine print on the label to be sure of what you're getting.

Spanish Tofu and Noodles

Any thin noodles will work in this delicately flavored dish, but my favorite type is the spaghetti-like Japanese Soba noodles. They're made with whole grain flour (usually buckwheat) and can be found in health food stores or Oriental groceries. *Makes 4 servings*

2 teaspoons olive oil
3 cloves garlic, finely chopped
1 cup chopped onions
½ cup chopped celery
1 cup chopped green pepper
1 cup sliced mushrooms
12 ounces medium or firm tofu, cut into ½-inch cubes
2 1-pound cans tomatoes, drained and chopped (Reserve liquid.)
1 cup liquid from tomatoes
2 teaspoons paprika
1 bay leaf
1/8 teaspoon saffron
¼ teaspoon pepper
Salt to taste
2 cups cooked very thin noodles or very thin spaghetti

Heat oil in a large nonstick skillet over medium heat. Add garlic, onions, celery, green pepper, mushrooms and tofu. Cook 15 minutes, stirring frequently, being careful not to break up the tofu.

Add tomatoes, the 1 cup of reserved tomato liquid, and spices. Cover. Reduce heat to low, and simmer 20 minutes.

Remove and discard bay leaf.

Add noodles. Toss until well mixed. Serve hot.

Each serving provides: 238 Calories, 7 g Fat, 0 mg Cholesterol, 34 g Carbohydrate, 401 mg Sodium, 4 g Fiber, 13 g Protein

GOOD HEALTH ALERT:

Walk to lose weight. A 200-pound person who starts walking a mile and a half a day and keeps on eating the same number of daily calories will lose, on average, 14 pounds in a year.

Peach-Glazed Tofu

This slightly sweet, very delicious dish will add a new dimension to your tofu repertoire. Serve it alongside a baked potato and add a green vegetable for a meal you'll love. *Makes 4 servings*

¼ cup plus 2 tablespoons reduced-calorie sweet and spicy French dressing (16 calories per tablespoon)
3 tablespoons peach jam
3 tablespoons very finely chopped onions

Cut tofu into slices 1-inch thick. Press slices between 2 pans for 1 hour to squeeze the water out and compress the tofu. (Place slices between 2 baking sheets, top them with something heavy, such as 8 one-pound cans of food or a pile of cookbooks. Prop up one end so the water can drain into the lower end of the pan.)

Preheat oven to 350º.

Lightly oil a 6 x 10-inch shallow baking pan, or spray with a nonstick cooking spray.

Cut pressed tofu into 1-inch cubes. Place in prepared pan.

Combine remaining ingredients and mix well. Spoon over tofu cubes.

Bake, uncovered, 45 minutes.

Place pan under the broiler and broil 2 to 3 minutes, until crisp and bubbly.

Each serving provides: 154 Calories, 5 g Fat, 0 mg Cholesterol, 18 g Carbohydrate, 197 mg Sodium, 3 g Fiber, 9 g Protein

Chocolate Raspberry Tofu Trifle

I've added cocoa to tofu and layered it with graham crackers and raspberry jam. The result is a dessert that's quick, easy, delicious, and healthy.

Makes 8 servings

1½ pounds soft tofu
¼ cup cocoa (unsweetened)
½ cup confectioners sugar
1½ teaspoons vanilla extract
¼ teaspoon almond extract
¼ cup reduced-sugar raspberry jam or fruit-only raspberry jam
8 2-½ x 5-inch graham crackers
Sliced almonds for garnish (optional)

Have a 6 x 10-inch pan ready.

Cut tofu into chunks and place half of the chunks in a blender container. Blend until smooth. Spoon into a medium bowl and repeat with remaining tofu. Add sugar, cocoa, and extracts. Mix well.

Spread jam on graham crackers, using 1-½ teaspoons on each cracker. Place 4 of the crackers in the bottom of prepared pan, jam side up. Spread ***half*** of the tofu mixture evenly over crackers. Top with remaining graham crackers and end with remaining tofu. Garnish with sliced almonds, if desired.

Cover and chill thoroughly. Serve cold.

Each serving provides: 151 Calories, 4 g Fat, 0 mg Cholesterol, 25 g Carbohydrate, 101 mg Sodium, 2 g Fiber, 6 g Protein

Howard's Cheesy Spinach Tofu Rounds

Attention Tofu and cheese lovers! This one's for you. A meal I look forward to enjoying (the patties are good alone but sitting in spaghetti sauce is a vegetarian delight).

Makes 8 servings

1 14 oz. package of Extra Firm Tofu
3/4 cup of shredded mozzarella cheese
½ cup of shredded Parmesan cheese
1 32 oz. jar of spaghetti sauce
1 9 oz. package of frozen spinach
4- 6 oz. goat cheese crumbles
1 package of breadcrumbs

Open the tofu and drain.

In a large mixing bowl mix the tofu and cheeses by hand.

Thaw the spinach in the microwave and squeeze out most of the water. Add the spinach to the tofu/cheese mixture and mix well. Add a small amount of bread crumbs into the mixture. Using a measuring cup, scoop out about 1/3 cup of the mixture and form into flat rounds.

Lightly coat the rounds with breadcrumbs.

Preheat a griddle to 350° and lightly coat the griddle with olive oil. Place the rounds on the griddle and cook, flipping occasionally, until the rounds are golden brown and the cheese is melting (about 10-12 minutes).

While the rounds are cooking heat the spaghetti sauce and spoon in to pasta bowls. When the rounds are done place them in the bowl on top of the spaghetti sauce. Sprinkle with crushed red pepper flakes and fresh grated Parmesan cheese and serve.

Each serving provides: 152 Calories, 24 g Fat, 42 mg Cholesterol, 39 g Carbohydrate, 949 mg Sodium, 6 g Fiber, 31 g Protein

Etcetera, Etcetera. Etcetera

This rather oddly named section contains all of the entrée recipes that didn't quite fit into any of the other sections. It consists of dishes such as meatless stews, vegetable pizza, vegetable quiche, and some interesting casseroles.

As with my other entrées, my goal has been to make dishes that are both nutritious and taste-tempting with a fat content as low as possible and with lots of high-fiber vegetables, grains, and legumes.

Be sure to check my other chapters for side dishes and salads that are hearty and filling enough to serve as entrées.

Hearty Vegetable Stew

Thick, hearty, and delicious, this stew is one of my family's favorite meals. Just add a salad and your meal is complete.

Makes 6 servings

- 1 tablespoon canola oil
- 2 cloves garlic, minced
- 1 cup water
- 1 bay leaf
- 4 cups mushrooms, cut into quarters
- 1 cup celery, cut into 1-inch thick slices
- 2 cups cooked kidney beans (12 ounces)
- 1 8-ounce can salt-free (or regular) tomato sauce
- 3 medium potatoes (18 ounces total), unpeeled, cut into 1-inch chunks
- 1 1-pound can tomatoes, undrained, coarsely chopped)
- Salt and pepper to taste
- 3 tablespoons all-purpose flour
- ¼ cup water
- ¼ cup red wine
- 1-½ cups sliced onions
- 1 cup carrots, cut into 1-inch thick slices
- 1 teaspoon dried thyme

Heat oil in a large, heavy saucepan over medium heat. Add onions, garlic, carrots, celery and mushrooms. Cook 10 minutes, stirring frequently. Add small amounts of water, if necessary, to prevent sticking.

Add remaining ingredients, ***except*** flour, ¼ cup water and wine. Cover, reduce heat to low, and simmer 30 minutes, or until vegetables are tender. Stir occasionally while cooking.

In a small bowl, gradually stir flour into ¼ cup water until smooth. Add to stew, along with wine. Cook, stirring, 5 more minutes. Remove and discard bay leaf before serving.

Each serving provides: 244 Calories, 3 g Fat, 0 mg Cholesterol, 45 g Carbohydrate, 166 mg Sodium, 4 g Fiber, 10 g Protein

Beans and Vegetables Bourguignonne

The major similarity between this recipe and our original beef version is the thick, rich, wonderfully spiced, tomato-wine sauce. The major difference is that the fat and cholesterol are gone!

Makes 6 servings

1 tablespoon canola oil
2 cloves garlic, finely chopped
2 cups mushrooms, cut into quarters
1 cup pearl onions, peeled
1 cup carrots, sliced ½-inch thick
1 cup celery, sliced ½-inch thick
1 cup turnips, cut into ½-inch chunks
2-¼ cups water
3 medium potatoes (18 ounces total), unpeeled, cut into 3/4-inch chunks
2 1-pound cans butter beans, rinsed and drained (This will yield 20 ounces, or 1-¼ pounds of beans.)
1 6-ounce can tomato paste
½ cup dry red wine
½ teaspoon dried thyme
¼ teaspoon ***each*** salt and pepper
1/16 teaspoon ground allspice
1 bay leaf

Heat oil in a large saucepan over medium heat. Add garlic, mushrooms, onions, carrots, celery, and turnips. Cook 5 minutes, stirring frequently. Add ½ cup of the water, cover and cook 10 minutes.

Add the remaining water and remaining ingredients, mixing well. Bring to a boil, then reduce heat and simmer, covered, 30 to 40 minutes, until vegetables are tender.

Remove and discard bay leaf.

Each serving provides: 241 Calories, 3 g Fat, 0 mg Cholesterol, 46 g Carbohydrate, 587 mg Sodium, 5 g Fiber, 9 g Protein

Split Pea and Vegetable Stew

This hearty stew makes a great Sunday night supper. Add a slice of crusty rye bread and dig in! *Makes 6 servings*

1 tablespoon canola oil
2 cloves garlic, finely chopped
2 cups sliced mushrooms
1 cup chopped onions
1 cup chopped carrots, in ½ inch pieces
½ cup chopped celery, in ½ inch pieces
2 cups water
1 cup split peas, uncooked (7½ ounces)
1 1-pound can tomatoes, chopped, undrained
3 medium potatoes (18 ounces total), unpeeled, cut into ½ inch chunks
1 teaspoon dried basil
1 bay leaf
½ teaspoon dried marjoram
¼ teaspoon dried thyme
¼ teaspoon ground cumin
Salt and pepper to taste

Heat oil in a large saucepan over medium heat. Add garlic, mushrooms, onions, carrots and celery. Cook 10 minutes, stirring frequently.

Add remaining ingredients. Bring mixture to a boil, stirring occasionally. Reduce heat to low, cover and simmer 1¼ hours.

Remove and discard bay leaf before serving.

Each serving provides: 252 Calories, 3 g Fat, 0 mg Cholesterol, 46 g Carbohydrate, 152 mg Sodium, 3 g Fiber, 12 g Protein

Turkish Stew

I have Sabrina to thank for sharing this wonderful idea with me. For a really authentic touch, serve this uniquely spiced stew over cooked couscous, add a salad topped with Tahini Dressing (see index for page #) and pass a basket of pita breads. *Makes 6 servings*

3 medium sweet potatoes (18 ounces total), peeled, cut into 1-inch chunks
2½ cups butternut squash, peeled, cut into 1-inch chunks (about a 1¼ pound squash)
1½ cups carrots, cut into ½ inch slices
1½ cups chopped onions
1 1-pound can chickpeas, rinsed and drained
(This will yield 10 ounces of chickpeas.)
1-2/3 cups water
1½ teaspoons chili powder

1½ teaspoons ground coriander
¼ teaspoon ground nutmeg
1/16 teaspoon saffron
1/16 teaspoon ground cloves

Combine all ingredients in a large saucepan. Bring to a boil over medium heat. Reduce heat to low, cover, and simmer 1 hour, or until vegetables are tender. Stir occasionally while cooking.

Each serving provides: 186 Calories, 2 g Fat, 0 mg Cholesterol, 39 g Carbohydrate, 121 mg Sodium, 4 g Fiber, 6 g Protein

Southwest Potato Lentil Stew

This hearty stew is thick with potatoes and lentils and spiced with chili powder. It goes great with a tossed salad and a piece of crusty bread, and makes a handy dinner for TV football games.

Makes 4 servings

½ cup lentils, uncooked (3-3/4 ounces)
2 medium potatoes (12 ounces total), unpeeled, cut into ½ inch pieces
1 cup chopped carrots
1 cup chopped onions
½ cup chopped celery
¼ cup chopped celery leaves
2 cloves garlic, finely chopped
2 cups tomato juice
3/4 cup water
2 teaspoons chili powder (or more if you're a chili lover)
½ teaspoon dried basil
½ teaspoon dried oregano
Salt to taste

In a large saucepan, combine all ingredients, mixing well. Bring to a boil over medium heat. Reduce heat to low, cover and simmer 40 to 45 minutes, until vegetables are tender. Stir several times while cooking and add small amounts of water if a thinner stew is desired.

Each serving provides: 210 Calories, 1 g Fat, 0 mg Cholesterol, 42 g Carbohydrate, 487 mg Sodium, 4 g Fiber, 11 g Protein

Very Veggie Enchiladas

These corn tortillas are stuffed with mushrooms, corn and beans and topped with a delectable sauce. They make a wonderful, filling, meatless dinner.

Makes 8 servings

Sauce:

2 teaspoons canola oil
¼ cup very finely chopped onions
¼ cup very finely chopped green pepper
3 cloves garlic, finely chopped
2 8-ounce cans salt-free (or regular) tomato sauce
1 teaspoon vinegar
½ teaspoon dried oregano
½ teaspoon ground cumin
Salt and pepper to taste

Enchiladas:

2 teaspoons canola oil
1 cup chopped onions
2 cloves garlic, chopped
1 1-pound can kidney beans, rinsed and drained (This will yield 10 ounces of beans.)
1 cup canned or frozen corn, drained
1 4-ounce can mushroom pieces, drained
8 corn tortillas
3 ounces shredded lowfat Cheddar cheese (3/4 cup)

Prepare sauce:

Heat oil in a small saucepan over medium heat. Add onions, green pepper and garlic. Cook, stirring frequently, until tender, about 5 minutes.

Stir in remaining sauce ingredients and remove from heat.

Prepare enchiladas:

Heat oil in a large nonstick skillet over medium heat. Add onions and garlic. Cook, stirring frequently, until onions are tender, about 5 minutes.

Place kidney beans in a bowl and mash slightly with a fork. Add to skillet along with corn and mushrooms. Add ½ cup of the sauce and mix well.

To assemble:

Preheat oven to 350°.

Lightly oil a 6 x 10-inch baking pan or spray with a nonstick cooking spray.

To soften tortillas, moisten them lightly on both sides with wet fingers. Stack them on a piece of aluminum foil, wrap them tightly, and bake 10 minutes.

Spread ½ cup of sauce in the bottom of prepared pan.

Spoon 1/3 cup of bean mixture onto each tortilla in a strip across the center. Roll up tightly and place tortillas, seam side down, on top of sauce in pan.

Spoon remaining sauce evenly over tortillas.

Cover tightly and bake 30 minutes.

Uncover, sprinkle evenly with cheese and return to oven for 5 minutes.

Serve hot.

Each serving provides: 214 Calories, 6 g Fat, 8 mg Cholesterol, 31 g Carbohydrate, 248 mg Sodium, 5 g Fiber, 10 g Protein

New England Dinner Au Gratin

Thanks to my friend, Betty, for this wonderful idea. Served over cooked brown rice, this filling dish tastes like a cross between a stir-fry and a stew. Or, if you prefer, spoon it into bowls and serve with thick, crusty rye bread. The flavor is wonderful.

Makes 6 servings

- 6 cups cabbage, coarsely chopped
- 3 medium potatoes (18 ounces total), unpeeled, cut into 1-inch cubes
- 2 cups carrots sliced ½ inch thick
- 1½ cups leeks, white part only, sliced ½ inch thick
- 1 teaspoon caraway seeds
- 2 teaspoons paprika
- ½ teaspoon garlic powder
- ¼ teaspoon salt
- ¼ teaspoon pepper
- 2 cups water
- 6 ounces shredded lowfat Cheddar cheese (1½ cups)

Place cabbage, potatoes, carrots and leeks in a 4-quart Dutch oven. Sprinkle spices over vegetables and mix well. Add water.

Bring mixture to a boil over medium heat, stirring occasionally. Cover, reduce heat to low, and simmer 30 minutes.

Preheat oven to 350°.

Spread cheese evenly over cooked vegetables. Place in oven and bake, uncovered, 25 minutes.

Serve as is or spoon over any cooked grain.

Each serving provides: 212 Calories, 6 g Fat, 20 mg Cholesterol, 28 g Carbohydrate, 328 mg Sodium, 4 g Fiber, 11 g Protein

Stuffed Cabbage Rolls

You'll love my slightly sweet, slightly sour version of an old favorite. I serve it over brown rice and, when I can, I cook it a day ahead. It tastes even better the next day.

Makes 6 servings

1 medium head of cabbage

Sauce:

2 15-ounce cans salt-free (or regular) tomato sauce
¼ cup lemon juice
3 tablespoons firmly packed brown sugar
1 cup chopped onions
1 cup chopped cabbage

Filling:

1½ cups finely shredded carrots
1½ cups finely shredded, unpeeled potatoes (9 ounces)
2 tablespoons lemon juice
1 tablespoon canola oil
¼ cup plus 2 tablespoons whole wheat flour
½ cup raisins
1 small apple, unpeeled, finely shredded
½ teaspoon ground cinnamon
¼ teaspoon ground ginger
Salt and pepper to taste

Carefully remove 12 outside leaves from head of cabbage. Chop 1 cup of the remaining cabbage to use in the sauce and reserve remaining cabbage for another use. Place whole cabbage leaves in a large pot of boiling water and boil 5 minutes.

Remove from water, place in a colander, and run under cold water for a few minutes. Drain.

To prepare sauce:

Combine all sauce ingredients in a small saucepan. Bring to a boil over medium heat. Reduce heat to low, cover, and simmer 15 minutes.

To prepare filling:

In a large bowl, combine all filling ingredients. Add 1/3 cup of the sauce. Mix well.

To assemble:

Preheat oven to 350º.

Lightly oil a 9 x 13-inch baking pan or spray with a nonstick cooking spray.

Place ¼ cup of filling near the base of each cabbage leaf.
Roll tightly, folding in sides as you roll.
Place rolls, seam side down, in prepared pan.
Spoon remaining sauce evenly over rolls.
Cover tightly and bake 1 hour.

Each serving provides: 245 Calories, 3 g Fat, 0 mg Cholesterol, 53 g Carbohydrate, 67 mg Sodium, 3 g Fiber, 6 g Protein

Bulgur Chili

Bulgur (cracked wheat) is a nutritious grain that cooks quickly and is available in most grocery stores. In this chili recipe, it adds a texture surprisingly like ground beef but without the fat and cholesterol.

Makes 4 servings

1 tablespoon plus 1 teaspoon olive oil
2 cloves garlic, chopped
1 cup chopped onions
1 cup chopped green pepper
2 cups sliced mushrooms
1 1-pound can kidney beans rinsed and drained (This will yield 10 ounces of beans.)
1 8-ounce can salt-free (or regular) tomato sauce
1 1-pound can tomatoes, chopped, undrained
½ cup bulgur, uncooked (3 ounces)
½ cup water
1 teaspoon dried oregano
1 teaspoon ground cumin
1 teaspoon chili powder

Heat oil in a large nonstick skillet over medium heat. Add garlic, onions, green pepper and mushrooms.
Cook 10 minutes, or until vegetables are tender, stirring occasionally.
Add remaining ingredients.
Reduce heat to low, cover, and cook 15 minutes.
Stir several times while cooking.

Each serving provides: 274 Calories, 7 g Fat, 0 mg Cholesterol, 46 g Carbohydrate, 358 mg Sodium, 4 g Fiber, 12 g Protein

Super Quick Chili

Calling students: this is so easy you can make it in a dorm room. I really love it. Get a few extra meals or invite a favorite friend to eat with you.

Makes 6 servings

2 1-pound cans stewed tomatoes
2 1-pound cans kidney beans, rinsed and drained
(This will yield 1-¼ pounds of beans.)
1 1-pound can corn, drained
1 6-ounce can tomato paste
3/4 cup jarred mild picante sauce (or hot picante sauce, if you dare!)
½ teaspoon chili powder
¼ teaspoon ground cumin
1/8 teaspoon cayenne pepper (optional)

Combine all ingredients in a large saucepan. Cook over medium heat until hot and bubbly.

Serve in bowls with crushed crackers or over rice.

Each serving provides: 223 Calories, 2 g Fat, 0 mg Cholesterol, 44 g Carbohydrate, 1,000 mg Sodium, 3 g Fiber, 12 g Protein

Mexican Pot Pie

Lots of vegetables and Mexican flavor with a corn bread crust: here's a hearty family meal bound to please.

Makes 6 servings

Filling:
1 tablespoon canola oil
2 cloves garlic, finely chopped
1 cup chopped onions
1 cup chopped green pepper
½ cup thinly sliced celery
½ cup thinly sliced carrots
1 10-ounce package frozen corn, thawed slightly
2 cups canned kidney beans, rinsed and drained (12 ounces)
1½ teaspoons ground cumin
1½ teaspoons chili powder
1 teaspoon dried oregano
2 8-ounce cans salt-free (or regular) tomato sauce
1 tablespoon cornstarch

Corn bread crust:

3/4 cup plus 2 tablespoons yellow cornmeal (4-½ ounces)
¼ cup plus 2 tablespoons whole wheat flour
1 teaspoon baking powder
1 cup water
1 tablespoon plus 1 teaspoon vegetable oil
1 4-ounce can green chilies, drained

Preheat oven to 350°.

Lightly oil a 9 x 13 inch baking pan or spray with a nonstick cooking spray.

Heat 1 tablespoon of vegetable oil in a large nonstick skillet over medium heat. Add garlic, onions, green pepper, celery, carrots, and corn.

Cover and cook until vegetables are tender, 10 to 15 minutes.

Stir occasionally and add a few tablespoons of water, if necessary, to prevent sticking.

Add remaining filling ingredients, stirring the cornstarch into the tomato sauce before adding.

Bring mixture to a boil.

Spoon into prepared baking pan.

To prepare crust:

In a small bowl, combine cornmeal, flour and baking powder, mixing well.

Combine water, oil, and chilies and stir into dry mixture, stirring just until all ingredients are moistened.

Drop by tablespoonfuls onto filling.

Spread mixture evenly with a spoon.

Bake, uncovered, 30 minutes.

Each serving provides: 321 Calories, 8 g Fat, 0 mg Cholesterol, 56 g Carbohydrate, 343 mg Sodium, 5 g Fiber, 11 g Protein

GOOD HEALTH ALERT:

The nutrients of most concern to those who eat no animal foods (including meat, fish, fowl, eggs and dairy products) are iron, calcium, zinc and vitamin B12. With some planning, however, these nutrients can be obtained in adequate amounts.

Skillet Pinto Pot Pie

This delicious and hearty home-style meal goes from burner, to oven, to table—all in one skillet.

Makes 6 servings

Filling:

1 tablespoon canola oil
2 cups sliced mushrooms
1 cup chopped onions
1 cup chopped sweet red pepper
1 teaspoon vegetable broth mix (see index for page #)
1 teaspoon dried oregano
¼ teaspoon dried rosemary, crumbled
¼ teaspoon salt
¼ teaspoon pepper
1 1-pound package frozen mixed broccoli, cauliflower, and carrots
2 1-pound cans pinto beans, rinsed and drained
(This will yield 20 ounces, or 1¼ pounds, of beans.)
2 tablespoons cornstarch
¼ cup water
2 teaspoons Dijon mustard
1½ cups evaporated skim milk

Biscuit topper:

½ cup all-purpose flour
½ cup plus 2 tablespoons whole wheat flour
2 teaspoons baking powder
1 teaspoon poppy seeds
1 teaspoon paprika
1/8 teaspoon salt
1/8 teaspoon garlic powder
2 tablespoons butter
½ cup skim milk

To prepare filling:

Heat oil in a 10-inch cast iron skillet over medium heat.

Add mushrooms, onions, red pepper, broth mix, and spices. Cook, stirring frequently, 5 minutes, or until vegetables are tender.

Add frozen vegetables and pinto beans. Cook, stirring frequently, 10 minutes.

In a small bowl, combine cornstarch, water, and mustard. Mix until cornstarch is dissolved. Add milk, mixing well. Pour milk mixture into skillet. Bring to a full boil.

Cook, stirring, 5 minutes.

Remove from heat.

Preheat oven to 400°.

To prepare biscuit topper:

In a large bowl, combine both flours, baking powder, poppy seeds and spices. Mix well.

Add butter. Mix with a fork or pastry blender until mixture resembles coarse crumbs. Add milk. Stir until dry ingredients are moistened.

With your hands, work dough into a ball. (Add a small amount of flour if dough is sticky.) Place dough between 2 pieces of waxed paper. Roll into a 10-inch circle. Remove 1 piece of waxed paper and invert dough onto skillet, covering vegetables.

Carefully remove remaining paper.

Prick top of dough about 8 times with a fork.

Bake 12 minutes.

Let stand 5 minutes before serving.

Each serving provides: 347 Calories, 8 g Fat, 3 mg Cholesterol, 53 g Carbohydrate, 866 mg Sodium, 5 g Fiber, 17 g Protein

GOOD HEALTH ALERT:

While sodium is associated with increasing blood pressure, nutrients that may help to lower it include potassium and magnesium.

Italian Polenta

Italian spiced cornmeal, topped with tomato sauce and mozzarella cheese, makes an easy and nutritious Italian dinner.

Makes 6 servings

Polenta:
3 cups water
1 cup yellow cornmeal (6 ounces)
¼ teaspoon salt
¼ cup finely chopped green onions (green part only)
1/8 teaspoon garlic powder

Sauce:
1 8-ounce can salt-free (or regular) tomato sauce
¼ teaspoon ***each*** dried oregano and dried basil
1/8 teaspoon garlic powder

Topping:
2 ounces shredded part-skim mozzarella cheese (3/4 cup)

Lightly oil an 8-inch square baking pan or spray with a nonstick cooking spray.

Bring 2 cups of the water to a boil in a small saucepan over medium heat. Place cornmeal and salt in a small bowl and gradually stir in remaining water. Mix well and stir into boiling water. Reduce heat to low and cook 15 minutes, stirring frequently, until mixture is very thick. Remove from heat and stir in onions and 1/8 teaspoon garlic powder.

Spread mixture in pan, cover, and chill 5 to 6 hours.

Remove polenta from refrigerator ½ hour before baking.

Preheat oven to 400°.

Bake polenta 15 minutes. While polenta is baking, prepare sauce by combining all sauce ingredients in a small bowl.

Remove polenta from oven and spread sauce over top. Sprinkle evenly with cheese.

Return to oven and bake 15 minutes longer.

Each serving provides: 156 Calories, 3 g Fat, 8 mg Cholesterol, 26 g Carbohydrate, 165 mg Sodium, 3 g Fiber, 6 g Protein

Pizza with The Works

You can make this easy pizza at home in less time than it takes to run out and buy one. It's so much lower in fat, too!

Makes 4 servings

Crust:

3/4 cup ***each*** whole wheat flour and all-purpose flour
1 teaspoon baking powder
¼ teaspoon salt
3/4 cup plus 1 tablespoon water

Sauce:

1 8-ounce can salt-free (or regular) tomato sauce
¼ teaspoon ***each*** dried oregano and dried basil
1/8 teaspoon garlic powder

Topping:

6 ounces shredded part-skim mozzarella cheese (1½ cups)
¼ cup chopped or thinly sliced onions
1 cup coarsely chopped mushrooms
½ cup chopped green pepper
20 small pitted black olives, sliced (6 tablespoons)

Preheat oven to 400°.

Lightly oil a 12-inch pizza pan, or spray with a nonstick spray.

In a large bowl, combine both types of flour, baking powder, and salt. Mix well.

Add water, mixing until all ingredients are moistened. With your hands, work dough into a ball. Place dough in prepared pan. Press in pan to form a crust, flouring your hands slightly. Bake 10 minutes. Remove pan from oven.

Combine tomato sauce and spices, mixing well. Spread evenly over baked crust, staying ½ inch away from edge of pan.

Sprinkle cheese and then vegetables evenly over sauce.

Bake 10 to 15 minutes, until cheese is melted.

Each serving provides: 318 Calories, 9 g Fat, 25 mg Cholesterol, 43 g Carbohydrate, 566 mg Sodium, 3 g Fiber, 17 g Protein

Veggie Quiche

Unlike the typical quiche made with cream and whole eggs, I use only skim milk and egg whites in mine. I've added lots of vegetables too. This is a truly delectable entrée for lunch or dinner, or a great brunch dish.

Makes 8 servings

Crust:

½ cup all-purpose flour
¼ cup whole wheat flour
¼ teaspoon baking powder
1/8 teaspoon salt
2 tablespoons plus 2 teaspoons butter
3 tablespoons plus 2 teaspoons ice water

Filling:

1 cup broccoli, cut into tiny flowerets
1 cup sliced mushrooms
½ cup sliced green onions
1 cup chopped fresh tomato
¼ teaspoon garlic powder
¼ teaspoon salt
1/8 teaspoon pepper
½ teaspoon dried rosemary, crumbled
4 ounces shredded lowfat Swiss cheese (1 cup)
1-1/3 cups water
2/3 cup nonfat dry milk
6 egg whites
1 teaspoon sherry

Preheat oven to 450°. Have a 9-inch pie pan ready.

To prepare crust:

In a medium bowl, combine both types of flour, baking powder and salt, mixing well. Add butter. Mix with a fork or a pastry blender until mixture resembles coarse crumbs.

Add water. Mix with a fork until dry ingredients are moistened. Work dough into a ball, using your hands. (Add a little more flour if dough is sticky, or a little more water if dough is too dry.) Roll dough between 2 sheets of waxed paper into an 11-inch circle. Remove top sheet of waxed paper and invert crust into prepared pan. Fit crust into pan, leaving an overhang. Carefully remove remaining waxed paper. Bend edges of crust under and flute dough with your fingers or a fork.

Prick the bottom and sides of crust with a fork about 25 times.

Bake 8 minutes.

To prepare filling:

Reduce oven temperature to 350°.

Heat a large nonstick skillet over medium-high heat. Add vegetables and spices. Cook, stirring frequently, until broccoli is tender-crisp, about 5 minutes. Spoon vegetables into prepared crust.

Spread cheese evenly over vegetables.

In a small bowl, combine water, dry milk, egg whites and sherry. Beat with a fork or wire whisk until blended. Pour over cheese and vegetables.

Bake 45 minutes, or until set.

Let stand 5 minutes before serving.

Each serving provides: 165 Calories, 7 g Fat, 11 mg Cholesterol, 15 g Carbohydrate, 260 mg Sodium, 3 g Fiber, 12 g Protein

GOOD HEALTH ALERT:

Foods made from soybeans, a staple of many meatless meals, may have unique health benefits. Recent studies have found lower rates of heart disease and some forms of cancer among those who regularly eat protein foods made from soybeans.

Mexicali Squares

It's a Mexican bean filling atop a corn bread crust. I serve it whenever the entire family is together. They all just smile!

Makes 6 servings

Topping:

1 tablespoon olive oil
1 clove garlic, finely chopped
1 cup chopped onions
1 cup chopped green pepper
1 1-pound can kidney beans, rinsed and drained (This will yield 10 ounces of beans.)
1 8-ounce can salt-free (or regular) tomato sauce
1 teaspoon dried oregano
1 teaspoon ground cumin
1 teaspoon chili powder

Crust:

3/4 cup plus 2 tablespoons yellow cornmeal (4-½ ounces)
1 teaspoon baking powder
2 egg whites
½ cup skim milk
2 tablespoons olive oil
1 cup canned or frozen corn, drained (Thaw corn if frozen.)

Preheat oven to 350°.

Lightly oil an 8-inch square baking pan or spray with a nonstick cooking spray.

To prepare topping:

Heat oil in a large nonstick skillet over medium heat. Add garlic, onions and green pepper. Cook 10 minutes, or until onions are tender and start to brown. Remove from heat and stir in remaining topping ingredients. Set aside.

To prepare crust:

In a small bowl, combine cornmeal and baking powder, mixing well.

In another bowl, combine egg whites, milk and oil. Beat with a fork or wire whisk until blended.

Stir into cornmeal, mixing just until all ingredients are moistened. Stir in corn.

Spread crust mixture evenly in prepared pan. (Mixture will be loose.)

Spoon topping evenly over crust.

Bake, uncovered, 35 minutes.
Let stand 5 minutes, then cut into squares to serve.

Each serving provides: 259 Calories, 8 g Fat, 0 mg Cholesterol, 38 g Carbohydrate, 213 mg Sodium, 4 g Fiber, 10 g Protein

Tortilla Lasagna

If there is such a thing as Mexican lasagna, this is it!

Makes 6 servings

- 3 8-ounce cans salt-free (or regular) tomato sauce
- ¼ cup finely chopped onions
- ½ cup finely chopped green pepper
- 15 small pitted black olives, sliced (¼ cup)
- 1 1-pound can kidney beans or pinto beans, rinsed and drained (This will yield 10 ounces of beans.)
- 1 teaspoon vinegar
- ¼ teaspoon garlic powder
- ½ teaspoon dried oregano
- ½ teaspoon ground cumin
- 6 6-inch corn tortillas, cut into quarters
- 1 cup shredded lowfat Cheddar cheese (4 ounces)

Preheat oven to 375°.

Lightly oil a 7 x 11-inch baking pan or spray with a nonstick cooking spray.

Spread ¼ cup of tomato sauce in the bottom of the prepared pan.

In a large bowl, combine remaining tomato sauce with remaining ingredients, ***except*** tortillas and cheese. Mix well.

Arrange 1/3 of the tortilla sections over sauce in pan. Spread 1 cup of sauce over tortillas. Sprinkle with 1/3 of the cheese.

Repeat with another 1/3 of the tortillas, 1 cup of sauce, and 1/3 of the cheese.

Repeat one more time, using remaining tortilla sections, sauce, and cheese.

Cover and bake 20 minutes. Uncover and continue baking 15 more minutes.

Let stand 5 minutes before serving.

Each serving provides: 235 Calories, 6 g Fat, 13 mg Cholesterol, 32 g Carbohydrate, 359 mg Sodium, 3 g Fiber, 13 g Protein

Spicy Tofu and Fruit

Slow cooking really brings out the spicy flavor and plumps up the fruit in this unusual dish. Serve it over cooked rice, add a side dish of fresh steamed green beans, and enjoy a gourmet delight.

Makes 6 servings

1½ pounds firm tofu, cut into 3/4-inch cubes
½ cup dried apricots, cut into quarters (12 apricot halves)
½ cup pitted prunes, cut into quarters (8 prunes)
¼ cup raisins
½ cup orange juice
¼ cup dry white wine
2 tablespoons wine vinegar
1 tablespoon cornstarch
2 tablespoons sugar
½ teaspoon ground cinnamon
½ teaspoon ground allspice

Place tofu, apricots, prunes and raisins in a large crockpot.
In a small bowl, combine remaining ingredients.
Mix to dissolve cornstarch.
Pour over tofu and fruit.
Cover and cook on low setting 8 hours.
Serve over cooked brown rice or any other grain.

Each serving provides: 273 Calories, 10 g Fat, 0 mg Cholesterol, 33 g Carbohydrate, 20 mg Sodium, 3 g Fiber, 19 g Protein

GOOD HEALTH ALERT:

Dry beans, in addition to being a treasure trove of protein and fiber, are a good source of folate.

Grains

Grains are one of the oldest foods in the history of mankind. While they are traditional in virtually every culture, today's American homemakers tend to ignore these valuable foods. In a society that is geared to a fast pace, many people are used to buying and preparing convenience foods and lean toward quick-cooking, refined grains rather than the healthier whole grains.

What makes a whole grain different from a refined one? The answer is simple – milling. In this process, the bran and the germ are removed, and with them much of the fiber, vitamins, and minerals of the grain. Ironically, in many cases these by-products are then packed in jars and sold back to us for added nutrition!

It is important to read labels and choose breads and cereals that contain whole grains. For example, when buying whole wheat bread, look for bread labels that list 100% whole wheat flour as the first ingredient. Also, choose brown rice over white rice. It's more nutritious and it has a wonderful flavor and texture.

In addition to adding fiber to our meals, whole grains are high in complex carbohydrates. Since carbohydrates actually fuel our bodies and give us energy, grains are a perfect addition to our daily meals. Grains are also low in fat, they're filling, and they're inexpensive.

So, be adventurous. If you haven't tried many different grains, take a trip to the nearest health food store. Many grocery stores are now carrying an expanded line of whole grains. Some examples are millet, couscous, bulgur, whole rye, whole oats, kasha and barley.

You'll find lots of delicious grain recipes in other chapters of this book as well. Be sure to check Soups, Salads and Salad Dressings, Breakfast Ideas, Entrées, Breads and Muffins and Desserts. Here are just a few of my other grain recipes – see index for page number:

- Kasha Tomato Soup – Thick and hearty.
- Carrot and Rice Salad – Tangy and colorful.
- Raisin Oat Muffins – Delicious.
- Blueberry Cornmeal Pancakes – Breakfast specials
- Raspberry-Almond Couscous "Cake" – A nutritious dessert.

Cheesy Squash and Rice Casserole

This unique blend of two kinds of squash with rice and cheese makes a dish so filling I often eat it as my main course.

Makes 6 servings

- 2 tablespoons canola oil
- 2 cloves garlic, finely chopped
- 1 cup finely chopped onions
- 2 cups zucchini squash, unpeeled, sliced into ¼-inch slices (3/4 pound)
- 2 cups yellow summer squash, unpeeled, sliced into ¼-inch slices (3/4 pound)
- ½ cup skim milk
- 2 ounces shredded part-skim mozzarella cheese (½ cup)
- 3/4 ounce grated Parmesan cheese (3 tablespoons)
- ¼ teaspoon pepper
- Salt to taste
- 3 cups cooked brown rice
- 3 tablespoons wheat germ (3/4 ounce)

Preheat oven to 400°.

Lightly oil an 8-inch square baking dish or spray with a nonstick cooking spray.

Heat oil in a large nonstick skillet over medium heat.

Add garlic and onions. Cook 5 minutes, until tender. Add squash. Cook 10 minutes, stirring frequently, until squash is slightly tender.

Remove from heat and stir in remaining ingredients, ***except*** wheat germ. Mix well.

Spoon mixture into prepared baking dish. Press down firmly into pan with the back of a spoon. Sprinkle with wheat germ.

Cover and bake 25 minutes. Serve hot.

Each serving provides: 239 Calories, 9 g Fat, 9 mg Cholesterol, 32 g Carbohydrate, 129 mg Sodium, 4 g Fiber, 10 g Protein

GOOD HEALTH ALERT:

A recent government panel increased the calcium recommendation for adult women from 800 mg to 1000 mg per day. Most of us do not meet the recommended intakes.

Savory Herbed Rice

The delicate blend of herbs makes this dish a very tasty accompaniment to any entrée.

Makes 4 servings

1-3/4 cups water
½ teaspoon dill weed
¼ teaspoon dried oregano
3/4 cup brown rice, uncooked (5 ounces)
½ teaspoon dried rosemary
¼ teaspoon dried basil
1/8 teaspoon dried thyme

In a medium saucepan, combine water and spices.

Bring to a boil over medium heat.

Add rice. When water boils again reduce heat to low, cover and simmer 45 minutes, until rice is tender and most of the liquid has cooked out.

Remove from heat, fluff rice with a fork, replace cover, and let stand 5 minutes before serving.

Each serving provides: 133 Calories, 1 g Fat, 0 mg Cholesterol, 28 g Carbohydrate, 3 mg Sodium, 3 g Fiber, 3 g Protein

Greek Spinach and Rice

The flavor combination in this easy side dish tastes a lot like Greek spinach pies.

Makes 4 servings

2 teaspoons olive oil
1 cup chopped onions
3 cloves garlic, finely chopped
1 10-ounce package frozen, chopped spinach, thawed and drained
2 tablespoons grated Parmesan cheese
2 cups cooked brown rice
Salt and pepper to taste

Heat oil in a medium saucepan over medium heat.

Add onions and garlic. Cook until onions are tender, about 5 minutes. Add small amounts of water, if necessary, to prevent sticking.

Add remaining ingredients and heat through, stirring.

Serve hot.

Each serving provides: 174 Calories, 4 g Fat, 2 mg Cholesterol, 29 g Carbohydrate, 105 mg Sodium, 3 g Fiber, 6 g Protein

Nice Spiced Rice

A delectable blend of spices makes this rice – nice!

Makes 4 servings

1 1-pound can tomatoes, chopped, drained (Reserve liquid.)
½ cup very finely chopped onions
¼ teaspoon ground cloves
¼ teaspoon garlic powder
½ teaspoon ground cumin
1/8 teaspoon pepper
1 bay leaf
Salt to taste
3/4 cup brown rice, uncooked (5 ounces)

Place drained tomatoes in a medium saucepan.

Add water to reserved tomato liquid to equal 2 cups. Add to saucepan. Add remaining ingredients, ***except*** rice.

Bring to a boil over medium heat.

Stir in rice, reduce heat to low, cover, and simmer 45 minutes, until most of the liquid has been absorbed.

Remove from heat, fluff rice with a fork, replace cover, and let stand 5 minutes before serving.

Remove and discard bay leaf before serving.

Each serving provides: 163 Calories, 1 g Fat, 0 mg Cholesterol, 34 g Carbohydrate, 189 mg Sodium, 4 g Fiber, 4 g Protein

Raggedy Rice Patties

The flavor of the browned rice and onions is indescribably delicious in this wonderful side dish that goes with everything. I like to top the patties with Chinese sweet and sour sauce, which can be found in the Oriental section of most grocery stores.

Makes 6 servings (2 patties each serving)

2 cups cooked brown rice
1 cup finely shredded carrots
½ cup very finely chopped onions
¼ teaspoon garlic powder
¼ teaspoon salt
¼ teaspoon pepper
¼ cup plus 2 tablespoons whole wheat flour
4 egg whites

**If using Chinese Sweet & Sour sauce, follow the nutritional information on the guidelines for that label.

In a large bowl, combine rice, carrots and onions. Sprinkle with garlic powder, salt, pepper and flour. Mix well. Add egg whites. Mix well.

Preheat a large nonstick skillet or griddle over medium heat. Oil it lightly or spray with a nonstick cooking spray.

Shape mixture into 12 balls, using ¼ cup for each one, and pressing together firmly. Place each ball on preheated griddle and flatten slightly, making 3 inch patties. When patties are nicely browned on the bottom, turn carefully and brown the other side. (Patties are somewhat raggedy and will hold together after the bottoms are browned.)

Serve hot.

Each serving provides: 122 Calories, 1 g Fat, 0 mg Cholesterol, 24 g Carbohydrate, 137 mg Sodium, 3 g Fiber, 5 g Protein

Apple Rice Casserole

This delicious side dish is a real change of pace. The rice soaks up the juice from the apples and becomes plump and sweet. I love the leftovers for breakfast – served hot or cold with a dollop of yogurt.

Makes 8 servings

- 2 cups cooked brown rice
- 3 small, sweet apples, peeled, coarsely shredded
- 1/3 cup apple juice
- 1 tablespoon firmly packed brown sugar
- 2 teaspoons lemon juice
- 1 teaspoon vanilla extract
- ½ teaspoon ground cinnamon
- 1/16 teaspoon ground nutmeg

Preheat oven to 350°.

Lightly oil a 1½ quart casserole or spray with a nonstick cooking spray.

In a large bowl, combine all ingredients. Mix well. Spoon into prepared pan.

Cover tightly and bake 45 minutes.

Serve hot.

Each serving provides: 88 Calories, 1 g Fat, 0 mg Cholesterol, 20 g Carbohydrate, 4 mg Sodium, 3 g Fiber, 1 g Protein

Mexican Rice

This spicy dish is as easy as opening a can, and the use of brown rice gives it a fiber and vitamin boost.

Makes 4 servings

1 15-ounce can stewed tomatoes
1-3/4 cups water
1 teaspoon chili powder
3/4 cup brown rice, uncooked (5 ounces)

In a medium saucepan, combine tomatoes, water and chili powder. Bring to a boil over medium heat.

Stir in rice, reduce heat to low, cover and simmer 45 minutes, until most of the liquid has been absorbed.

Remove from heat, fluff rice with a fork, replace cover, and let stand 5 minutes before serving.

Each serving provides: 161 Calories, 1 g Fat, 0 mg Cholesterol, 35 g Carbohydrate, 279 mg Sodium, 3 g Fiber, 4 g Protein

Mushroom Couscous Pilaf

This tastes so much like stuffing, you may want to add it to your holiday menu, but don't wait for a holiday to try it. Look for couscous in most large grocery stores.

Makes 6 servings

1 tablespoon canola oil
1 cup chopped onions
3 cloves garlic, chopped
½ teaspoon dried basil
¼ teaspoon pepper
2½ cups boiling water (or vegetable broth)
4 cups coarsely chopped mushrooms
1 cup chopped celery
½ teaspoon dried oregano
¼ teaspoon salt
1 cup couscous (6 ounces), uncooked

Heat oil in a large nonstick skillet over medium heat. Add mushrooms, onions, celery and garlic. Cook 25 minutes, stirring frequently, until most of the liquid has cooked out.

Preheat oven to 350°.

Lightly oil an 8-inch square baking dish or spray with a nonstick cooking spray.

Remove mushroom mixture from heat and stir in spices and couscous. Mix well. Spoon mixture into prepared dish. Stir in boiling water.

Cover and bake 35 minutes.
Fluff with a fork before serving.

Each serving provides: 154 Calories, 3 g Fat, 0 mg Cholesterol, 27 g Carbohydrate, 113 mg Sodium, 3 g Fiber, 5 g Protein

Barley Vegetable Casserole

The only thing better than the aroma of this casserole baking is its wonderful flavor.

Makes 6 servings

2 tablespoons butter
2/3 cup barley, uncooked (4-½ ounces)
1 cup chopped onions
1 cup chopped cauliflower (¼-inch pieces)
1 cup chopped mushrooms
1 cup finely shredded carrots
2½ cups water
2 teaspoons instant vegetable broth mix (See index for page #)
¼ teaspoon garlic powder
1/8 teaspoon pepper

Preheat oven to 350°.
Lightly oil a 1-3/4-quart casserole or spray with a nonstick cooking spray.
Melt 1 tablespoon of the butter in a large nonstick skillet over medium heat.
Add barley and cook 2 to 3 minutes, stirring frequently, until lightly browned.
Place in prepared casserole.

Melt remaining margarine in skillet. Add onions and cauliflower. Cook, stirring frequently, 5 minutes. Add mushrooms and carrots. Cook 5 more minutes, stirring frequently. Add vegetables to casserole.

In a small bowl, combine water, broth mix, garlic powder and pepper. Mix well and add to casserole.

Mix well, cover, and bake 1 hour and 15 minutes, until barley is tender and most of the liquid has been absorbed. Stir several times while baking.

Let stand 5 minutes, then mix and serve.

Each serving provides: 135 Calories, 4 g Fat, 0 mg Cholesterol, 21 g Carbohydrate, 268 mg Sodium, 3 g Fiber, 4 g Protein

Baked Bulgur with Pecans

This easy cracked wheat side dish combines the flavor of basil with the crunch of pecans. It really dresses up any meal and is a perfect addition to a buffet dinner. *Makes 6 servings*

1 cup bulgur (cracked wheat), uncooked (6 ounces)
½ teaspoon dried basil
1/8 teaspoon salt
1/8 teaspoon pepper
2 cups boiling water
¼ cup chopped pecans (1 ounce)

Preheat oven to 350°.

Lightly oil a 1 quart baking dish or spray with a nonstick cooking spray.

Place bulgur, basil, salt and pepper in prepared baking dish. Add boiling water and mix well. Cover tightly and bake 20 minutes.

Fluff with a fork, add pecans, and mix well. Serve hot.

Each serving provides: 129 Calories, 4 g Fat, 0 mg Cholesterol, 22 g Carbohydrate, 51 mg Sodium, 4 g Fiber, 4 g Protein

Bulgur Pilaf

This delicious grain cooks quickly and has a wonderful texture. I've added a few spices for an easy pilaf that goes with everything. *Makes 4 servings*

1 tablespoon plus 1 teaspoon canola oil
½ cup chopped onions
2/3 cup bulgur (cracked wheat), uncooked (4 ounces)
1-1/3 cups water
½ teaspoon paprika
1/16 teaspoon dried thyme
1 tablespoon dried parsley flakes
¼ teaspoon dried oregano

Heat oil in a small saucepan over medium heat. Add onions and bulgur. Cook 5 minutes, stirring constantly.

Stir in remaining ingredients and bring to a boil. Cover, reduce heat to low, simmer 15 minutes, until water has been absorbed. Fluff with a fork before serving.

Each serving provides: 145 Calories, 5 g Fat, 0 mg Cholesterol, 23 g Carbohydrate, 6 mg Sodium, 3 g Fiber, 4 g Protein

Southern Spoon Bread

Spoon bread is a favorite side dish in the South. It's a cross between a soft, moist corn bread and a soufflé. I grew up calling it Mamaliga, as it was named in Romania. Dip in!

Makes 6 servings

3/4 cup plus 2 tablespoons yellow cornmeal (4-½ ounces)
¼ teaspoon salt
1-½ cups evaporated skim milk
2 tablespoons butter
4 egg whites
1 teaspoon sugar
1 teaspoon baking powder
1-½ cups canned corn, drained

Preheat oven to 375°.

Oil a 1-3/4-quart baking dish or spray with a nonstick cooking spray.

Combine cornmeal and salt in a medium saucepan. Gradually stir in milk, making a smooth mixture. Cook over medium heat, stirring constantly, until mixture is thick, about 5 minutes. Remove from heat.

Stir in butter, 2 of the egg whites, sugar, baking powder and corn. Mix well.

In a small, deep bowl, beat remaining egg whites on high speed of an electric mixer until stiff. Fold into cornmeal mixture, gently but thoroughly.

Spoon mixture into prepared pan.

Bake, uncovered, 40 minutes, until mixture is set and top begins to brown.

Serve right away.

Each serving provides: 209 Calories, 5 g Fat, 3 mg Cholesterol, 32 g Carbohydrate, 316 mg Sodium, 2 g Fiber, 10 g Protein

GOOD HEALTH ALERT:
Carotenes provide color to food. Picking fruits and vegetables with rich, deep colors (orange, red and green) is an easy way to know you're getting lots of these health-promoting nutrients.

Kasha and Apple Bake

Kasha (buckwheat groats) is a rich-flavored grain that goes well with the sweetness of apples. This pudding-like casserole can be served as a side dish, for breakfast, or topped with vanilla ice milk for an unusual dessert.

Makes 6 servings

½ cup kasha, uncooked (3 ounces)
¼ cup firmly packed brown sugar
1 teaspoon ground cinnamon
½ teaspoon ground nutmeg
1/8 teaspoon ground ginger
1/8 teaspoon ground allspice
3 small, sweet apples, unpeeled, finely chopped into 1/8- to ¼-inch pieces (2-½ cups)
2-½ cups water
3 egg whites
1 teaspoon vanilla extract
1 cup nonfat dry milk

Preheat oven to 350°.

Lightly oil an 8-inch square baking pan or spray with a nonstick cooking spray.

In a medium saucepan, combine kasha, brown sugar, spices, apples and water. Bring to a boil over medium heat. Boil 2 minutes, stirring frequently. Remove from heat.

Place egg whites in a small bowl. Stir in vanilla extract. Add dry milk and mix until blended. Add to kasha mixture, mixing well. Place mixture in prepared pan.

Bake, uncovered, 25 minutes, until set.

Serve warm.

Each serving provides: 164 Calories, 1 g Fat, 2 mg Cholesterol, 33 g Carbohydrate, 94 mg Sodium, 4 g Fiber, 7 g Protein

GOOD HEALTH ALERT:
Protein can rob the body of calcium. Choosing meatless meals, which tends to lower protein intake, may be a good way to improve bone health.

Toasted Kasha Patties

The toasty taste of kasha really comes through in these delicious, fragrant patties.

Makes 4 servings
(2 patties each serving)

- 2 teaspoons canola oil
- ½ cup kasha (buckwheat groats), uncooked (3 ounces)
- ½ cup very finely chopped onions
- 2 cups water
- ½ teaspoon salt
- 3 tablespoons whole wheat flour
- 1 egg white
- 1/8 teaspoon pepper

Heat oil in a large nonstick skillet over medium heat. Add kasha and onions. Cook 5 minutes, stirring constantly. Remove from heat.

Bring water to a boil over medium heat. Stir in salt and kasha mixture. Reduce heat to low, cover, and simmer 15 minutes, until water has been absorbed. Remove from heat and stir in flour. Let cool 5 to 10 minutes.

Add egg white and pepper, mixing well.

Shape mixture into patties, using 1/3 cup for each one, and wetting your hands slightly to keep mixture from sticking.

Heat skillet again over medium heat. Place patties in skillet and flatten to ½ inch thick, using a spatula. Cook until nicely browned on both sides, turning several times. (Makes 8 patties.)

Serve hot.

Each serving provides: 124 Calories, 3 g Fat, 0 mg Cholesterol, 22 g Carbohydrate, 290 mg Sodium, 3 g Fiber, 4 g Protein

GOOD HEALTH ALERT:
If you're allergic to your cat, dog or pet piglet, stop suffering the ravages of animal dander: install an air filter in your home.

Millet Primavera

If you haven't tried millet, it's definitely worth a trip to the health food store. This nutritious grain has a subtle flavor and wonderful texture all its own. My friend, Betty, gave me the idea for this recipe, and I love it.

Makes 6 servings

1½ cups water
½ cup uncooked millet (3 ounces)
1 tablespoon canola oil
1½ cups sliced mushrooms
½ cup chopped sweet red pepper
3 cloves garlic, very finely chopped
1 10-ounce package frozen peas and carrots thawed
½ cup thinly sliced green onion (green part only)
½ teaspoon dried oregano
½ teaspoon dried basil
2 tablespoons grated Parmesan cheese
1 teaspoon vegetable broth mix dissolved in ½ cup water (see index for page #)

Bring water to a boil in a medium saucepan. Add millet, reduce heat to low, cover, and cook 25 minutes, until water has been absorbed.

While millet is cooking, heat oil in a large nonstick skillet over medium heat.

Add mushrooms, red pepper, garlic, and peas and carrots.

Cook, stirring frequently, 8 to 10 minutes, until vegetables are tender.

Stir in remaining ingredients. Add cooked millet and mix well.

Serve hot.

Each serving provides: 118 Calories, 4 g Fat, 1 mg Cholesterol, 18 g Carbohydrate, 176 mg Sodium, 3 g Fiber, 5 g Protein

Mediterranean Millet

Saffron adds a delicate flavor to this tasty side dish, and the currants provide a tiny burst of tartness in every bite.

Makes 6 servings

1 tablespoon canola oil
1 cup coarsely shredded carrots
2 cloves garlic, very finely chopped
1/8 teaspoon saffron
Salt and pepper to taste
½ cup millet, uncooked (3 ounces)
1 cup chopped onions
2 cups sliced mushrooms
1-3/4 cups water
1/8 teaspoon ground allspice
¼ cup plus 2 tablespoons currants

Heat oil in a medium saucepan over medium heat. Add onions, carrots, mushrooms and garlic. Cook, stirring frequently, until onions are tender, 5 to 10 minutes.

Add water and spices. Bring mixture to a boil. Stir in millet and currants. Cover, reduce heat to low, and simmer 25 to 30 minutes, until water has been absorbed. Stir once during cooking.

Each serving provides: 124 Calories, 3 g Fat, 0 mg Cholesterol, 22 g Carbohydrate, 10 mg Sodium, 3 g Fiber, 3 g Protein

Crockpot Grains, Etc.

Just throw it all in the crockpot in the morning and return home to a hearty dish of grains and beans. This serves 8 as a side dish and 4 to 6 as a filling main course. (You can use any combination of grains. Just use about 1 cupful altogether.) *Makes 8 servings*

¼ cup millet, uncooked (1-½ ounces)
¼ cup barley, uncooked (1½ oz)
1/3 cup brown rice, uncooked (2 ounces)
1 cup chopped onions
1 cup chopped green pepper
½ cup finely chopped carrots
1 1-pound can kidney beans or any other beans, drained
(This will yield 10 ounces of beans.)
1 8-ounce can salt-free (or regular) tomato sauce
1 1-pound can tomatoes, chopped, drained (Reserve liquid.)
1-½ cups canned or frozen corn, drained
1 teaspoon dried oregano
1 teaspoon dried basil
½ teaspoon garlic powder
Salt and pepper to taste

Combine all ingredients in a crockpot. Add water to reserved tomato liquid to equal 2½ cups. Stir into grain mixture.

Cover and cook on low setting 8 hours.

Stir before serving.

Each serving provides: 168 Calories, 2 g Fat, 0 mg Cholesterol, 33 g Carbohydrate, 177 mg Sodium, 6 g Fiber, 7 g Protein

Vegetables

Vegetables are low in calories, high in fiber, and loaded with vitamins and minerals. The variety of available vegetables is vast. Sadly, many people eat the same few types of vegetables day after day, never venturing past the frozen green beans or the peas and carrots. With their excellent nutritional value and endless variety, vegetables can play a major role in our daily meals.

Health experts tell us that we need to eat a variety of vegetables in order to benefit from the different nutrients that each one has to offer. In order to do this, a good rule of thumb is to include vegetables of all different colors when planning your meals. That way you will get the nutritional benefits of all of them.

I often use vegetables as a filler. If I want larger portions, I simply add more vegetables. That way I get more food and more nutrition. Vegetables add flair to recipes too. My Veggie Quiche and Pizza with The Works, for example, would be rather boring without the added color, texture and flavor of vegetables.

For the best flavor and nutritional value, cook vegetables until just tender-crisp, and for added fiber, leave the skin on whenever possible. My first preference is for fresh vegetables, with frozen ones my next choice. Canned vegetables tend to be overcooked and many of them contain added salt.

In my vegetable recipes that call for oil, I use a minimal amount and choose a monounsaturated oil such as canola oil or olive oil. When sautéing vegetables, I prefer to use a nonstick skillet and a small amount of oil. I recommend adding small amounts of water, if necessary, to keep the vegetables from sticking.

Be sure to check my other chapters for more vegetable recipes. You'll find lots of them in Appetizers, Dips, and Spreads, Soups, Salads and Salad Dressings, Starchy Vegetables, Sandwiches and Burgers, Entrées, and even Desserts. Also, be sure to check Spice It Right for ideas on adding spices to vegetables. Here is just a sampling of some of my other tasty vegetable dishes – see index for page number:

- Zucchini-Pimento Hot Bites – A delicious appetizer.
- Convenience Vegetable Soup – Easy and satisfying.
- Yellow Submarine – A sandwich chock full of veggies.
- Millie's Everything" Salad – Lots of color and flavor.
- Cheddar-Broccoli Bread Roll – Swirls of broccoli and cheese in a biscuit dough.

Many Layered Vegetable Bake

My good friend, Tulli, gave me the idea for this delicious vegetable combo. It's a great oven-to-table dish that your family and guests will love.

Makes 8 servings

1 cup sliced carrots, 1/8-inch thick
1 10-ounce package frozen French-style green beans thawed and drained
1 cup thinly sliced sweet red pepper
1 cup thinly sliced onions
2 cups sliced mushrooms
¼ teaspoon garlic powder
1 teaspoon dried parsley flakes
1/8 teaspoon salt
1/8 teaspoon pepper
1 1-pound can stewed tomatoes

Preheat oven to 375°.

Lightly oil a 2-quart casserole or spray with a nonstick cooking spray.

Layer vegetables in casserole in the following order: carrots, green beans, red pepper, onions, and mushrooms.

Sprinkle spices evenly over vegetables.

Spoon stewed tomatoes and their liquid evenly over vegetables, breaking up any large pieces of tomato.

Cover tightly and bake 1 hour.

Each serving provides: 47 Calories, 0 g Fat, 0 mg Cholesterol, 11 g Carbohydrate, 186 mg Sodium, 4 g Fiber, 2 g ProteinParty Vegetable Loaf

GOOD HEALTH ALERT:

Nuts, in addition to providing protein, are a rich source of monounsaturated fat.

Party Vegetable Loaf

Pretty as a picture and delicious, too. Your guests will rave over this layered beauty!

Makes 8 servings

Layer #1:

2 10-ounce packages frozen peas
2 teaspoons canola oil
2 egg whites
¼ cup all-purpose flour
1/8 teaspoon garlic powder
1 tablespoon minced onion flakes
Salt and pepper to taste

Layer #2:

2 10-ounce packages frozen cauliflower
2 teaspoons canola oil
2 egg whites
¼ cup all-purpose flour
1/8 teaspoon garlic powder
1 teaspoon grated fresh lemon peel
1 tablespoon minced onion flakes
Salt and pepper to taste

Layer #3:

1½ 1-pound packages frozen sliced carrots
2 teaspoons canola oil
2 egg whites
¼ cup all-purpose flour
1 teaspoon grated fresh orange peel
Salt and pepper to taste

Preheat oven to 350°.

Lightly oil a 5 x 9-inch loaf pan or spray with a nonstick cooking spray. Place a 9-inch-wide piece of waxed paper in the pan, lining the sides and bottom. Oil or spray again.

Prepare Layer #1:

Cook peas according to package directions. Drain. Place peas and remaining ingredients in a blender container. Blend until smooth. Spread evenly in pan.

Prepare Layer #2:

Cook cauliflower according to package directions. Drain. Place cauliflower in blender container with remaining ingredients. Blend until smooth. Spread evenly over layer of peas.

Prepare Layer #3:

Cook carrots according to package directions. Drain. Place carrots in blender container with remaining ingredients. Blend until smooth. Spread evenly over cauliflower layer.

Bake, uncovered, 55 minutes.

Let stand 10 minutes, then invert onto a serving plate.

Peel off waxed paper. Cut into slices to serve.

Each serving provides: 194 Calories, 4 g Fat, 0 mg Cholesterol, 31 g Carbohydrate, 188 mg Sodium, 3 g Fiber, 10 g Protein

Oriental Green Beans with Peanut Sauce

This is a quick and easy way to turn ordinary green beans into an extraordinary Oriental dish.

Makes 4 servings

- 1 10-ounce package frozen French-style green beans
- 2 tablespoons peanut butter
- 1 tablespoon lemon juice
- 2 teaspoons honey
- ¼ teaspoon ground ginger
- 1 tablespoon soy sauce
- 1 tablespoon water
- ¼ teaspoon garlic powder

Cook green beans according to package directions.

While beans are cooking, combine remaining ingredients in a small bowl. Mix with a fork or wire whisk until well blended.

When beans are finished cooking, drain them and place in a serving bowl. Spoon peanut sauce evenly over beans and serve right away.

Each serving provides: 86 Calories, 4 g Fat, 0 mg Cholesterol, 10 g Carbohydrate, 298 mg Sodium, 1 g Fiber, 4 g Protein

Ten-Layer Casserole

A great last-minute dinner; just layer it, bake it and enjoy it. I always keep small packages of cooked brown rice in the freezer for just this type of meal.

Makes 6 servings

2 8-ounce cans salt-free (or regular) tomato sauce
2 tablespoons firmly packed brown sugar
2 tablespoons sweet pickle relish
½ teaspoon garlic powder
1 teaspoon dry mustard
2 cups cooked brown rice
1 1-pound can whole kernel corn, drained
2 1-pound cans kidney beans, rinsed and drained
(This will yield 20 ounces, or 1¼ pounds of beans.)
1 cup very finely chopped onions

Preheat oven to 350°.

Lightly oil a 1-3/4-quart deep-sided baking dish or casserole, or spray with a nonstick cooking spray.

In a small bowl, combine tomato sauce, brown sugar, relish, garlic powder and dry mustard. Mix well.

Spread ***half*** of the rice in the bottom of the prepared baking dish. Top with ***half*** the corn. Spoon ***half*** of the beans evenly over the corn. Top with ***half*** of the onions and then ***half*** of the sauce.

Top with remaining rice, then corn, then beans, then onions, then remaining sauce.

Cover and bake 1 hour.

Each serving provides: 284 Calories, 3 g Fat, 0 mg Cholesterol, 55 g Carbohydrate, 254 mg Sodium, 4 g Fiber, 12 g Protein

Stir-Fried Green Beans with Pine Nuts

Stir-frying leaves green beans wonderfully crunchy, and the addition of pine nuts adds even more crunch.

Makes 4 servings

2 teaspoons sesame oil
3/4 pound fresh green beans, cut into 1-inch pieces (about 2-½ cups)
3 cloves garlic, finely chopped
¼ cup pine nuts (1 ounce)
1 tablespoon reduced-sodium (or regular) soy sauce
¼ cup water
1 cup chopped onions
1/8 teaspoon pepper

Heat oil in a large nonstick skillet or wok over medium-high heat. Add green beans, garlic, onions, and pine nuts. Cook, stirring constantly with a tossing motion, 5 to 7 minutes, until onions start to brown.

Stir in soy sauce, pepper and water. Reduce heat to medium-low, cover, and cook 5 minutes, stirring once during cooking time.

Each serving provides: 102 Calories, 6 g Fat, 0 mg Cholesterol, 11 g Carbohydrate, 157 mg Sodium, 3 g Fiber, 4 g Protein

Mushrooms in Sherry Vinaigrette

This tangy dish has two lives. First, serve it hot as a wonderfully tasty side dish or as a topping for any of our meatless burgers. Then, chill the leftovers and enjoy them cold.

Makes 4 servings

- 1 tablespoon Dijon mustard
- 3 tablespoons wine vinegar
- 2 tablespoons canola oil
- 1 tablespoon sherry
- 1 teaspoon dried parsley flakes
- ½ teaspoon dried oregano
- 1/8 teaspoon salt
- 1/8 teaspoon pepper
- 1/8 teaspoon garlic powder
- 4 cups sliced mushrooms

In a medium bowl, combine all ingredients, ***except*** mushrooms. Mix very well. Add mushrooms, stirring until evenly coated.

Preheat a large nonstick skillet over medium-high heat. Add mushrooms and sauce. Cook, stirring, until mushrooms are tender, about 5 minutes.

Serve hot or chill and serve cold.

Each serving provides: 91 Calories, 7 g Fat, 0 mg Cholesterol, 5 g Carbohydrate, 187 mg Sodium, 1 g Fiber, 1 g Protein

GOOD HEALTH ALERT:

Exercising longer rather than harder appears to be a better way to burn stored fat.

Orange Broccoli

I've added orange juice to this Oriental version of stir-fried broccoli. You're guaranteed to love it.

Makes 4 servings

- ½ cup orange juice
- 1 tablespoon reduced-sodium (or regular) soy sauce
- ¼ teaspoon ground ginger
- ¼ teaspoon garlic powder
- 2 teaspoons honey
- 1 tablespoon cornstarch
- 1 tablespoon sesame oil
- 4 cups broccoli, cut into small flowerets

In a small bowl, combine orange juice, soy sauce, ginger, garlic powder, honey and cornstarch. Mix until cornstarch is dissolved. Set aside.

Heat oil in a large nonstick skillet over medium heat. Add broccoli. Cook, stirring frequently, until broccoli is bright green, about 2 minutes.

Stir orange juice mixture and pour over broccoli. Cook, stirring for a few minutes, until broccoli is evenly coated and sauce is thick and clear.

Each serving provides: 90 Calories, 4 g Fat, 0 mg Cholesterol, 13 g Carbohydrate, 174 mg Sodium, 2 g Fiber, 3 g Protein

Broccoli with Mushrooms and Walnuts

Stir-fried and laced with Cheddar cheese and sherry, this is my very favorite way to serve broccoli. Your family will love it, and your guests will rave.

Makes 6 servings

- ½ cup water
- 2 tablespoons reduced-sodium (or regular) soy sauce
- 1 tablespoon sherry
- 1 tablespoon cornstarch
- 1 teaspoon instant vegetable broth mix (see index for page #)
- ½ teaspoon dried oregano
- ¼ teaspoon garlic powder
- 1/8 teaspoon pepper
- 1 tablespoon canola oil
- 1 cup onions, cut lengthwise into ¼-inch slices
- 3 cups sliced mushrooms
- 4 cups (packed) broccoli, cut into flowerets

3 tablespoons chopped walnuts (3/4 ounce)
3 ounces lowfat Cheddar cheese (3/4 cup)

In a small bowl, combine water, soy sauce, sherry, cornstarch, broth mix, oregano, garlic powder and pepper. Stir to dissolve cornstarch. Set aside.

Heat oil in a large nonstick skillet or wok over medium-high heat. Add onions and mushrooms. Cook 5 minutes, stirring.

Add broccoli and walnuts. Cook, stirring, 3 minutes, or until broccoli turns bright green.

Stir soy sauce mixture and pour over vegetables. Cook, stirring, until vegetables are glazed and liquid has thickened and turned clear.

Remove from heat, sprinkle evenly with cheese, cover, and let stand 5 minutes before serving.

Each serving provides: 136 Calories, 7 g Fat, 10 mg Cholesterol, 10 g Carbohydrate, 424 mg Sodium, 3 g Fiber, 8 g Protein

King Cabbage

Thick slices of cabbage, crowned with onions and melted cheese, make this a "king" of a vegetable dish. *Makes 4 servings*

1 small cabbage (3/4 pound), sliced ½-inch thick
2 teaspoons sugar
1 teaspoon caraway seeds
1 medium onion, thinly sliced (about 1 cup)
1/8 teaspoon salt
1/8 teaspoon pepper
2 ounces part-skim mozzarella cheese
(or lowfat Swiss or Muenster, if you prefer) (½ cup)

Preheat oven to 350°.

Lightly oil an 8-ounce square baking dish or spray with a nonstick cooking spray.

Place cabbage slices in bottom of prepared pan. Sprinkle evenly with ***half*** of the sugar and ***half*** of the caraway seeds. Place onion slices over cabbage. Sprinkle with remaining sugar, caraway seeds, and salt and pepper.

Cover and bake 1 hour. Uncover, sprinkle with cheese, and return to oven for 5 minutes to melt cheese.

Each serving provides: 82 Calories, 3 g Fat, 8 mg Cholesterol, 10 g Carbohydrate, 151 mg Sodium, 2 g Fiber, 5 g Protein

Spiced German Cabbage and Apples

This tangy blend of red cabbage, apples, and spices is colorful as well as delicious.

Makes 6 servings

- 1 tablespoon canola oil
- 1 cup thinly sliced onions
- 4 cups shredded red cabbage
- 3 small, tart apples, peeled, coarsely shredded
- 3 tablespoons firmly packed brown sugar
- 3 tablespoons wine vinegar
- ½ teaspoon ground cinnamon
- 1/8 teaspoon ground allspice

Heat oil in a large nonstick skillet over medium heat. Add onions and cook until tender, about 10 minutes.

Add cabbage and apples to skillet. Toss with onions.

In a small bowl, combine remaining ingredients. Add to skillet. Cook, stirring frequently, 10 to 15 minutes, or until cabbage is tender.

Serve hot.

Each serving provides: 96 Calories, 3 g Fat, 0 mg Cholesterol, 19 g Carbohydrate, 9 mg Sodium, 2 g Fiber, 1 g Protein

Gourmet Turnip Medley

This is a great-tasting dish, either by itself or spooned over cooked rice. The blend of spices is just perfect.

Makes 6 servings

- 1 tablespoon canola oil
- 3 cloves garlic, coarsely chopped
- 1 cup coarsely chopped onions
- 1-½ cups turnips, peeled, cut into ½-inch cubes
- 1 cup carrots, cut into ½-inch slices
- 2 cups mushrooms, cut into quarters
  (If the mushrooms are large, cut them into eighths.)
- ½ teaspoon dried thyme
- ¼ teaspoon dried tarragon
- 1 bay leaf
- 1 teaspoon dried parsley flakes
  Salt and pepper to taste
- ½ cup water

Heat oil in a large saucepan over medium heat. Add all ingredients, ***except*** water. Cook 5 minutes, stirring frequently.

Add water, reduce heat to low, cover, and cook 20 minutes, or until vegetables are tender.

Remove and discard bay leaf before serving.

Each serving provides: 55 Calories, 2 g Fat, 0 mg Cholesterol, 8 g Carbohydrate, 30 mg Sodium, 2 g Fiber, 1 g Protein

Asparagus Française

Asparagus, Dijon mustard, and Parmesan cheese are all perfect for each other. You won't believe how elegant this easy dish is.

Makes 4 servings

1 10-ounce package frozen asparagus spears
1 tablespoon wine vinegar
¼ teaspoon garlic powder
1 tablespoon parsley flakes
1 teaspoon Dijon mustard
1 tablespoon plus 1 teaspoon canola oil
2 teaspoons grated Parmesan cheese
Pepper to taste

Cook asparagus according to package directions. Drain.

While asparagus is cooking, combine wine vinegar, garlic powder, parsley, Dijon and oil. Whisk with a fork or wire whisk until blended.

Transfer cooked asparagus to serving plate. Spoon sauce over asparagus. Sprinkle with Parmesan cheese and pepper.

Each serving provides: 64 Calories, 5 g Fat, 1 mg Cholesterol, 3 g Carbohydrate, 60 mg Sodium, 1 g Fiber, 3 g Protein

GOOD HEALTH ALERT:

Eat that parsley. Fresh parsley contains relatively high amounts of beta carotene (which the body converts to Vitamin A) and Vitamin C. You have to eat about seven sprigs of it to get 10% of the RDA for these nutrients, so try parsley as a salad green, not just as a garnish.

Asparagus and Onion Sauté

Made with fresh asparagus, this elegant side dish is at home at a family meal or at a fancy dinner party. For the best flavor and tenderness, choose thin stalks of asparagus.

Makes 4 servings

2 teaspoons canola oil
2 cups chopped onions
2 cloves garlic, minced
2 cups fresh asparagus, cut into 1-inch pieces (about ½ pound)
1 teaspoon dried oregano
¼ cup dry white wine
1 tablespoon lemon juice
Salt to taste
Few drops bottled hot pepper sauce

Heat oil in a large nonstick skillet over medium heat. Add onions and garlic. Cook until tender, stirring occasionally, about 10 minutes. Add small amounts of water, if necessary, to prevent sticking.

Add asparagus and remaining ingredients. Cover and cook 10 minutes, or until asparagus is just tender-crisp. Stir occasionally while cooking.

Each serving provides: 76 Calories, 3 g Fat, 0 mg Cholesterol, 9 g Carbohydrate, 7 mg Sodium, 1 g Fiber, 3 g Protein

Dusty Cauliflower

This is truly cauliflower at its best! For a spectacular variation, try "Dusty Mushrooms." Simply replace the cauliflower with 4 cups of fresh mushrooms, cut into halves or quarters.

Makes 4 servings

4 cups cauliflower, cut into small flowerets
2 tablespoons canola oil
3 tablespoons oat bran (3/4 ounce)
3 tablespoons dry bread crumbs
1 tablespoon plus 1 teaspoon grated Parmesan cheese
1/8 teaspoon pepper
Dash garlic powder

Preheat oven to 400°.

Lightly oil a 10 x 15-inch baking pan or spray with a nonstick cooking spray.

Place cauliflower in a large bowl. Drizzle with oil and toss until cauliflower is evenly coated.

Combine remaining ingredients and sprinkle over cauliflower. Toss until coated.

Spread cauliflower in prepared pan. Sprinkle with any remaining crumbs.

Bake 18 to 20 minutes, until lightly browned.

Each serving provides: 124 Calories, 8 g Fat, 2 mg Cholesterol, 12 g Carbohydrate, 81 mg Sodium, 1 g Fiber, 4 g Protein

Cauliflower Curry

You can easily turn this Indian-style vegetable into a delicious entrée by adding beans or cubes of tofu and serving it over brown rice.

Makes 6 servings

1 1-pound can tomatoes, undrained, chopped
1/3 cup water
1 teaspoon curry powder
½ teaspoon turmeric
½ teaspoon ground cumin
¼ teaspoon garlic powder
1/16 teaspoon ground cinnamon
1 bay leaf
4 cups cauliflower, cut into flowerets

In a large nonstick skillet, combine tomatoes, water, and spices. Bring to a boil over medium-low heat. Cover and simmer 5 minutes, stirring occasionally.

Add cauliflower, cover, and cook 10 minutes, or until cauliflower is tender-crisp. Stir occasionally.

Remove and discard bay leaf before serving.

Each serving provides: 34 Calories, 0 g Fat, 0 mg Cholesterol, 7 g Carbohydrate, 134 mg Sodium, 1 g Fiber, 2 g Protein

GOOD HEALTH ALERT:
Vitamin B2 (riboflavin) is usually obtained from foods of animal origin. Alternative sources include asparagus, almonds, broccoli and fortified breakfast cereals.

Honey Baked Carrots and Apples

Simple to make, this sweet blend of carrots and apples makes any meal a special event.

Makes 4 servings

3 cups coarsely shredded carrots
2 small, sweet apples, peeled, coarsely shredded
½ teaspoon ground cinnamon
1 tablespoon honey
¼ cup orange juice

Topping:
1 tablespoon wheat germ
¼ teaspoon ground cinnamon
2 teaspoons butter

Preheat oven to 350º.

Lightly oil a 1-quart baking dish or spray with a nonstick cooking spray.

In a large bowl, combine carrots, apples, cinnamon, honey, and orange juice. Mix well.

Spoon into prepared baking dish. Press mixture down gently with the back of a spoon.

For topping:

In a small bowl or custard cup, combine wheat germ and cinnamon. Sprinkle evenly over carrots. Dot with butter.

Bake, uncovered, 40 minutes.

Serve hot.

Each serving provides: 110 Calories, 2 g Fat, 0 mg Cholesterol, 23 g Carbohydrate, 52 mg Sodium, 3 g Fiber, 2 g Protein

Pineapple Glazed Carrots

Sweet and spicy, this is a delicious way to eat your vegetables. The leftovers are good cold, too.

Makes 4 servings

2 teaspoons canola oil
2 tablespoons water
1/8 teaspoon ground cinnamon
2/3 cup pineapple juice
1 tablespoon cornstarch
1/8 teaspoon ground nutmeg

1/16 teaspoon ground allspice
4 cups carrots, cut into matchstick-size pieces
1 tablespoon reduced-sodium (or regular) soy sauce

Heat oil in a large nonstick skillet over medium-high heat. Add carrots. Cook, stirring frequently, 8 to 10 minutes, until carrots are tender-crisp and start to brown.

While carrots are cooking, combine remaining ingredients in a small bowl. Stir to dissolve cornstarch. Add to cooked carrots. Cook, stirring constantly, 1 minute, or until sauce is thick and carrots are coated.

Each serving provides: 100 Calories, 3 g Fat, 0 mg Cholesterol, 19 g Carbohydrate, 189 mg Sodium, 1 g Fiber, 2 g Protein

Parmesan-Dill Brussel Sprouts

If possible, use freshly squeezed lemon juice to top this and other vegetables. It tastes so much better than the bottled kind and adds such a wonderful, fresh flavor.

Makes 4 servings

1 tablespoon lemon juice
2 teaspoons butter
1 10-ounce package frozen brussel sprouts
Salt and pepper to taste
1 tablespoon grated Parmesan cheese
½ teaspoon dried dill weed

Cook brussel sprouts according to package directions. Drain. Add remaining ingredients and toss to combine.

Each serving provides: 53 Calories, 3 g Fat, 1 mg Cholesterol, 6 g Carbohydrate, 54 mg Sodium, 2 g Fiber, 3 g Protein

GOOD HEALTH ALERT:

Consider frozen broccoli. Ounce for ounce, it often contains one-third more beta carotene than fresh broccoli. That's because frozen broccoli generally contains more of the tender buds or florets, which are richer in beta carotene than the stalks.

Clove Spiced Tomatoes

The unusual blend of spices makes this one of my very favorite vegetable dishes.

Makes 4 servings

2 1-pound cans tomatoes, undrained, coarsely chopped
½ cup chopped onions
¼ teaspoon ground cloves
1 small bay leaf
2 tablespoons firmly packed brown sugar
1/8 teaspoon pepper
Salt to taste
4 slices whole wheat bread (1-ounce slices), cut into cubes

In a medium saucepan, combine all ingredients, ***except*** bread cubes. Bring to a boil over medium heat. Reduce heat to low and simmer, uncovered, 30 minutes. Stir occasionally while cooking.

Remove and discard bay leaf.

Preheat oven to 375º.

Lightly oil a 1-½-quart baking dish or spray with a nonstick cooking spray.

Add bread cubes to tomato mixture and place in prepared baking dish.

Bake, uncovered, 1 hour.

Serve hot.

Each serving provides: 148 Calories, 2 g Fat, 1 mg Cholesterol, 31 g Carbohydrate, 553 mg Sodium, 1 g Fiber, 5 g Protein

Classy Stewed Tomatoes

These dressed-up stewed tomatoes are delicious spooned over cooked rice or macaroni.

Makes 6 servings

3 cups sliced mushrooms
2 tablespoons sherry
¼ teaspoon garlic powder
1 tablespoon plus 1 teaspoon cornstarch
1 1-pound can stewed tomatoes, drained (Reserve liquid.)
1½ ounces shredded lowfat Cheddar cheese (¼ cup plus 2 tablespoons)

In a medium saucepan, combine mushrooms, sherry, and garlic powder. Cook over medium heat, stirring frequently, 3 to 5 minutes, or until mushrooms are tender.

Dissolve cornstarch in a reserved tomato liquid and add it to mushrooms, along with tomatoes. Cook, stirring, until mixture comes to a boil. Boil 2 minutes, stirring.

Spoon into a serving bowl and sprinkle evenly with Cheddar cheese.

Each serving provides: 66 Calories, 1 g Fat, 5 mg Cholesterol, 9 g Carbohydrate, 244 mg Sodium, 2 g Fiber, 3 g Protein

Italian Eggplant

This wonderful dish consists of layers of eggplant in a thick, cheesy sauce. Serve it plain or over pasta or rice. *Makes 4 servings*

Sauce:

2 8-ounce cans salt-free (or regular) tomato sauce
1½ teaspoons dried oregano
½ teaspoon dried basil
¼ teaspoon garlic powder
1/8 teaspoon pepper

Eggplant:

1 medium eggplant (1 pound), peeled, sliced into ½ inch slices
1 cup part-skim ricotta cheese
2 ounces shredded part-skim mozzarella cheese (½ cup)
1 tablespoon grated Parmesan cheese

Preheat oven to 400°.

Combine sauce ingredients in a small bowl and set aside.

Place eggplant slices on a lightly oiled baking sheet and bake 15 minutes.

Reduce oven temperature to 350°.

Lightly oil an 8-inch square baking pan or spray with a nonstick cooking spray.

Spoon 2/3 cup of the sauce in the bottom of prepared pan. Top with ½ of the eggplant slices. Drop ricotta cheese by spoonfuls onto eggplant. Top with another 2/3 cup of the sauce. Add remaining eggplant slices, pressing them down gently. Sprinkle with mozzarella cheese, then top with remaining sauce.

Sprinkle top with Parmesan cheese.

Bake, uncovered, 35 minutes.

Let stand 5 minutes before serving.

Each serving provides: 193 Calories, 8 g Fat, 28 mg Cholesterol, 18 g Carbohydrate, 195 mg Sodium, 2 g Fiber, 14 g Protein

Cheddar Eggplant Boats

The eggplant shells make such pretty serving bowls. Everyone will be impressed with the look – and the taste – of this elegant dish. I often serve it as an entrée.

Makes 4 servings

1 1¼ pound eggplant (or 2 small eggplants)
2 teaspoons olive oil
1 cup chopped onions
1 cup chopped mushrooms
¼ teaspoon garlic powder
½ teaspoon dried oregano
½ teaspoon dried basil
1/16 teaspoon pepper
1 teaspoon reduced-sodium (or regular) soy sauce
1 cup cooked brown rice
2 ounces shredded lowfat Cheddar cheese (½ cup)

Cut eggplant in half, lengthwise. Carefully scoop out pulp, leaving a ¼ inch shell. Chop pulp into ¼ inch pieces.

Heat oil in a large nonstick skillet over medium heat. Add eggplant pulp, onions and mushrooms. Add spices and soy sauce. Cook 10 to 15 minutes, stirring frequently, until vegetables are tender. Remove from heat and stir in rice and ***half*** of the Cheddar cheese.

Preheat oven to 350º.

Lightly oil a shallow baking dish or spray with a nonstick cooking spray.

Spoon cooked mixture into eggplant shells. Sprinkle remaining cheese evenly over tops.

Cook, uncovered, 30 minutes.

(Eggplant shells tend to be bitter, so use them for serving and then discard.)

Each serving provides: 178 Calories, 6 g Fat, 10 mg Cholesterol, 25 g Carbohydrate, 160 mg Sodium, 4 g Fiber, 8 g Protein

GOOD HEALTH ALERT:

Brush your teeth – for at least two minutes – brush the teeth, the junction of the teeth and gums, the tongue and the roof of your mouth. You don't need a fancy, angled toothbrush – just a sturdy, soft-bristled one that you replace each month.

Swiss Spinach Casserole

You can turn this delicately flavored casserole into a filling main dish by serving it over a baked potato. Add a salad and your meal is complete.

Makes 4 servings

- 1 10-ounce package frozen, chopped spinach, thawed and drained well
- 1 tablespoon all-purpose flour
- ¼ cup finely chopped onions
- ½ cup water
- 2/3 cup nonfat dry milk
- 1 egg white
- 2/3 cup lowfat cottage cheese
- 2 ounces lowfat Swiss cheese, shredded (½ cup)
- 1/8 teaspoon garlic powder
- 1/8 teaspoon pepper
- Salt to taste

Preheat oven to 350º.
Lightly oil a 1-quart baking dish or spray with a nonstick cooking spray.
Place drained spinach in a large bowl. Sprinkle with flour and mix well.
Add remaining ingredients. Mix well. Pour into prepared baking dish.
Bake, uncovered, 40 minutes.
Let stand 5 minutes before serving.

Each serving provides: 145 Calories, 3 g Fat, 14 mg Cholesterol, 13 g Carbohydrate, 305 mg Sodium, 1 g Fiber, 17 g Protein

GOOD HEALTH ALERT:

If you have frequent headaches, look at what you eat. Foods and beverages may play a role in some headaches, especially migraines. Most of the suspects, such as chocolate, ripe cheeses, and freshly baked yeast products, contain a naturally occurring chemical called tyramine, which may constrict or dilate blood vessels in the brain.

Lemon Pepper Spinach Puff

You'll love the unusual combination of flavors in this easy, cheesy dish.

Makes 6 servings

1 tablespoon canola oil
½ cup chopped onions
½ cup chopped sweet red pepper
2 cloves garlic, finely chopped
1 cup lowfat cottage cheese
3 egg whites
1 teaspoon grated fresh lemon peel
1/8 teaspoon pepper
Dash nutmeg
1 10-ounce package frozen, chopped spinach, thawed and drained very well (Squeeze out water.)
¼ teaspoon cream of tartar

Preheat oven to 350º.

Lightly oil a 1-quart baking dish or spray with a nonstick spray.

Heat oil in a small nonstick skillet over medium heat. Add onions, red pepper and garlic. Cook 5 to 10 minutes, until tender. Remove from heat.

In a blender container, combine cottage cheese, 1 of the egg whites, lemon peel, pepper and nutmeg. Blend until smooth. Pour into a large bowl and stir in onion mixture and spinach. Mix well.

Place remaining 2 egg whites in a medium, deep bowl. Beat on medium speed of an electric mixer until frothy. Add cream of tartar and beat on high speed until egg whites are stiff. Fold egg whites into spinach mixture, gently but thoroughly. Spoon into pan.

Bake 40 minutes, until set and lightly browned.

Serve right away.

Each serving provides: 75 Calories, 3 g Fat, 2 mg Cholesterol, 5 g Carbohydrate, 216 mg Sodium, 2 g Fiber, 8 g Protein

GOOD HEALTH ALERT:
Never go to the grocery store hungry or without a list.

Sicilian Stuffed Squash

I used lowfat Cheddar cheese in these superb stuffed zucchini, but mozzarella or Swiss cheese will also be successful.

Makes 4 servings

- 2 zucchini squash, 10 to 12 ounces each
- 2 teaspoons olive oil
- ½ cup chopped onions
- 1 clove garlic, chopped
- ¼ teaspoon dried basil
- 1/8 teaspoon pepper
- 1 ounce shredded lowfat Cheddar cheese (¼ cup)
- 1 slice whole wheat bread (1 ounce), crumbled
- 1 egg white

Preheat oven to 350º.

Lightly oil a large, shallow baking pan or spray with a nonstick cooking spray.

Place both whole squash in 1 inch of boiling water in a large saucepan. Cover and steam 10 minutes. Remove from pan.

Cut each squash in half lengthwise and scoop out pulp, leaving a ¼-inch shell. Chop pulp.

Heat oil in a medium nonstick skillet over medium heat. Add onions and garlic and cook 5 minutes, stirring frequently. Add zucchini pulp and continue to cook 2 more minutes. Remove from heat and stir in basil and pepper. Then add cheese, bread, and egg white. Mix well.

Divide mixture evenly and spoon into zucchini shells. Place on prepared pan.

Bake, uncovered, 30 minutes.

Each serving provides: 94 Calories, 4 g Fat, 5 mg Cholesterol, 10 g Carbohydrate, 114 mg Sodium, 2 g Fiber, 6 g Protein

GOOD HEALTH ALERT:

Check out broccoli. It's a powerhouse of nutrition. One cup (chopped) supplies 90% of the daily RDA for Vitamin A in the form of beta carotene, 200% of the RDA for Vitamin C, significant amounts of niacin, calcium, thiamin and phosphorus, and 25% of your daily fiber needs. Not only that, but other substances in broccoli, such as sulforaphane, may also protect against cancer. All this for only 45 calories.

Baked Zucchini Sticks

Baked vegetables are easy and delicious – and these are so attractive. My favorite way to serve them is topped with my Herbed Tomato Sauce (see index for page #).

Makes 4 servings

2 zucchini (8 ounces each), unpeeled, cut lengthwise into eighths (or 4 small zucchini, cut lengthwise into quarters)
3 tablespoons wheat germ (3/4 ounce)
¼ teaspoon garlic powder
¼ teaspoon paprika
½ teaspoon dried oregano

Preheat oven to 450°.

Lightly oil a baking sheet or spray with a nonstick cooking spray.

Arrange zucchini, cut sides up, on a plate or a sheet of waxed paper. Let stand 5 minutes.

In a small bowl, combine remaining ingredients, mixing well. Spread onto a plate. Dip cut sides of zucchini into wheat germ mixture, pressing lightly so crumbs stick to zucchini. Place zucchini, cut sides up, on baking sheet. Sprinkle with any remaining crumbs.

Bake 15 minutes, until tender-crisp.

Each serving provides: 38 Calories, 1 g Fat, 0 mg Cholesterol, 6 g Carbohydrate, 4 mg Sodium, 2 g Fiber, 3 g Protein

Potato and Broccoli Dijon

Baked potatoes topped with Cheddar cheese and broccoli and sparked with Dijon mustard are a real gourmet treat. I serve this filling dish as an entrée for 4 or a side dish for 8.

Makes 4 servings

1 10-ounce package frozen, chopped broccoli, cooked and drained
1 tablespoon plus 1 teaspoon reduced-calorie mayonnaise
2 teaspoons Dijon mustard
4 ounces lowfat Cheddar cheese, shredded
4 medium potatoes (6 ounces each), baked

Preheat oven to 375°.

Lightly oil a shallow baking pan, or spray with a nonstick cooking spray.

Place cooked broccoli in a medium bowl.

In a small bowl or custard cup, combine mayonnaise and mustard.

Add to broccoli, along with cheese. Mix well.

Make a lengthwise slip in each potato. Squeeze the ends, making an opening in the top of each one. Divide broccoli mixture evenly and pile on top of each potato.

Place potatoes in prepared baking pan.

Bake, uncovered, 15 to 20 minutes, until cheese is hot and bubbly.

Each serving provides: 249 Calories, 7 g Fat, 22 mg Cholesterol, 34 g Carbohydrate, 328 mg Sodium, 2 g Fiber, 13 g Protein

Tex-Mex Zucchini

This is a great new way to enjoy zucchini. If you like your Mexican food spicy, add more chili powder.

Makes 4 servings

2 teaspoons olive oil
1 cup chopped onions
1 cup chopped sweet red pepper
2 cloves garlic, finely chopped
1 pound zucchini, unpeeled, cut in half lengthwise, then into ¼-inch slices (about 2-½ cups)
1 1-pound can tomatoes, chopped, drained (Reserve ¼ cup liquid.)
¼ teaspoon ground coriander
½ teaspoon ground cumin
½ teaspoon chili powder
Salt to taste

Heat oil in a large nonstick skillet over medium heat. Add onions, red pepper and garlic. Cook until tender, about 10 minutes.

Stir in zucchini, tomatoes, and reserved tomato liquid. Sprinkle spices evenly over vegetables. Mix well.

Cover and cook 5 minutes, until zucchini is tender-crisp.

Each serving provides: 83 Calories, 3 g Fat, 0 mg Cholesterol, 13 g Carbohydrate, 194 mg Sodium, 2 g Fiber, 3 g Protein

Squash Medley

You won't find vegetables boring with this pretty and tasty blend of squash, onions, tomatoes, and spices.

Makes 6 servings

1 tablespoon olive oil
1 cup sliced onions
2 cloves garlic, minced
1 cup sliced yellow summer squash, unpeeled, ¼ inch thick
1 cup sliced zucchini, unpeeled, ¼ inch thick
1 cup sliced mushrooms
2 1-pound cans tomatoes, undrained, coarsely chopped
1 teaspoon dried basil
½ teaspoon dried oregano

Heat oil in a large nonstick skillet over medium heat. Add onions and garlic. Cook, stirring occasionally, until onions are tender, about 10 minutes.

Add remaining ingredients. Cover, reduce heat to medium-low, and cook until vegetables are tender, about 15 minutes.

Serve hot.

Each serving provides: 72 Calories, 3 g Fat, 0 mg Cholesterol, 11 g Carbohydrate, 249 mg Sodium, 2 g Fiber, 3 g Protein

"Cheese" Cookies

This recipe was borrowed from a low carb cookbook and turned out to be an excellent addition for my meatless compilation. You'll make these often – enjoy!

Makes 1 serving

1 tablespoon grated cheese

Using 1 tablespoon of grated Parmesan cheese (only), place on a baking pan sprayed with non-stick product. As you put the contents of the tablespoon down, put the cheese mound in a cookie shape.

Place in a 350° oven for 5-6 minutes.

Watch closely as these "cookies" spread and brown quickly.

Make as many as you want and fill up the baking pan.

These cheese "cookies" are excellent with a salad or soup and is an excellent source of protein.

Each serving provides: 93 Calories, 1.5 g Fat, 5 mg Cholesterol, 0 g Carbohydrate, 105 mg Sodium, 0 g Fiber, 2 g Protein

Mexican Pizza

A genuine favorite!

Makes 8 servings

1 1-pound can kidney beans, rinsed and drained (This will yield 10 ounces of beans.)
2 teaspoons canola oil
1/4 teaspoon ***each*** ground cumin and chili powder
1/4 teaspoon garlic powder
1 4-ounce can chopped green chilies, drained
8 flour tortillas
1 cup jarred salsa (or taco sauce, or spaghetti sauce)
1/2 cup finely chopped green pepper
1/2 cup finely chopped onions
10 small, pitted black olives, sliced (3 tablespoons)
4 ounces shredded part-skim mozzarella cheese (1 cup)

Preheat oven to 400°.

Lightly oil a large baking sheet or spray with a nonstick spray.

Place kidney beans and oil in a medium bowl and mash with a fork or a potato masher. Sprinkle evenly with cumin, chili powder, and garlic powder. Mix well. Add canned chilies and mix again.

Place 4 of the tortillas on the prepared sheet. Divide bean mixture evenly and spread over the 4 tortillas, staying 1-inch away from the edges of the tortillas. Top each one with another tortilla.

Spread 1/4 cup of the salsa over the top of each tortilla. Sprinkle evenly with green pepper, onions, and olives. Divide cheese evenly and sprinkle over the top.

Each serving provides: 223 Calories, 4 g Fat, 8 mg Cholesterol, 35 g Carbohydrate, 644 mg Sodium, 5 g Fiber, 10 g Protein

Bake 15 minutes. Cut in half to serve.

GOOD HEALTH ALERT:

Get free nutrition advice from a registered dietician by calling the American Dietetic Association's Nutrition Hotline at 1-800-366-1655.

Dinner in a Nest

It's all here – onions, beans, tomato sauce, and cheese – in a potato nest.

Makes 6 servings

2 large potatoes (18 ounces total), unpeeled, coarsely shredded
1 tablespoon canola oil
2 cups chopped onions
1 1-pound can Great Northern beans, rinsed and drained (This will yield 10 ounces of beans.)
1 8-ounce can salt-free (or regular) tomato sauce
¼ teaspoon dried basil
¼ teaspoon dried oregano
1/8 teaspoon garlic powder
4 ounces shredded part-skim mozzarella cheese (1 cup)

Preheat oven to 400°.

Oil a 10-inch pie pan or spray with a nonstick cooking spray.

Arrange potatoes in bottom and sides of pan, forming a thick crust, or nest.

Press potatoes firmly in place. Bake 20 minutes.

While potatoes are baking, heat oil in a large nonstick skillet over medium heat. Add onions. Cook, stirring frequently, until onions are nicely browned, about 15 minutes. Remove from heat and stir in beans.

When potatoes are finished baking, remove from oven. Spread bean mixture evenly into potato nest. Combine tomato sauce and spices and spoon evenly over bean mixture. Top with cheese.

Return to oven and bake 10 minutes, until cheese is melted.

Each serving provides: 211 Calories, 6 g Fat, 11 mg Cholesterol, 29 g Carbohydrate, 242 mg Sodium, 4 g Fiber, 11 g Protein

GOOD HEALTH ALERT:
Tomatoes are the superstar in the fruit and veggie pantheon. They contain lycopene, a powerful cancer fighter. They're also rich in Vitamin C.

Vegetable Bread Stuffing

For Thanksgiving or anytime, you'll love the delicate blend of spices in this vegetable-packed stuffing.

Makes 8 servings

- 12 slices whole wheat bread (1-ounce slices), cut into cubes
- 1 tablespoon plus 1 teaspoon butter
- 3 cloves garlic, finely chopped
- 1 cup chopped onions
- 1 cup chopped celery
- 1 cup carrots, coarsely shredded
- 2 cups sliced mushrooms
- ½ teaspoon ***each*** poultry seasoning and ground sage
- ¼ teaspoon dried thyme
- ¼ teaspoon pepper
- 2 tablespoons dried parsley flakes
- Salt to taste
- 2 cups water

Preheat oven to 350º.

Lightly oil a 2-quart casserole or spray with a cooking spray.

Place bread cubes on a baking sheet in a single layer. Bake 10 minutes. Set aside to cool.

In a large nonstick skillet, melt butter over medium heat. Add garlic, onions, celery and carrots. Cook, stirring frequently, until vegetables are tender, about 10 minutes. Add mushrooms and spices. Cook 10 more minutes, stirring frequently. Remove from heat.

Add bread cubes, tossing to combine bread and vegetables. Gradually add water, tossing, until bread is moistened. (Add more water if a moister stuffing is preferred.)

Spoon stuffing into prepared pan. Cover and bake 1 hour.

Each serving provides: 134 Calories, 3 g Fat, 1 mg Cholesterol, 24 g Carbohydrate, 313 mg Sodium, 3 g Fiber, 5 g Protein

Ratatouille Pot Pie

Chunks of vegetables in a thick, spicy sauce, topped with a crusty biscuit topping – yum! You can turn this scrumptious side dish into a filling meal by simply adding a can of drained kidney beans along with the tomato sauce.

Makes 8 servings

1 tablespoon olive oil
1-½ cups onions, sliced ¼-inch thick
1 cup green pepper, sliced ¼-inch thick
3 cloves garlic, finely chopped
3 cups eggplant, peeled, cut into 1-inch cubes
2 cups zucchini, unpeeled, cut into 1-inch chunks
1½ teaspoons dried oregano
1 teaspoon dried basil
Salt and pepper to taste
2 8-ounce cans salt-free (or regular) tomato sauce
1 tablespoon plus 1 teaspoon cornstarch

Biscuit topper:

3/4 cup all-purpose flour
3/4 cup whole wheat flour
1 tablespoon baking powder
¼ teaspoon salt
3 tablespoons butter
½ cup plus 2 tablespoons skim milk

Crumb topping:

1 teaspoon olive oil
1-½ teaspoons wheat germ
1-½ teaspoons grated Parmesan cheese

Heat oil in a 10-inch cast iron (or other ovenproof) skillet over medium heat. Add onions, green pepper and garlic. Cook 5 minutes, stirring frequently.

Add eggplant, zucchini and spices. Cook 10 minutes, stirring frequently. Add small amounts of water, if necessary, to prevent sticking.

In a small bowl, combine tomato sauce and cornstarch. Stir to dissolve cornstarch. Remove skillet from heat and stir in tomato sauce.

Preheat oven to 450°.

Prepare biscuit topper:

In a large bowl, combine both flours, baking powder and salt. Mix well.

Add butter. Mix with a fork or pastry blender until mixture resembles coarse crumbs.

Add milk. Stir until dry ingredients are moistened.

Place dough on a floured piece of waxed paper and knead a few times until dough holds together in a ball. (Add a small amount of flour if dough is sticky.)

Place another piece of waxed paper over dough and roll into a 10 inch circle. Remove the top piece of paper and invert dough onto eggplant mixture. Carefully remove remaining paper.

Crumb topping:

Drizzle 1 teaspoon olive oil over dough. Spread it evenly over dough with your fingertips.

Combine wheat germ and grated cheese and sprinkle evenly over dough. With a sharp knife, cut a few slits in the dough to allow steam to escape.

Bake 20 minutes.

Let stand 5 minutes before serving.

Each serving provides: 204 Calories, 7 g Fat, 1 mg Cholesterol, 30 g Carbohydrate, 310 mg Sodium, 5 g Fiber, 6 g Protein

Onion Bread Custard

This is a unique and delectable side dish – onions and bread cubes baked in a savory, herbed custard. It also makes a wonderful brunch dish.

Makes 6 servings

- 1 tablespoon canola oil
- 1 clove garlic, finely chopped
- ¼ teaspoon dried thyme
- 1 cup nonfat dry milk
- 6 egg whites
- 2½ cups thinly sliced onions
- 1 teaspoon ground sage
- 6 slices whole wheat bread (1-ounce slices), cut into cubes
- 2 cups water
- 2 teaspoons Dijon mustard

Lightly oil an 8-inch square baking pan or spray with a nonstick cooking spray.

Heat oil in a large nonstick skillet over medium heat. Add onions and garlic. Cook 8 to 10 minutes, until onions are tender. Stir frequently, separating onions into rings. Remove from heat.

Sprinkle sage and thyme over onions. Mix well, distributing spices evenly. Add bread cubes. Toss to combine. Place in prepared pan.

In a medium bowl, combine remaining ingredients. Beat with a fork or wire whisk until well blended. Pour over onion mixture. Press mixture down gently with the back of a spoon. Let stand 30 minutes before baking.

Preheat oven to 350º. Bake 45 minutes, until custard is set and top is lightly browned. Let stand 5 minutes before serving.

Each serving provides: 173 Calories, 4 g Fat, 3 mg Cholesterol, 24 g Carbohydrate, 349 mg Sodium, 2 g Fiber, 11 g Protein

Starchy Vegetable

This section includes white potatoes, sweet potatoes, corn, peas, and all varieties of winter squash. Like the other vegetables, these are packed with vitamins, minerals, and fiber. These vegetables are higher in carbohydrates and calories than other vegetables. I have also included in this section several side dishes that use legumes. **Diabetics need to review their specific guidelines and review their recommended carbohydrate intake on a daily basis.**

In all of the recipes that call for either white potatoes or sweet potatoes, I specify the amount in ounces. Please keep in mind that a medium potato weighs approximately 7 ounces.

Whenever possible, I recommend leaving the skin on white potatoes and sweet potatoes. The skin not only provides extra nutrients and fiber, but it is also quite tasty. Don't think that potatoes are only for dinner. A steamy baked white potato or sweet potato makes a nutritious and filling breakfast. Incidentally, in case your mother told you that potatoes are fattening," the real culprit is the fatty toppings that are often put on potatoes (such as bacon, cheese, butter and sour cream). Potatoes themselves are low in fat and high in fiber and carbohydrates.

Examples of winter squash are butternut, hubbard, and acorn. I love the versatility of these types of squash—although higher in carbohydrates, these are so essentially good for you that I encourage you to use them freely and feel good about giving "you" some great ingredients with these choices. They can be served as a side dish, added to soups, stews and casseroles, and, with a little cinnamon and brown sugar, can even pass as dessert. Unlike most other vegetables, the skin on winter squash is inedible. It can be removed either before or after cooking the squash.

Corn and peas are familiar, but I have created some new and tasty ways to prepare them. I invite you to try my recipes and to be creative with these delicious vegetables. Be sure to check my other chapters because I use many starchy vegetables in Soups, Salads and Salad Dressings, Grains, and Entrées. Also see Spice It Right (see index for page number) for ideas that will help you add spices that will complement your foods. Here are just a few of my other recipes that use starchy vegetables – see index for page number:

- Millet Butternut Soup – Butternut squash in a thick soup.
- Very Veggie Enchiladas – Corn and beans in tortillas.
- Mexicali Squares – Corn and cornmeal crust topped with Mexican-flavored vegetables.
- Hearty Vegetable Stew – Potatoes and lots of goodies.
- French Potato Salad – My own spicy version.

Raspberry-Filled Sweet Potato Croquettes

There's a burst of raspberry flavor in the center of each one of these delicious croquettes – and they're very easy to make.

Makes 6 servings

1 18-ounce can sweet potatoes (vacuum packed)
2 tablespoons firmly packed brown sugar
¼ teaspoon orange extract
1 teaspoon vanilla extract
½ teaspoon ground cinnamon
2 tablespoons reduced-sugar raspberry jam (8-10 calories per tablespoon) or fruit-only raspberry jam
½ cup plus 1 tablespoon Grape Nuts® cereal, crushed slightly* (2¼ ounces)
1½ teaspoons canola oil

Preheat oven to 350º.

Lightly oil a shallow baking pan or spray with a cooking spray.

In a large bowl, combine sweet potatoes, brown sugar, orange extract, vanilla extract, and cinnamon. Mash with a fork or potato masher until mixture is smooth and thoroughly blended.

Divide mixture into 12 equal portions. Shape each portion into a ½-inch thick patty. With your thumb, make an indentation in the center of the patty. Spoon ½ teaspoon of the jam into the indentation. Carefully form the sweet potato around the jam, molding it into the shape of a ball.

Roll each ball in crushed cereal. Place in prepared pan and drizzle lightly with the oil, using 1/8 teaspoon on each croquette.

Bake, uncovered, 30 minutes.

*An easy way to crush cereal is to place it in a plastic bag and crush it with a rolling pin.

Each serving provides: 153 Calories, 1 g Fat, 0 mg Cholesterol, 33 g Carbohydrate, 110 mg Sodium, 4 g Fiber, 3 g Protein

GOOD HEALTH ALERT:

Odd as it sounds, wearing a hat will keep your feet warm in winter. Hatless, you'll lose a lot of your total body heat through your head.

Apricot Baked Sweets

Chunks of sweet potatoes, baked with apricots and orange juice, make a wonderful, sweet addition to any meal – especially at holiday time.

Makes 6 servings

3 medium sweet potatoes (18 ounces total), unpeeled, cut into 1-inch chunks
½ cup chopped dried apricots (12 apricot halves)
1 tablespoon pure maple syrup
½ cup orange juice
1 teaspoon grated fresh orange peel
Ground cinnamon

Preheat oven to 350°.

Lightly oil a 9-inch pie pan or spray with a nonstick cooking spray.

Place sweet potatoes and apricots in a large bowl.

In a small bowl, combine maple syrup, orange juice, and orange peel. Pour over sweet potatoes. Mix well.

Transfer mixture to prepared pie pan. Make sure that apricots are evenly distributed. Sprinkle with cinnamon.

Cover and bake 45 minutes.

Each serving provides: 124 Calories, 0 g Fat, 0 mg Cholesterol, 29 g Carbohydrate, 12 mg Sodium, 3 g Fiber, 2 g Protein

Pineapple Upside-Down Sweet Potatoes

This dish makes such a pretty presentation. You invert the pan to reveal pineapple and brown sugar on the top.

Makes 6 servings

Topping:

2 tablespoons butter, melted
2 tablespoons firmly packed brown sugar
1 tablespoon maple syrup
Ground cinnamon
1-½ cups canned pineapple chunks (unsweetened), drained

Filling:

1 18-ounce can sweet potatoes (vacuum packed)
1-½ teaspoons vanilla extract
3/4 teaspoon ground cinnamon
1 tablespoon firmly packed brown sugar

Preheat oven to 350°.

Lightly oil a 9-inch pie pan or spray with a nonstick cooking spray.

Combine butter, brown sugar, and maple syrup in prepared pan. Mix well and spread evenly over bottom of pan. Sprinkle lightly with cinnamon. Arrange pineapple chunks in a single layer over butter mixture.

In a large bowl, combine all filling ingredients. Mash with a fork or a potato masher until smooth and thoroughly combined.

Spoon sweet potato mixture over pineapple chunks. Smooth the top with the back of a spoon.

Cover with aluminum foil and bake 45 minutes.

Let pan sit 1 minute, then remove foil, run a knife around the edge of the pan, and invert onto a serving plate.

Each serving provides: 187 Calories, 4 g Fat, 0 mg Cholesterol, 37 g Carbohydrate, 93 mg Sodium, 3 g Fiber, 2 g Protein

Orange Sweet Potatoes

Shredded sweet potatoes, oranges, and raisins make this side dish a real sweet treat.

Makes 6 servings

- 2 tablespoons butter
- 3 medium sweet potatoes (18 ounces total), unpeeled, coarsely shredded
- 1 cup orange juice
- 1 teaspoon grated fresh orange peel
- 1½ teaspoons ground cinnamon
- 3 tablespoons firmly packed brown sugar
- 2 small oranges, peeled and sectioned (Discard white membrane)
- ¼ cup raisins
- ½ teaspoon vanilla extract

Melt butter in a large nonstick skillet over medium heat. Add sweet potatoes, orange juice, orange peel, and cinnamon. Cook, stirring frequently, 5 minutes.

Reduce heat to medium low, cover, and cook 15 minutes, or until sweet potatoes are tender, stirring occasionally.

Add remaining ingredients. Cook, stirring, until heated through.

Each serving provides: 188 Calories, 2 g Fat, 0 mg Cholesterol, 42 g Carbohydrate, 60 mg Sodium, 3 g Fiber, 2 g Protein

Sweet Potato and Banana Puff

This sweet, delectable dish puffs up like a soufflé, then sinks as it cools, so you'll want to serve it right away.

Makes 8 servings

- 4 medium sweet potatoes (1-½ pounds total)
- 2 medium, ripe bananas
- ¼ cup orange juice
- 2 tablespoons firmly packed brown sugar
- 1 teaspoon vanilla extract
- 1¼ teaspoons rum extract
- ¼ teaspoon ground cinnamon
- 1/8 teaspoon ground nutmeg
- 2 egg whites
- ¼ teaspoon cream of tartar

Prick sweet potatoes several times with a sharp knife and bake them in a 350° oven 1 hour, or until tender. Remove sweet potatoes from oven. Increase oven temperature to 400°.

Lightly oil a 2-quart casserole or soufflé dish or spray with a nonstick cooking spray.

Peel sweet potatoes and place them in a large bowl. Add bananas, orange juice, brown sugar, extracts and spices. Mash with a fork or potato masher until combined. Then beat on medium speed of an electric mixer until smooth. Wash and dry beaters.

Place egg whites in a small, deep bowl. Beat on medium speed until frothy. Add cream of tartar and beat on high speed until egg whites are stiff.

Using a folding motion, fold egg whites into sweet potato mixture, gently but thoroughly. Spoon into prepared pan.

Bake 30 to 35 minutes, until top is puffed and starts to brown.

Each serving provides: 116 Calories, 0 g Fat, 0 mg Cholesterol, 26 g Carbohydrate, 23 mg Sodium, 3 g Fiber, 2 g Protein

GOOD HEALTH ALERT:

Get your fiber from your food, not supplements. Most fiber pills actually have little fiber in them: five pills contain about 2.5 grams of fiber – about one-tenth of the recommended daily intake. You can easily get all the fiber you need from food, at a lower cost.

Sweet Stuffed Sweets

These delicious pineapple-flavored sweet potatoes can be stuffed a day ahead and baked when needed.

Makes 4 servings

2 large sweet potatoes (9 ounces each)
½ cup canned crushed pineapple (unsweetened), drained
¼ teaspoon vanilla extract
1/8 teaspoon ground cinnamon
1 teaspoon firmly packed brown sugar

Topping:
1 tablespoon chopped pecans (optional)
2 teaspoons wheat germ
1/8 teaspoon ground cinnamon

Preheat oven to 375°.

Prick sweet potatoes several times with a sharp knife and bake them 45 minutes, or until tender.

Cut potatoes in half lengthwise. Carefully scoop out the pulp with a spoon, leaving a ¼-inch shell.

In a medium bowl, combine potato pulp with crushed pineapple, vanilla, cinnamon, and brown sugar. Mix with a fork until well blended.

Divide mixture evenly and fill the potato shells, smoothing the tops with the back of a spoon.

Sprinkle with pecans (if desired), pressing them gently into the potatoes. Combine wheat germ and cinnamon and sprinkle evenly over potatoes.

Place potatoes in a shallow baking pan.

Bake 15 minutes.

Each serving provides: 125 Calories, 0 g Fat, 0 mg Cholesterol, 29 g Carbohydrate, 13 mg Sodium, 4 g Fiber, 2 g Protein

GOOD HEALTH ALERT:
Rounding out the top 10 nutrition all-stars among fruits and vegetables, along with broccoli and kale, are cantaloupe, carrots, mangoes, pumpkin, red bell peppers, spinach, strawberries, and sweet potatoes.

Sweet Potatoes and Onions

The unusual blend of cinnamon and thyme gives this dish a special flair.
Makes 4 servings

1 tablespoon plus 1 teaspoon canola oil
1 cup chopped onions
2 medium sweet potatoes (12 ounces total), peeled, cut into ½-inch cubes
½ teaspoon ground cinnamon
¼ teaspoon dried thyme
½ cup water

Preheat a large nonstick skillet over medium heat. Add all ingredients, ***except*** water, and cook 10 minutes, or until onions are tender, stirring frequently.

Add water, reduce heat to low, cover, and cook 15 minutes, or until sweet potatoes are tender. Stir occasionally while cooking and add water in small amounts, if necessary, to prevent sticking.

Each serving provides: 119 Calories, 5 g Fat, 0 mg Cholesterol, 18 g Carbohydrate, 9 mg Sodium, 2 g Fiber, 1 g Protein

Chili Fried Corn

I've taken a plain can of corn and jazzed it up! You can use mild green chilies or, if you dare, use the hot ones. *Makes 4 servings*

2 teaspoons canola oil
1 cup chopped onions
1 1-pound can corn, drained
1 4-ounce can chopped green chilies (mild or hot), drained
½ cup shredded lowfat Cheddar cheese (2 ounces)

Heat oil in a large nonstick skillet over medium-high heat. Add onions. Cook, stirring frequently, until onions start to brown, about 3 minutes. Add corn and chilies. Cook, stirring frequently, 5 minutes. Remove skillet from heat and sprinkle cheese evenly over corn. Cover and let stand 5 minutes to melt cheese.

Each serving provides: 142 Calories, 6 g Fat, 10 mg Cholesterol, 18 g Carbohydrate, 274 mg Sodium, 2 g Fiber, 7 g Protein

Creamy Corn and Spinach

You won't believe the wonderful, delicate flavor of this unusual combination. I serve it as a side dish and use the leftovers for a quick, hot lunch: just spread on toast and broil until hot and bubbly.

Makes 6 servings

2 teaspoons canola oil
1 cup chopped onions
1 1-pound can cream-style corn
1 10-ounce package frozen chopped spinach, thawed and drained well
Salt to taste
¼ teaspoon pepper

Topping:
2 tablespoons wheat germ
2 tablespoons grated Parmesan cheese
2 teaspoons butter

Preheat oven to 375°.

Lightly oil a 1-quart baking dish or spray with a nonstick cooking spray.

Heat oil in a medium nonstick skillet over medium heat. Add onions and cook, stirring frequently, until onions are lightly browned and edges begin to crisp, about 10 minutes. Add small amounts of water, if necessary, to prevent sticking.

Place browned onions in a large bowl. Add corn, spinach, salt, and pepper. Mix well. Spoon into prepared baking dish.

Combine wheat germ and Parmesan cheese and sprinkle evenly over casserole. Dot with butter.

Bake, uncovered, 30 minutes.

Each serving provides: 111 Calories, 3 g Fat, 1 mg Cholesterol, 19 g Carbohydrate, 297 mg Sodium, 3 g Fiber, 4 g Protein

Creole Corn

Sliced olives add zip to this unusual, yet easy, corn dish. It's a delicious accompaniment to any of our sandwiches or meatless burgers.

Makes 4 servings

1 tablespoon canola oil
½ cup chopped onions
1 cup chopped celery
2 cloves garlic, finely chopped
1 1-pound can tomatoes, chopped, undrained
1 10-ounce package frozen corn
10 small stuffed green olives, chopped or thinly sliced (3 tablespoons)
1 small bay leaf
1 teaspoon sugar
1 teaspoon dried parsley
1/16 teaspoon dried thyme
1/8 teaspoon salt
1/8 teaspoon pepper

Heat oil in a medium saucepan over medium heat. Add onions, celery, and garlic. Cook, stirring frequently, until tender, about 10 minutes. Add small amounts of tomato liquid, as necessary to prevent sticking. Add remaining ingredients and bring mixture to a boil. Cover, reduce heat to medium-low, and simmer 10 minutes, or until corn is tender. Remove and discard bay leaf before serving.

Each serving provides: 141 Calories, 5 g Fat, 0 mg Cholesterol, 24 g Carbohydrate, 437 mg Sodium, 2 g Fiber, 4 g Protein

Carrot and Potato Pudding

The earthy flavor of the potatoes, along with the sweetness of the carrots, makes this a very tasty accompaniment to any meal. *Makes 6 servings*

2 cups finely shredded carrots
¼ cup firmly packed brown sugar
3 tablespoons margarine, melted
1 teaspoon ground cinnamon
1 teaspoon ground nutmeg
1 teaspoon baking soda
¼ cup plus 2 tablespoons whole wheat or all-purpose flour
2 medium potatoes (12 ounces total), unpeeled, finely shredded

Preheat oven to 350º.

Lightly oil a 1-quart baking dish or spray with a nonstick cooking spray. In a large bowl, combine all ingredients, mixing well. Place in prepared baking dish and press mixture down into pan with the back of a spoon. Cover and bake 30 minutes. Uncover and continue baking 30 more minutes.

Each serving provides: 138 Calories, 6 g Fat, 0 mg Cholesterol, 19 g Carbohydrate, 221 mg Sodium, 3 g Fiber, 3 g Protein

Bel Air Potatoes

Similar to hash browns, but laced with cheese, these potatoes are great for breakfast, lunch or dinner. The secret to their flavor is to let the onions get brown and crispy.

Makes 6 servings

1 tablespoon canola oil
3 cups chopped onions
½ cup plain nonfat yogurt or plain Greek yogurt
3 ounces shredded lowfat Cheddar cheese (3/4 cup)
1/8 teaspoon pepper
3 medium cooked potatoes (18 ounces total), cut into ½-inch cubes

(You can bake or boil the potatoes. If you bake them, remove the skin afterward.)

Heat oil in a large nonstick skillet over medium heat. Add onions. Cook, stirring frequently, until onions are browned, about 15 minutes.

While onions are cooking, combine yogurt, Cheddar cheese, and pepper in a small bowl. Set aside.

Add potatoes to browned onions. Cook, stirring, until potatoes are heated through. Remove from heat. Stir in yogurt mixture, mixing well.

Each serving provides: 176 Calories, 5 g Fat, 10 mg Cholesterol, 25 g Carbohydrate, 120 mg Sodium, 4 g Fiber, 7 g Protein

Potatoes Cacciatore

This flavorful dish serves 8 as a side dish or 6 as a delicious entrée. Sprinkle it lightly with Parmesan cheese or part-skim mozzarella. If you like, add a salad with Italian dressing, and enjoy. *Makes 8 servings*

- 2 teaspoons olive oil
- 2 cups sliced onions (Cut onions in half lengthwise, then slice each half crosswise into ¼ inch slices.)
- 2 cloves garlic, finely chopped
- 1 1-pound can tomatoes, undrained, chopped
- 1 8-ounce can salt-free (or regular) tomato sauce
- ¼ teaspoon pepper
- ½ teaspoon dried oregano
- ½ teaspoon dried basil
- ½ teaspoon dried rosemary, crumbled
- 4 medium baking potatoes (1½ pounds total), unpeeled, sliced crosswise into ¼ inch slices

Preheat oven to 375º.

Lightly oil a 9 x 13-inch baking pan or spray with nonstick cooking spray.

Heat oil in a large nonstick skillet over medium heat. Add onions and garlic and cook 5 minutes, stirring frequently, until onions are tender. Remove from heat and add remaining ingredients, ***except*** potatoes. Mix well.

Place a layer of potatoes in prepared pan. Spoon half of the tomato mixture evenly over potatoes. Add another layer of potatoes and end with remaining tomato mixture.

Cover pan tightly with aluminum foil.

Bake 50 minutes.

Each serving provides: 110 Calories, 2 g Fat, 0 mg Cholesterol, 22 g Carbohydrate, 106 mg Sodium, 4 g Fiber, 3 g Protein

Red Potatoes with Lemon "Butter"

These potatoes make a wonderful side dish for any meal. They're at home with a family dinner or an elegant dinner party.

Makes 4 servings

- 8 small, new red potatoes (18 ounces total)
- 1 tablespoon lemon juice
- 1 tablespoon dried chives
- 2 tablespoons butter
- 1 teaspoon grated fresh lemon peel
- Salt and pepper to taste

Preheat oven to 425°.

Prick potatoes and place directly on oven rack.

Bake 30 minutes, or until tender. (Potatoes may take more or less time, depending on their size.) While potatoes are baking, melt butter and place in a small bowl or custard cup. Add lemon juice and lemon peel.

To serve:

Cut potatoes in half and place cut side up on a serving platter. Drizzle evenly with butter mixture. Sprinkle with chives, salt, and pepper.

Serve right away.

Each serving provides: 155 Calories, 6 g Fat, 0 mg Cholesterol, 23 g Carbohydrate, 78 mg Sodium, 3 g Fiber, 3 g Protein

Lemon Dill Potatoes

These tangy stuffed potatoes can be made ahead and reheated when needed. They're perfect party food. *Makes 4 servings*

2 medium baking potatoes (6 ounces each), baked
1 tablespoon plus 1 teaspoon reduced-calorie margarine
2 tablespoons plain nonfat yogurt or plain Greek yogurt
1 teaspoon lemon juice
½ teaspoon dill weed
1/8 teaspoon garlic powder
Salt and pepper to taste
Paprika

Preheat oven to 375°.

Lightly oil a shallow baking pan or spray with nonstick cooking spray.

Cut baked potatoes in half lengthwise. Carefully scoop out the pulp with a spoon, leaving a ¼ inch shell.

In a large bowl, combine potato pulp with remaining ingredients, ***except*** paprika. Mash with a fork or potato masher until well blended. (Sometimes baked potatoes are dry and may need a little more yogurt or a few teaspoons of skim milk.) Divide mixture evenly and fill the potato shells, smoothing the top with the back of a spoon. Place in prepared pan. Sprinkle with paprika.

Bake, uncovered, 20 minutes, until lightly browned.

Each serving provides: 83 Calories, 2 g Fat, 0 mg Cholesterol, 15 g Carbohydrate, 56 mg Sodium, 3 g Fiber, 2 g Protein

Hawaiian Stir-Fry

I love this tasty stir-fry over rice or very thin noodles. Sometimes I add tofu and my meal is complete.

Makes 4 servings

Pineapple sauce:

2/3 cup pineapple juice
2 tablespoons reduced-sodium (or regular) soy sauce
½ teaspoon ground ginger
½ teaspoon garlic powder
1 tablespoon plus 1 teaspoon cornstarch
1 teaspoon sugar

Vegetables:

1 tablespoon plus 1 teaspoon canola oil
1 cup onions, sliced ¼ inch thick
1 cup green pepper, sliced ¼ inch thick
½ cup carrots, sliced ¼ inch thick
1 cup broccoli, cut into small flowerets
1 cup cauliflower, cut into small flowerets
½ cup sliced water chestnuts
1 cup sliced mushrooms
1½ cups coarsely shredded Chinese cabbage

In a small bowl, combine all sauce ingredients, mixing until cornstarch is dissolved. Set aside.

Heat oil in a large nonstick skillet or wok over medium-high heat. Add onions, green pepper and carrots. Cook 3 to 4 minutes, stirring constantly with a tossing motion.

Add broccoli, cauliflower, and water chestnuts. Cook, stirring, 2 to 3 minutes, until broccoli is bright green.

Add mushrooms and cabbage. Cook, stirring, 1 minute.

Stir sauce and add to vegetables. Cook, stirring, until sauce is thickened and vegetables are glazed, about 1 minute.

Each serving provides: 146 Calories, 5 g Fat, 0 mg Cholesterol, 23 g Carbohydrate, 322 mg Sodium, 2 g Fiber, 4 g Protein

Potatoes Florentine

Spinach and spices add a Greek note to potatoes in this unique dish.

Makes 6 servings

3 medium potatoes (18 ounces total), unpeeled, coarsely shredded
1 10-ounce package frozen chopped spinach, thawed and drained well
2/3 cup lowfat cottage cheese
3 egg whites
1 cup skim milk
¼ teaspoon garlic powder
1/16 teaspoon ground nutmeg
1 tablespoon sherry
Salt and pepper to taste

Topping:
1 tablespoon grated Parmesan cheese
1 tablespoon dry bread crumbs
1 tablespoon canola oil

Preheat oven to 350°.

Lightly oil an 8-inch square baking pan or spray with a nonstick cooking spray.

In a large bowl combine potatoes and spinach.

In a small bowl, combine cottage cheese, egg whites, and milk. Beat with a fork or wire whisk and add to potato mixture. Add garlic powder, nutmeg, sherry, salt, and pepper. Mix well. Place in prepared pan.

Combine Parmesan cheese and bread crumbs and sprinkle evenly over top of potatoes. Drizzle with oil.

Bake, covered, 30 minutes. Uncover and bake 30 more minutes.

Each serving provides: 146 Calories, 3 g Fat, 3 mg Cholesterol, 20 g Carbohydrate, 215 mg Sodium, 3 g Fiber, 10 g Protein

Baked Potato Onion Wrap-Ups

An idea remembered from Summer Camp, these potatoes have become a real family favorite. *Makes 4 servings*

4 medium baking potatoes (6 ounces each), unpeeled
4 medium onions (Try to find onions that are about the same diameter as the potatoes.)

Preheat oven to 350º.

Slice each potato, crosswise, into 4 thick slices. Slice each onion, crosswise, into 3 thick slices. Put potatoes together, placing an onion slice between each of the potato slices. Wrap potato tightly in foil. Bake 1 hour.

Each serving provides: 153 Calories, 0 g Fat, 0 mg Cholesterol, 34 g Carbohydrate, 14 mg Sodium, 3 g Fiber, 5 g Protein

Nacho Potatoes

Serve these spicy potatoes just as they are or topped with your favorite salsa. Kids (of all ages) will love them. *Makes 4 servings*

2 medium baking potatoes (12 ounces total), unpeeled, cut into 1-inch chunks
3 tablespoons water
½ teaspoon chili powder
¼ teaspoon ground cumin
Salt to taste
4 ounces shredded lowfat Cheddar cheese (1 cup)
1 4-ounce can chopped green chilies (hot *or* mild), drained

Preheat oven to 350º.

Lightly oil a 9-inch pie pan or spray with a nonstick cooking spray. Place water in prepared pan and add potato chunks. Sprinkle evenly with chili powder, cumin, and salt. Bake, covered, 45 minutes.

In a small bowl, combine cheese and chilies, mixing well. Spoon mixture evenly over baked potatoes. Return to oven, uncovered, 5 minutes, or until cheese is melted.

Each serving provides: 161 Calories, 5 g Fat, 20 mg Cholesterol,17 g Carbohydrate, 382 mg Sodium, 3 g Fiber, 10 g Protein

Taco Fries

Imagine French fried potatoes, rolled in taco seasoning, and cooked until crisp. Well, here they are. The only difference is that these are baked, not fried. Look out – they're spicy!

Makes 4 servings

- 2 medium baking potatoes (18 ounces total), unpeeled, cut into french fry-like strips
- 1 packet taco seasoning mix

Preheat oven to 450°.

Lightly oil a baking sheet or spray with a nonstick cooking spray.

Place potato strips in a paper or plastic bag. Add taco seasoning mix, close bag, and shake until potatoes are coated. Place on prepared baking sheet.

Bake 20 to 30 minutes, turning potatoes several times until desired crispness is reached.

Each serving provides: 124 Calories, 0 g Fat, 0 mg Cholesterol, 27 g Carbohydrate, 555 mg Sodium, 2 g Fiber, 4 g Protein

GOOD HEALTH ALERT:
Always drink before, during and after exercise: plain water is fine. During physical activity you may become significantly dehydrated before you feel thirsty. As you exercise, it's possible to lose up to two quarts of water before you notice your fluid loss. If you drink only when you're thirsty, you may not be drinking enough.

Scalloped Potatoes

I removed the butter and the cream, but not the flavor, from an old-time favorite.

Makes 4 servings

2 medium potatoes (12 ounces total), unpeeled, sliced 1/8-inch thick
3 tablespoons all-purpose flour
1 cup onions, sliced 1/8-inch thick
1 cup skim milk
Salt to taste
¼ teaspoon pepper
3/4 ounce grated Parmesan cheese (3 tablespoons)
Paprika

Preheat oven to 350°.

Lightly oil a 1-½-quart baking dish or spray with a nonstick cooking spray.

Place ***half*** of the potatoes in layers in the prepared baking dish. Sprinkle evenly with ***half*** the flour, and top with ***half*** the onions.

Repeat, using remaining potatoes, flour, and onions.

In a small bowl, combine milk, salt, pepper, and Parmesan cheese. Spoon over potato mixture. Sprinkle evenly with paprika.

Cover and bake 1 hour. Uncover and continue to bake 15 more minutes.

Each serving provides: 145 Calories, 2 g Fat, 5 mg Cholesterol, 25 g Carbohydrate, 138 mg Sodium, 2 g Fiber, 7 g Protein

Bombay Peas and Potatoes

Curry lovers will delight in this delicious blend of vegetables and spices. It's pretty and colorful, too.

Makes 8 servings

2 teaspoons canola oil
1 cup chopped onions
2 cloves garlic, chopped
1 1-pound can tomatoes, chopped, undrained
2 medium potatoes (18 ounces total), unpeeled, cut into ½-inch cubes
1 teaspoon curry powder
¼ teaspoon chili powder
½ teaspoon turmeric

1 bay leaf
1 cup water
1 cup fresh or frozen peas (If using frozen peas, there's no need to thaw.)

Heat oil in a large nonstick skillet over medium heat. Add onions and garlic. Cook 10 minutes, or until onions begin to brown.

Add remaining ingredients, ***except*** peas. Mix well. Bring mixture to a boil stirring frequently. Then cover, reduce heat to low, and simmer 15 minutes.

Stir in peas, cover, and cook 20 more minutes, or until potatoes are tender.

Remove and discard bay leaf before serving.

Each serving provides: 94 Calories, 2 g Fat, 0 mg Cholesterol, 18 g Carbohydrate, 99 mg Sodium, 3 g Fiber, 3 g Protein

Peppers, Peas, and Rice

This delicious side dish has a slightly Oriental flavor. I like to serve it with Shanghai Grilled Tofu (see index for page #).

Makes 6 servings

1 tablespoon sesame oil
1½ cups chopped green pepper
3 tablespoons soy sauce
3 tablespoons water
2 tablespoons firmly packed brown sugar
1/8 teaspoon garlic powder
1 10-ounce package frozen peas
1½ cups cooked brown rice

Heat oil in a large nonstick skillet over medium heat. Add green pepper. Cook 10 minutes, stirring frequently.

In a small bowl, combine soy sauce, water, brown sugar, and garlic powder. Add to skillet, along with peas, mixing well. Reduce heat to medium low, cover, and cook 10 minutes, or until peas are just tender.

Stir in rice. Heat through.

Each serving provides: 139 Calories, 3 g Fat, 0 mg Cholesterol, 24 g Carbohydrate, 572 mg Sodium, 4 g Fiber, 4 g Protein

Fruit and Nut Stuffed Squash

This makes a beautiful party dish as well as a sweet and filling family treat.

Makes 4 servings

2 acorn squash, 10 ounces each
3/4 cup water
1 teaspoon grated fresh orange peel
2 tablespoons firmly packed brown sugar
2 small, sweet apples, unpeeled, chopped into 1/8- to ¼-inch pieces
½ cup chopped, dried apricots (12 apricot halves)
2 tablespoons chopped walnuts (½ ounce)
Ground cinnamon

Preheat oven to 400°.

Have a large shallow baking pan ready.

Cut squash in half, lengthwise, and remove seeds. Place cut side down in pan. Pour water around squash to a depth of ½ inch. (This is in addition to the 3/4 cup of water in the recipe.)

Cover with aluminum foil and bake 20 minutes.

While squash is baking, bring 3/4 cup water to a boil in a small saucepan. Add orange peel, brown sugar, apples, and apricots. Cook 5 minutes, stirring occasionally. Remove from heat, cover, and set aside.

Turn squash halves over. Stir nuts into apple mixture, divide mixture evenly, and fill squash cavities. Spoon any remaining apple-cooking water over filling. Sprinkle squash and filling liberally with cinnamon.

Bake, covered, 30 minutes, or until squash is tender.

Each serving provides: 148 Calories, 3 g Fat, 0 mg Cholesterol, 33 g Carbohydrate, 7 mg Sodium , 4 g Fiber, 2 g Protein

Orange Honey Butternut

A 2-pound butternut squash will give you about 2 cups of cooked squash for this tasty side dish.

Makes 4 servings

2 cups cooked, mashed butternut squash*
3 tablespoons oat bran (3/4 ounce)
3 tablespoons honey
1/3 cup nonfat dry milk
1-½ teaspoons grated fresh orange peel
½ teaspoon ground cinnamon

Preheat oven to 350°.

Lightly oil a 1-quart baking dish or spray with a nonstick cooking spray.

In a large bowl, combine all ingredients, mixing well. Place in prepared pan.

Bake, uncovered, 30 minutes.

Serve hot. (I also like the leftovers cold.)

*Cut a 2-pound squash into 2-inch chunks, remove seeds, and cook in 1-inch of boiling water, covered, for 20 minutes, or until tender. Drain, cook, and peel squash.

Each serving provides: 124 Calories, 1 g Fat, 1 mg Cholesterol, 31 g Carbohydrate, 36 mg Sodium, 4 g Fiber, 4 g Protein

New England Baked Limas

The ketchup makes these tangy and the maple syrup makes them sweet.

Makes 4 servings

1 10-ounce package frozen baby lima beans
½ cup chopped onions
3 tablespoons pure maple syrup
3 tablespoons ketchup
1/8 teaspoon pepper
1/8 teaspoon garlic powder
½ cup water
1 small bay leaf, broken in half

Preheat oven to 350°.

Lightly oil a 1-quart baking dish or spray with a nonstick cooking spray.

Cook lima beans according to package directions. Drain.

In a medium bowl, combine remaining ingredients. Add limas, mixing well. Pour into prepared pan.

Bake, covered, 30 minutes. Uncover and bake 30 more minutes, stirring several times.

Remove and discard bay leaf before serving.

Each serving provides: 152 Calories, 0 g Fat, 0 mg Cholesterol, 32 g Carbohydrate, 174 mg Sodium, 4 g Fiber, 6 g Protein

Honey Glazed Chickpeas

Try this slightly sweet side dish in place of a potato for a nice change of pace. I mash the leftovers and use them as a sandwich filling.

Makes 4 servings

1 1-pound can chickpeas, rinsed and drained (This will yield 10 ounces of peas.)
2 teaspoons canola oil
½ teaspoon ground cinnamon
¼ cup honey

Preheat oven to 350°.

Lightly oil a 1-quart shallow baking dish or spray with a nonstick cooking spray.

In a small bowl, combine all ingredients, mixing well. Place in prepared baking dish.

Bake, uncovered, 1 hour, stirring once after 30 minutes.

Remove from oven, stir, and serve.

Each serving provides: 171 Calories, 4 g Fat, 0 mg Cholesterol, 30 g Carbohydrate, 141 mg Sodium, 3 g Fiber, 5 g Protein

GOOD HEALTH ALERT:
Load up on Vitamin C. We need at least 90 mg of Vitamin C per day and the best way to get this is by eating at least five servings of fresh fruit and vegetables every day.

Breads and Muffins

Breads and muffins are definitely among the favorite American foods. One reason, of course, is their heartiness and flavor. Another reason is their versatility. They can be made with fruits or vegetables, and have a place at breakfast, lunch, dinner, and even dessert. They make great snacks and party food, and as a sandwich make a meal. They even make great gifts.

Most of our breads and muffins are made with a large percentage of whole wheat flour. This, along with the addition of fruits, vegetables, and other grains, adds vitamins, minerals, and fiber to these delectable favorites.

To limit the amounts of fat and cholesterol, my recipes use only skim milk and lowfat dairy products, and egg whites in place of whole eggs. (I also found that I could use a 3 ounce piece of tofu, blended with the liquid ingredients until smooth, in place of either 1 whole egg or 2 egg whites.) I have kept the use of oil to a minimum and, instead, give my breads and muffins a moist texture by using ingredients such as fruit juice, skim milk, nonfat yogurt or applesauce. When I do use oil, I choose a monounsaturated oil such as canola oil. I use a very small amount of sugar or other sweetener in these recipes. Instead, I rely on other ingredients such as vanilla extract and fruits for sweetness and spices and extracts for added flavor.

All of my breads are quick breads (baked without yeast); my muffins are baked in a standard 2½ inch muffin pan. If you wish to use larger or smaller cups, the baking times may need to be altered. Remember when baking that oven temperatures vary and my cooking times are suggested times. Most breads and muffins can be tested for doneness by inserting a toothpick in the center. It will come out clean when the bread or muffins are done.

Most quick breads and muffins are at their best when eaten the same day, preferably while still warm. It is important to remember that home-baked goods, unlike most commercially baked goods, contain no preservatives and, therefore, have a shorter shelf life. On the second day it is best to store them in the refrigerator (or freezer) and either toast them or reheat them in a microwave briefly before serving.

I invite you to be creative with my bread and muffin recipes. For example, vary extracts and spices to create new flavors – or use your creations in any of my bread puddings. Whatever you do – enjoy!

Apple Raisin Spice Bread

You won't believe a bread can be so tasty, tender, and moist.

Makes 8 servings

3 small, sweet apples, unpeeled, coarsely shredded (2 cups)
½ cup plus 2 tablespoons raisins
3/4 cup boiling water
1½ cups whole wheat flour
½ teaspoon baking powder
1 teaspoon baking soda
1 teaspoon ground cinnamon
½ teaspoon ground allspice
1/8 teaspoon ground cloves
1 tablespoon plus 1 teaspoon canola oil
¼ cup skim milk
2 egg whites
1 teaspoon vanilla extract
¼ cup firmly packed brown sugar

In a small bowl, combine apples and raisins. Add boiling water, cover, and let stand until cool.

Preheat oven to 350º.

Lightly oil a 4 x 8-inch loaf pan or spray with a cooking spray.

In a large bowl, combine flour, baking powder, baking soda, and spices. Mix well.

In another bowl, combine remaining ingredients. Beat with a fork or wire whisk until blended. Add to dry ingredients, along with apple mixture. Mix until all ingredients are moistened. Place mixture in prepared pan.

Bake 45 minutes, until a toothpick inserted in the center of the bread comes out clean. Cool in pan on wire rack 5 minutes, then turn out onto rack to finish cooling.

Each serving provides: 182 Calories, 3 g Fat, 0 mg Cholesterol, 37 g Carbohydrate, 152 mg Sodium, 4 g Fiber, 5 g Protein

GOOD HEALTH ALERT:

Good sources of zinc, a nutrient of concern to those who avoid meat, include beans, whole grains and wheat germ.

Cocoa Nut Bread

Toasting really brings out the flavor of this sweet, crunchy bread. My favorite way to serve it is topped with orange marmalade.

Makes 12 servings

½ cup plus 3 tablespoons all-purpose flour
1 cup whole wheat flour
½ cup wheat germ (2-¼ ounces)
1 teaspoon baking powder
1 teaspoon baking soda
2 tablespoons cocoa (unsweetened)
¼ cup plus 2 tablespoons chopped walnuts, pecans, almonds, ***or*** unsalted peanuts (1-½ ounces)
1-¼ cups skim milk
1 tablespoon lemon juice
2 egg whites
3 tablespoons canola oil
2 teaspoons vanilla extract
¼ cup plus 2 tablespoons honey

Preheat oven to 350°.

Lightly oil a 5 x 9-inch loaf pan or spray with a nonstick cooking spray.

In a large bowl, combine both flours, wheat germ, baking powder, baking soda, cocoa, and nuts. Mix well.

Place milk in a small bowl. Add lemon juice and let stand 1 minute. Add remaining ingredients. Beat with a fork or wire whisk until blended. Add to dry mixture, mixing until all ingredients are moistened. Place mixture in prepared pan.

Bake 35 to 40 minutes, until a toothpick inserted in the center of the bread comes out clean.

Cool in pan on wire rack 10 minutes, then transfer bread to rack to finish cooling.

Each serving provides: 182 Calories, 7 g Fat, 1 mg Cholesterol, 27 g Carbohydrate, 129 mg Sodium, 4 g Fiber, 6 g Protein

Raisin Bran Bread

Now you can enjoy the flavor of bran muffins in a loaf. Sweetened with molasses and laced with cinnamon, this bread is at its best served while still warm, or toasted and spread with your favorite jam. (By bran, I mean wheat bran.)

Makes 8 servings

½ cup all-purpose flour
½ cup plus 2 tablespoons whole wheat flour
3/4 cup bran (1-½ ounces)
1½ teaspoons baking powder
1 teaspoon baking soda
1½ teaspoons ground cinnamon
½ cup raisins
2 tablespoons plus 2 teaspoons canola oil
2 egg whites
1 cup skim milk
¼ cup molasses
1 teaspoon vanilla extract

Preheat oven to 350º.

Lightly oil a 4 x 8-inch loaf pan or spray with a nonstick cooking spray.

In a large bowl, combine both flours, bran, baking powder, baking soda, and cinnamon. Mix well. Stir in raisins.

In another bowl, combine remaining ingredients. Beat with a fork or wire whisk until blended. Add to dry mixture, mixing until all ingredients are just moistened. Place mixture in prepared pan.

Bake 35 minutes, until a toothpick inserted in the center of the bread comes out clean.

Cool in pan or wire rack 5 minutes, then turn out onto rack to finish cooling.

Each serving provides: 183 Calories, 5 g Fat, 1 mg Cholesterol, 32 g Carbohydrate, 216 mg Sodium, 5 g Fiber, 5 g Protein

Apricot Fruit n' Nut Bread

This delicious, moist bread is chock full of fruit, fiber, and flavor. It's a great holiday bread.

Makes 8 servings

3/4 cup all-purpose flour
3/4 cup whole wheat flour
1 teaspoon baking powder
1 teaspoon baking soda
1 teaspoon ground cinnamon
½ cup chopped dried apricots (12 apricot halves)
1/3 cup chopped dried figs (2 large figs)
2 tablespoons raisins
2 tablespoons chopped walnuts (½ ounce)
1 cup apricot nectar
¼ cup water
2 egg whites
2 tablespoons plus 2 teaspoons canola oil
2 teaspoons vanilla extract

Preheat oven to 350º.

Lightly oil a 4 x 8-inch loaf pan or spray with a nonstick cooking spray.

In a large bowl, combine both flours, baking powder, baking soda, and cinnamon. Mix well. Add apricots, figs, raisins, and nuts.

In another bowl, combine remaining ingredients. Beat with a fork or wire whisk until blended. Add to dry mixture, mixing until all ingredients are moistened. Place mixture in prepared pan.

Bake 35 minutes, until a toothpick inserted in the center of the bread comes out clean.

Cool in pan on wire rack 10 minutes, then turn out onto rack to finish cooling.

Each serving provides: 223 Calories, 6 g Fat, 0 mg Cholesterol, 39 g Carbohydrate, 174 mg Sodium, 5 g Fiber, 5 g Protein

Molasses Buttermilk Nut Bread

This moist, dense, rich-flavored bread is completely eggless! It's one of my friend Suzi's favorites, and when you try it you'll see why. Makes 12 servings

2¼ cups whole wheat flour
1 teaspoon baking powder
½ teaspoon salt
1 teaspoon baking soda
1 teaspoon ground cinnamon
¼ cup finely chopped walnuts (1 ounce)
1/3 cup plus 2 tablespoons molasses
¼ cup canola oil
1-1/3 cups buttermilk (nonfat)
1½ teaspoons vanilla extract
1 tablespoon grated fresh orange peel

Preheat oven to 375°.

Lightly oil a 5 x 9-inch loaf pan or spray with a nonstick cooking spray.

In a large bowl, combine flour, baking soda, baking powder, cinnamon, and salt. Mix well. Add walnuts.

In another bowl, combine remaining ingredients. Beat with a fork or wire whisk until blended. Add to dry mixture, mixing just until all ingredients are moistened. Place mixture in prepared pan.

Let stand 15 minutes ***before*** baking.

Bake 35 to 40 minutes, until a toothpick inserted in the center of the bread comes out clean.

Cool in pan on a wire rack for 5 minutes, then turn out onto rack to finish cooling.

Each serving provides: 177 Calories, 7 g Fat, 1 mg Cholesterol, 27 g Carbohydrate, 227 mg Sodium, 3 g Fiber, 4 g Protein

Orange Marmalade Bread

Orange lovers, you're in for a real treat. This bread is delicious as is, but toasting it really brings out the rich orange flavor. Makes 8 servings

3/4 cup all-purpose flour
2 teaspoons baking powder
½ teaspoon ground cinnamon
2 tablespoons sugar
3/4 cup whole wheat flour
1 teaspoon baking soda
2 egg whites
2 tablespoons canola oil
¼ cup reduced-sugar orange marmalade
(8 calories per teaspoon)
1 cup orange juice
1 teaspoon vanilla extract
½ teaspoon orange extract

Preheat oven to 350°.

Lightly oil a 4 x 8-inch loaf pan or spray with a nonstick cooking spray.

In a large bowl, combine both flours, baking powder, baking soda, and cinnamon. Mix well.

In another bowl, combine remaining ingredients. Beat with a fork or wire whisk until blended. Add to dry mixture, mixing until all ingredients are moistened. Place in prepared pan.

Bake 35 minutes, until a toothpick inserted in the center of the bread comes out clean.

Cool in pan 5 minutes, then transfer to a rack to finish cooling.

Each serving provides: 157 Calories, 4 g Fat, 0 mg Cholesterol, 27 g Carbohydrate, 224 mg Sodium, 2 g Fiber, 4 g Protein

Lemony Bean Bread

When they rave about this moist and tender bread, they'll be amazed that the secret is beans! There's also lots of protein and fiber. *Makes 8 servings*

- 3/4 cup all-purpose flour
- 2 teaspoons baking powder
- 3 egg whites
- 1 cup cooked kidney beans, drained (6 ounces)
- ½ cup orange juice
- 1 teaspoon vanilla extract
- 1 teaspoon grated fresh lemon peel
- 3/4 cup whole wheat flour
- ½ teaspoon ground cinnamon
- ¼ cup firmly packed brown sugar
- 2 tablespoons plus 2 teaspoons canola oil
- 1 teaspoon lemon extract

Preheat oven to 350°.

Lightly oil a 4 x 8-inch loaf pan or spray with a nonstick cooking spray.

In a large bowl, combine both types of flour, baking powder, and cinnamon. Mix well.

In a blender container, combine remaining ingredients. Blend until mixture is smooth and beans are puréed. Add to dry mixture. Mix until all ingredients are moistened. Place mixture in prepared pan.

Bake 35 to 40 minutes, until a toothpick inserted in the center of the bread comes out clean. Cool in pan on a wire rack 5 minutes, then turn out onto rack to finish cooling.

Each serving provides: 193 Calories, 5 g Fat, 0 mg Cholesterol, 31 g Carbohydrate, 131 mg Sodium, 4 g Fiber, 6 g Protein

Orange Currant Wheel

Similar to scones, but without the kneading, this pull-apart bread is as pretty as a picture. It's not too sweet and it goes with any meal, from breakfast to midnight snacks.

3/4 cup all-purpose flour
3/4 cup whole wheat flour
1½ teaspoons baking powder
¼ teaspoon salt
1 tablespoon sugar
2 tablespoons plus 2 teaspoons butter
¼ cup currants (or raisins or any chopped, dried fruit)
½ cup milk
2 teaspoons lemon juice
2 egg whites
2 teaspoon grated fresh orange peel

Topping:
2 teaspoons sugar
1/8 teaspoon ground cinnamon

Preheat oven to 400°.

Lightly oil a baking sheet or spray with a nonstick cooking spray.

In a large bowl, combine both types of flour, baking powder, salt, and sugar. Mix well.

Add butter. Mix with a fork or pastry blender until mixture resembles coarse crumbs. Stir in currants.

Place milk in a small bowl. Add lemon juice and let stand 1 minute. Add egg whites and orange peel. Beat with a fork or wire whisk until blended. Add to dry mixture, mixing until all ingredients are moistened.

Turn dough out onto prepared baking sheet. Wetting your hands slightly, flatten dough into an 8-inch circle. With a sharp knife, cut the dough into 8 pie-shaped wedges. (Do not separate the sections.)

Combine topping ingredients and sprinkle evenly over top of bread.

Bake 15 minutes, until bottom of bread is lightly browned. Transfer to a wire rack and serve warm.

Each serving provides: 148 Calories, 4 g Fat, 0 mg Cholesterol, , 24 g Carbohydrate, 215 mg Sodium, 3 g Fiber, 4 g Protein

Acapulco Corn Bread

You'll love the bits of vegetables and tangy bite of this unusual bread.

Makes 12 servings

1¼ cups yellow cornmeal (7-½ ounces)
¼ cup plus 2 tablespoons whole wheat flour
1 tablespoon baking powder
½ teaspoon baking soda
1 tablespoon sugar
½ teaspoon onion powder
1/8 teaspoon salt
3/4 teaspoon chili powder
½ teaspoon ground cumin
1 cup skim milk
1 tablespoon lemon juice
2 egg whites
3 tablespoons canola oil
¼ cup finely chopped green pepper
¼ cup finely chopped plum tomatoes, drained on towels
¼ cup finely chopped green onions (green part only)

Preheat oven to 375°.

Lightly oil an 8-inch square baking pan or spray with a nonstick cooking spray.

In a large bowl, combine dry ingredients and spices. Mix well.

Place milk in a medium bowl. Add lemon juice and let stand 1 minute. Add egg whites and oil. Beat with a fork or wire whisk until blended. Stir in green pepper, tomato, and onions.

Add milk mixture to dry ingredients. Mix until all ingredients are just moistened. Pour into prepared pan. Bake 20 minutes.

Let stand 5 minutes, then cut into squares and serve warm.

Each serving provides: 125 Calories, 4 g Fat, 0 mg Cholesterol, 19 g Carbohydrate, 187 mg Sodium, 4 g Fiber, 3 g Protein

Cottage Cheese Dill Bread

This quick, herbed bread is at home with breakfast, lunch, or dinner. Serve it warm for the best flavor. *Makes 8 servings*

½ cup all-purpose flour	1 cup whole wheat flour
1 teaspoon baking powder	1 teaspoon baking soda
1 tablespoon dried dill weed	1 tablespoon dried chives
3 egg whites	1 cup lowfat cottage cheese
1 tablespoon plus 1 teaspoon canola oil	½ cup water

Preheat oven to 350°.

Lightly oil a 4 x 8-inch loaf pan or spray with a nonstick cooking spray.

In a large bowl, combine both types of flour, baking powder, baking soda, dill, and chives. Mix well.

In a blender container, combine remaining ingredients. Blend until smooth. Add to dry mixture. Mix until all ingredients are moistened.

Spoon into prepared pan. Smooth the top very lightly with the back of a spoon. Bake 35 minutes, until a toothpick inserted in the center of the bread comes out clean.

Cool in pan on wire rack 5 minutes, then turn out onto rack to cool slightly.

Serve warm.

Each serving provides: 127 Calories, 3 g Fat, 1 mg Cholesterol, 18 g Carbohydrate, 293 mg Sodium, 2 g Fiber, 8 g Protein

Cheddar Broccoli Bread Roll

I've rolled broccoli and Cheddar cheese in biscuit dough to create both a visual and a culinary masterpiece. *Makes 12 servings*

1 10-ounce package frozen, chopped broccoli
3/4 cup ***each*** all-purpose flour and whole wheat flour
1 tablespoon baking powder
½ teaspoon garlic powder
¼ teaspoon salt
3 tablespoons butter
½ cup plus 2 tablespoons skim milk
3 ounces shredded lowfat Cheddar cheese (3/4 cup)

Cook broccoli according to package directions. Drain.

Preheat oven to 375°. Have an ungreased baking sheet ready.

In a large bowl, combine both flours, baking powder, garlic powder, and salt.

Mix well. Add margarine. Mix with a fork or pastry blender until mixture resembles coarse crumbs. Add milk. Stir until all ingredients are moistened.

Place dough on a floured surface and knead a few times until dough holds together in a ball. (Add a small amount of flour if dough is sticky.) Roll dough, or press with your hands, into an 8 x 14-inch rectangle.

Sprinkle cheese evenly over dough, staying 1 inch away from edges. Spread broccoli evenly over cheese.

Starting with one long side, tightly roll up dough like a jelly roll. Pinch the ends and seam together. Place on ungreased baking sheet.

Bake 20 to 25 minutes, until bottom of bread is nicely browned.

Remove to a rack to cool for 5 minutes, then slice and serve warm.

Each serving provides: 114 Calories, 4 g Fat, 5 mg Cholesterol, 14 g Carbohydrate, 248 mg Sodium, 3 g Fiber, 5 g Protein

Herb Biscuits

Serve these biscuits piping hot, right out of the oven. They include a flavorful blend of herbs that complement any meal. *Makes 8 servings*

3/4	cup all-purpose flour	3/4	cup whole wheat flour
1	tablespoon baking powder	¼	teaspoon salt
½	teaspoon dried marjoram	½	teaspoon dill weed
¼	teaspoon dried thyme	1/8	teaspoon garlic powder
3	tablespoons butter	½	cup plus 2 tablespoons skim milk

Preheat oven to 450°.

Have an ungreased baking sheet ready.

In a large bowl, combine both flours, baking powder, salt, and spices. Mix well.

Add butter. Mix with a fork or pastry blender until mixture resembles coarse crumbs.

Add milk. Stir until dry ingredients are moistened.

Place dough on a floured surface and knead a few times until dough holds together in a ball. (Add a small amount of flour if dough is sticky.) Roll dough, or press with your hands, to ½ inch thickness. Using a 3 inch biscuit cutter or glass, cut 8 biscuits. (Scraps can be put together and rolled again.)

Place biscuits on baking sheet. Bakc 10 minutes, or until lightly browned.

Remove to a wire rack. Serve hot.

Each serving provides: 127 Calories, 5 g Fat, 0 mg Cholesterol, 18 g Carbohydrate, 288 mg Sodium, 2 g Fiber, 3 g Protein

Rum n' Raisin Muffins

I think the combination of rum flavor and raisins is heavenly.

Makes 8 servings

Topping:

1-½ teaspoons sugar
1/8 teaspoon ground cinnamon

Muffins:

3/4 cup all-purpose flour
3/4 cup whole wheat flour
2 teaspoons baking powder
½ teaspoon baking soda
1 cup plain nonfat yogurt or plain Greek yogurt
2 tablespoons canola oil
¼ cup firmly packed brown sugar
2 egg whites
1 teaspoon vanilla extract
2 teaspoons rum extract
2 teaspoons grated fresh lemon peel
½ cup raisins

Preheat oven to 400°.

Lightly oil 8 muffin cups or spray with a nonstick cooking spray.

Combine topping ingredients in a small bowl. Set aside.

In a large bowl, combine both flours, baking powder, and baking soda. Mix well.

In another bowl, combine remaining ingredients, ***except*** raisins. Beat with a fork or wire whisk until blended. Add to dry mixture, along with raisins, mixing just until all ingredients are moistened.

Divide mixture evenly into prepared muffin cups. Sprinkle topping evenly over muffins.

Bake 15 minutes, or until a toothpick inserted in the center of a muffin comes out clean.

Remove muffins to a rack to cool.

Each serving provides: 194 Calories, 4 g Fat, 1 mg Cholesterol, 34 g Carbohydrate, 197 mg Sodium, 3 g Fiber, 6 g Protein

Eggless Honey Wheat Muffins

These eggless muffins are not as sweet as most muffins, but they're tender and moist and they go with everything. If you want, you can add fruit, nuts, or extracts to jazz them up.

Makes 8 servings

Topping:

2 teaspoons sugar
¼ teaspoon ground cinnamon

Muffins:

1-½ cups whole wheat flour
¼ teaspoon salt
1-½ teaspoons baking powder
½ teaspoon ground cinnamon
1-¼ cups skim milk
3 tablespoons honey
2 tablespoons plus 2 teaspoons canola oil
2 teaspoons vanilla extract
2 teaspoons grated fresh orange peel

Preheat oven to 400°.

Lightly oil 8 muffin cups or spray with a nonstick cooking spray.

Combine topping ingredients in a small bowl. Set aside.

In a large bowl, combine flour, salt, baking powder, and cinnamon. Mix well.

In a small bowl, combine remaining ingredients. Beat with a fork or wire whisk until blended. Add to dry mixture. Mix until all ingredients are mois-tened. Divide mixture evenly into prepared muffin cups. Sprinkle evenly with topping.

Bake 18 to 20 minutes, until a toothpick inserted in the center of a muffin comes out clean.

Remove muffins to a rack and serve warm for best flavor.

Each serving provides: 163 Calories, 5 g Fat, 1 mg Cholesterol, 27 g Carbohydrate, 169 mg Sodium, 2 g Fiber, 4 g Protein

Cinna Muffins

These tender muffins, laced with cinnamon, can be enjoyed plain or they can easily be made into Cinnamon-Nut Muffins, Cinnamon-Raisin Muffins, or any variation you can imagine. Just add your favorite touch.

Makes 8 servings

Topping:

2 teaspoons wheat germ
¼ teaspoon ground cinnamon
½ teaspoon sugar

Muffins:

3/4 cup all-purpose flour
2 teaspoons baking powder
2¼ teaspoons ground cinnamon
1 tablespoon lemon juice
¼ cup firmly packed brown sugar
2 teaspoons vanilla extract
3/4 cup whole wheat flour
½ teaspoon baking soda
3/4 cup plus 2 tablespoons skim milk
2 tablespoons canola oil
2 egg whites

Preheat oven to 400°.

Lightly oil 8 muffin cups or spray with a nonstick cooking spray.

Combine topping ingredients in a small bowl. Set aside.

In a large bowl, combine both flours, baking powder, baking soda, and cinnamon. Mix well.

Pour milk into a small bowl and add lemon juice. Let stand 1 minute. Add remaining ingredients. Beat with a fork or wire whisk until blended. Add to dry mixture, mixing just until all ingredients are moistened.

Divide mixture evenly into prepared muffin cups. Sprinkle topping evenly over muffins.

Bake 15 minutes, or until a toothpick inserted in the center of a muffin comes out clean.

Remove muffins to a rack to cool.

Each serving provides: 160 Calories, 4 g Fat, 1 mg Cholesterol, 27 g Carbohydrate, 189 mg Sodium, 3 g Fiber, 5 g Protein

Raisin Oat Muffins

These muffins have a sweet oaty taste and a velvety texture all their own. Like most muffins, they're best when served warm.

Makes 10 servings

2-½ cups rolled oats (7-½ ounces)
1 tablespoon baking powder
½ cup plus 2 tablespoons raisins
1 cup skim milk
1 tablespoon lemon juice
1/3 cup firmly packed brown sugar
1 tablespoon plus 2 teaspoons canola oil
2 egg whites
2 teaspoons vanilla extract

Preheat oven to 375°.

Lightly oil 10 muffin cups or spray with a nonstick cooking spray.

Place oats in a blender container and blend until the consistency of flour. Place in a large bowl and add baking powder. Mix well. Stir in raisins.

Place milk in a medium bowl. Add lemon juice and let stand 1 minute. Add remaining ingredients. Beat with a fork or wire whisk until blended. Add to dry mixture, mixing until all ingredients are moistened.

Divide batter evenly into prepared muffin cups.

Bake 20 minutes, until a toothpick inserted in the center of a muffin comes out clean.

Remove muffins to a rack to cool.

Each serving provides: 172 Calories, 4 g Fat, 0 mg Cholesterol, 30 g Carbohydrate, 156 mg Sodium, 3 g Fiber, 5 g Protein

Lemon Poppy Seed Muffins

You'll love the very lemony taste of these moist muffins. They work just as well without the poppy seeds, but I like the subtle crunch that they add.

Makes 8 servings

3/4 cup all-purpose flour
3/4 cup whole wheat flour
2 teaspoons baking powder
½ teaspoon baking soda
1 tablespoon poppy seeds
1 cup plain nonfat yogurt or plain Greek yogurt
2 tablespoons canola oil
¼ cup sugar
2 egg whites
1 teaspoon vanilla extract
½ teaspoon lemon extract
2 teaspoons grated fresh lemon peel

Preheat oven to 400°.

Lightly oil 8 muffin cups or spray with a nonstick cooking spray.

In a large bowl, combine both flours, baking powder, baking soda, and poppy seeds. Mix well.

In another bowl, combine remaining ingredients. Beat with a fork or wire whisk until blended. Add to dry mixture, mixing just until all ingredients are moistened.

Divide mixture evenly into prepared muffin cups.

Bake 15 minutes, or until a toothpick inserted in the center of a muffin comes out clean.

Remove muffins to a rack to cool.

Each serving provides: 165 Calories, 4 g Fat, 1 mg Cholesterol, 26 g Carbohydrate, 194 mg Sodium, 3 g Fiber, 5 g Protein

Orange Pineapple Muffins

These moist, sweet muffins have a hint of orange and lots of pineapple bits. Why not pop one in a lunch box in place of a cupcake?

Makes 8 servings

3/4 cup all-purpose flour
3/4 cup whole wheat flour
1 teaspoon baking powder
1 teaspoon baking soda
½ teaspoon ground cinnamon
2 cups crushed pineapple, drained very well
¼ cup orange juice
2 egg whites
1 tablespoon plus 1 teaspoon canola oil
1½ teaspoons vanilla extract
1 teaspoon grated fresh orange peel
¼ cup sugar

Preheat oven to 375°.

Lightly oil 8 muffin cups or spray with a nonstick cooking spray.

In a large bowl, combine both flours, baking powder, baking soda, and cinnamon. Mix well.

Measure 1 full cup of the drained pineapple. Place in blender container and blend for a few seconds. Then add remaining ingredients, ***except*** remaining pineapple, to blender. Blend until smooth.

Add blended mixture to dry ingredients, along with remaining pineapple. Mix until all ingredients are moistened. Spoon batter into prepared muffin cups.

Bake 20 minutes, until a toothpick inserted in the center of a muffin comes out clean.

Remove muffins to a rack to cool.

Each serving provides: 174 Calories, 3 g Fat, 0 mg Cholesterol, 35 g Carbohydrate, 171 mg Sodium, 3 g Fiber, 4 g Protein

Apricot Pumpkin Pecan Muffins

These delectable muffins make a wonderful homemade holiday gift. They're always a hit.

Makes 8 servings

½ cup all-purpose flour
1 cup whole wheat flour
2 teaspoons baking powder
½ teaspoon baking soda
1 teaspoon ground cinnamon
1/16 teaspoon ground cloves
½ cup chopped dried apricots (12 apricot halves)
2 tablespoons chopped pecans (½ ounce)
½ cup orange juice
2 tablespoons canola oil
¼ cup firmly packed brown sugar
2 egg whites
½ cup canned pumpkin
1½ teaspoons vanilla extract

Preheat oven to 400°.

Lightly oil 8 muffin cups or spray with a nonstick cooking spray.

In a large bowl, combine both flours, baking powder, baking soda, cinnamon, and cloves. Mix well. Mix in apricots and pecans.

In another bowl, combine remaining ingredients. Beat with a fork or wire whisk until blended. Add to dry mixture, mixing until all ingredients are moistened.

Divide mixture evenly into prepared muffin cups.

Bake 15 minutes, until a toothpick inserted in the center of a muffin comes out clean.

Remove muffins to a rack to cool.

Each serving provides: 180 Calories, 5 g Fat, 0 mg Cholesterol, 31 g Carbohydrate, 176 mg Sodium, 4 g Fiber, 4 g Protein

Chunky Apple Molasses Spice Muffins

Guess what the chunks are? Lots of chewy dried apples!

Makes 8 servings

1 cup whole wheat flour
½ cup all-purpose flour
1½ teaspoons baking soda
1 teaspoon ground cinnamon
¼ teaspoon ground cloves
¼ teaspoon ground allspice
½ teaspoon ground nutmeg
1 cup dried apples (3 ounces), cut into small pieces
1 cup applesauce (unsweetened)
2 egg whites
¼ cup skim milk
2 tablespoons canola oil
¼ cup molasses
1½ teaspoons vanilla extract

Preheat oven to 400°.

Lightly oil 8 muffin cups or spray with a nonstick cooking spray.

In a large bowl, combine both flours, baking soda, and spices. Mix well. Stir in dried apples.

In another bowl, combine remaining ingredients. Beat with a fork or wire whisk until blended. Add to dry mixture, mixing until all ingredients are moistened.

Divide mixture evenly into prepared muffin cups.

Bake 15 to 18 minutes, until a toothpick inserted in the center of a muffin comes out clean.

Remove muffins to a rack to cool.

Each serving provides: 186 Calories, 4 g Fat, 0 mg Cholesterol, 35 g Carbohydrate, 184 mg Sodium, 4 g Fiber, 4 g Protein

Cranberry Nut Muffins

These moist muffins were invented to use up some leftover cranberry sauce. They've now become one of my very favorite muffins.

Makes 8 servings

3/4 cup all-purpose flour
3/4 cup whole wheat flour
1½ teaspoons baking powder
1 teaspoon baking soda
½ teaspoon ground cinnamon
2 tablespoons chopped walnuts (½ ounce)
2 egg whites
2 tablespoons sugar
2 tablespoons canola oil
1 cup canned whole-berry cranberry sauce
¼ cup orange juice
1 teaspoon vanilla extract
½ teaspoon orange extract

Preheat oven to 400°.

Lightly oil 8 muffin cups or spray with a nonstick cooking spray.

In a large bowl, combine both flours, baking powder, baking soda, and cinnamon. Mix well. Add chopped nuts.

In another bowl, combine remaining ingredients. Beat with a fork or wire whisk until blended. Add to dry mixture, mixing until all ingredients are moistened.

Divide mixture evenly into prepared muffin cups.

Bake 15 minutes, until a toothpick inserted in the center of a muffin comes out clean.

Remove muffins to a rack to cool.

Each serving provides: 198 Calories, 5 g Fat, 0 mg Cholesterol, 35 g Carbohydrate, 208 mg Sodium, 5 g Fiber, 4 g Protein

Two Berry Muffins

What's a two berry? Just bite into one of these tender muffins and you'll find out!

Makes 8 servings

1 cup all-purpose flour	½ cup whole wheat flour
2 teaspoons baking powder	1 teaspoon baking soda
3/4 cup skim milk	1 tablespoon lemon juice
2 tablespoons canola oil	¼ cup sugar
2 egg whites	2 teaspoons vanilla extract

¼ teaspoon lemon extract

½ cup fresh or frozen blueberries (If using frozen blueberries, there's no need to thaw.)

½ cup fresh or frozen raspberries (If using frozen raspberries, thaw them first and drain on paper towels.)

Preheat oven to 400°.

Lightly oil 8 muffin cups or spray with a nonstick cooking spray.

In a large bowl, combine both flours, baking powder, and baking soda. Mix well.

Place milk in another bowl. Add lemon juice and let stand 1 minute. Add remaining ingredients, ***except*** berries. Beat with a fork or wire whisk until blended. Add to dry mixture, stirring until all ingredients are moistened.

Gently fold in berries.

Divide mixture evenly into prepared muffin cups.

Bake 15 minutes, until a toothpick inserted in the center of a muffin comes out clean.

Remove muffins to a rack to cool.

Each serving provides: 163 Calories, 4 g Fat, 0 mg Cholesterol, 28 g Carbohydrate. 237 mg Sodium, 3 g Fiber, 4 g Protein

Fruits

Fruits are extremely versatile. They can be appetizers, salads, desserts, or snacks. They can be served for breakfast, lunch, or dinner, or anywhere in between. They are portable, too, and can be taken along for a snack on-the-run. Fruits are very healthy and are high in carbohydrates and supply us with vitamins, minerals, and fiber.

In my recipes I use fresh fruits as much as I can and, for added fiber, I leave the skin on whenever possible. My second choice is frozen, unsweetened, fruit. When I use canned fruits, I choose the ones that are packed in water or unsweetened fruit juice. I highly recommend that, if you have a freezer, you take advantage of the fruits that are in season and freeze them for later enjoyment.

I try to choose the sweetest varieties of fruits for my recipes, thereby reducing the amount of sugar needed. For example, a dish made with Golden Delicious apples will generally require less sugar than the same dish made with Granny Smith apples. I also choose very ripe fruit because it is generally sweeter than fruit that is less ripe.

It's fun to be creative with fruits. There are so many interesting combinations to discover, and so many attractive ways to serve them. Take a variety of fruits, for example, and simply layer them in a clear bowl and you have a beautiful dish. Alternate layers of berries and nonfat vanilla yogurt in parfait glasses and sprinkle the tops lightly with crushed cereal. Fruit lends itself beautifully to just such a simple presentation.

Over the past three plus years Web MD, Weight Watchers® and diabetes educators have given fresh fruit and those canned in their own juice (not syrup of any kind) a green light to use as a better snack anytime rather than so many sugared alternatives. So, use them as a plus to a meal in addition to salads and certainly as an in-between delight. Using them excessively is not recommended.

There are many more fruit ideas in the other chapters of my book. Be sure to check Appetizers, Dips and Spreads, Breakfast Ideas, Salads and Salad Dressings, Grains, Vegetables, Starchy Vegetables, Breads and Muffins, and Desserts. Here are just a few of my other delicious fruit recipes – see index for page number:

- Orange-Fig Spread – Delicious on crackers or bread.
- Pineapple Slaw – Tired of the same old cole slaw?
- Cranberry Vinaigrette – Cranberry juice adds a new flavor to a familiar dressing.
- Apple Rice Casserole – A delicious side dish.
- Apricot Fruit n' Nut Bread – Chock full of fruit.
- Raspberry-Glazed Apple Pie – A delectable combination.

Tropical Fruit Cup with Raspberry Sauce

Kiwis and papayas are often overlooked in the grocery store. Here's a delicious reason to try them.

Makes 6 servings

Fruit cup:

1 medium, ripe papaya, peeled, cut into 1-inch chunks
2 ripe kiwis, peeled, cut in half lengthwise, the cut into ¼ inch slices
1 cup fresh or canned (unsweetened) pineapple chunks
(If using canned pineapple, drain before using.)
2 cups strawberries, cut in half
1 medium, almost ripe banana, peeled, sliced into ¼inch slices

Raspberry sauce:

1 10-ounce package frozen raspberries (unsweetened), thawed
3 tablespoons confectioners sugar

In a large bowl, combine all cut-up fruit.

Place raspberries and their juice in a blender container. Blend until puréed. Pour through a strainer into a small bowl. Add sugar, stirring until it dissolves.

Both fruit and sauce can be chilled until serving time.

To serve, stir fruit and divide evenly into 6 serving bowls. Top each serving with 2½ tablespoons of raspberry sauce.

Each serving provides: 121 Calories, 1 g Fat, 0 mg Cholesterol, 30 g Carbohydrate, 4 mg Sodium, 3 g Fiber, 2 g Protein

Fruit to Go

This is an ideal picnic treat. The fruit is neatly packed in its own disposable carrying case!

Makes 4 servings

1 medium-size honeydew melon (or other type of melon)
1 cup sliced strawberries
1 cup raspberries
1 tablespoon confectioners sugar
2 teaspoons lemon juice

Carefully slice off top of melon to make a lid about 2 inches thick. Scoop out and discard melon seeds. Scoop out flesh, using a spoon or melon baller. Place 2 cups of the melon balls in a large bowl, reserving remaining melon. Add remaining ingredients and mix well.

Spoon fruit into melon shell. (You may be able to add some of the reserved melon balls, depending on the size of the melon.) Tap melon on table top several times to help pack fruit down.

Replace lid, wrap melon tightly, and chill several hours or overnight. (Enjoy remaining reserved melon separately.)

To serve, simply spoon fruit out of melon onto serving plates.

Each serving provides: 126 Calories, 1 g Fat, 0 mg Cholesterol, 32 g Carbohydrate, 27 mg Sodium, 3 g Fiber, 2 g Protein

Spiced Peaches

Here's a delicious way to use that pumpkin pie spice that sits in the pantry from Thanksgiving to Thanksgiving. You'll love what it does to peaches. Try these hot or cold, spooned over vanilla lowfat ice cream or frozen yogurt.

Makes 4 servings

½ cup water
½ teaspoon vanilla extract
½ teaspoon pumpkin pie spice
2 tablespoons firmly packed brown sugar
4 medium peaches, peeled and sliced thin (Canned peaches will also work, but fresh or frozen peaches are best. If using frozen peaches, thaw before using.)

In a small saucepan, combine water, vanilla, pumpkin pie spice, and brown sugar.

Bring to a boil over medium heat.

Add peaches. Simmer 3 to 5 minutes. (Firm peaches will take 5 minutes, while very ripe peaches only need 3 minutes.)

Serve hot or cold.

Each serving provides: 66 Calories. 0 g Fat. 0 mg Cholesterol. 17 g Carbohydrate, 2 mg Sodium, 2 g Fiber, 1 g Protein

Cranberry Pineapple Relish

This is an easy and tasty addition to a Thanksgiving dinner – or any dinner. Freeze cranberries when they are plentiful and you can enjoy them all year long.

Makes 16 servings
(About ¼ cup each serving)

- 2 cups cranberries
- 4 small, sweet apples, cored, unpeeled
- 1 cup canned crushed pineapple (unsweetened), undrained
- ¼ cup honey or sugar
- ¼ teaspoon ground cinnamon
- ¼ cup chopped walnuts (1 ounce)

Combine all ingredients in a food processor. Process until mixture is chopped, but not puréed. (A blender will also work, but you'll have to blend the mixture in small batches to prevent it from becoming puréed.)

Chill.

Each serving provides: 59 Calories, 1 g Fat, 0 mg Cholesterol, 13 g Carbohydrate, 1 mg Sodium, 3 g Fiber, 0 g Protein

GOOD HEALTH ALERT:
It's safe to eat the food in a dented can if the vacuum seal isn't broken; but if the can is leaky with a stained label, rust or dented seam or if the ends bulge (a possible sign of botulism), don't buy the can. If it's already in your cupboard, don't eat the food – don't even open the can.

Cranbrosia

Cranberry juice cocktail adds a lovely color, as well as a lively new flavor, to ambrosia. I like to serve it topped with lightly sweetened yogurt or my Tofu Crème Topping. *Makes 6 servings*

2 small oranges, peeled and sectioned (Discard white membrane.)
1 medium, ripe banana, sliced in half lengthwise, then into ¼ inch slices
1 cup fresh or canned (unsweetened) pineapple chunks
2 teaspoons shredded coconut (unsweetened)
2/3 cup cranberry juice cocktail
1 tablespoon plus 1 teaspoon sugar

In a medium bowl, combine fruit and coconut. Toss gently.

In a small bowl, combine cranberry juice and sugar. Stir to dissolve sugar. Pour over fruit.

Chill several hours or overnight.

To serve, divide evenly into 6 serving bowls. Add topping if desired.

Each serving provides: 91 Calories, 1 g Fat, 0 mg Cholesterol, 23 g Carbohydrate, 1 mg Sodium, 2 g Fiber, 1 g Protein

Orange Prune Compote

Serve this delicious compote warm or cold. It's great by itself or over cottage cheese, yogurt, or your favorite breakfast cereal.

Makes 6 servings

1 cup pitted prunes, cut into quarters (16 prunes)
1 cup orange juice
1 tablespoon firmly packed brown sugar
¼ teaspoon ground cinnamon
½ teaspoon grated fresh orange peel
½ teaspoon vanilla extract
2 small oranges peeled and sectioned (Discard white membrane.)

In a small saucepan, combine prunes, orange juice, brown sugar, cinnamon, and orange peel. Bring to a boil over medium heat. Reduce heat to low, cover, and simmer 15 minutes. Remove pan from heat and stir in vanilla and orange sections. Serve warm or chill and serve cold.

Each serving provides: 112 Calories, 0 g Fat, 0 mg Cholesterol, 28 g Carbohydrate, 2 mg Sodium, 3 g Fiber, 1 g Protein

Pineapple Orange Tapioca

Smooth and fruity, this easy pudding is a great dessert or after-school snack.

Makes 4 servings

1 cup orange juice
1/3 cup nonfat dry milk
2 tablespoons quick-cooking tapioca
1 cup canned crushed pineapple (unsweetened), undrained
¼ cup water
1 tablespoon sugar

In a blender container, combine all ingredients, ***except*** tapioca. Blend for a few seconds, until mixture is just blended. Pour mixture into small saucepan and stir in tapioca. Let stand 5 minutes. Bring to a boil over medium heat, stirring frequently. Remove from heat and cool in pan 20 minutes. Then stir and divide evenly into 4 custard cups. Chill.

Each *serving provides: 114 Calories, 0 g Fat, 1 mg Cholesterol, 27 g Carbohydrate, 32 mg Sodium, 1 g Fiber, 3 g Protein*

Orange Berry Fruit Cup

Oranges and blueberries complement each other naturally. They're a winning combination in this easy dish.

Makes 4 servings

2 cups fresh orange sections
1 cup fresh or frozen blueberries
(If using frozen berries, there's no need to thaw.)
¼ cup orange juice
1 tablespoon sugar
1 teaspoon lime juice (or lemon juice)
½ teaspoon vanilla extract
1/8 teaspoon orange extract

In a medium bowl, toss orange sections with blueberries. In a small bowl, combine remaining ingredients. Add to fruit, mixing well. Chill several hours or overnight. Divide into 4 serving bowls or tall-stemmed sherbet glasses and serve cold.

Each serving provides: 84 Calories, 0 g Fat, 0 mg Cholesterol, 21 g Carbohydrate, 3 mg Sodium, 2 g Fiber, 1 g Protein

Pears L'Orange

These pears, with a hint of orange and vanilla, are scrumptious by themselves, or as a topping for cottage cheese or vanilla ice milk.

Makes 4 servings

2/3 cup apple juice
1 teaspoon vanilla extract
1 teaspoon grated fresh orange peel
2 teaspoons sugar
4 small pears, peeled, cored, and sliced into 1/8 inch slices

In a large nonstick skillet, combine apple juice, orange peel, vanilla, and sugar. Add pears. Bring to a boil over medium heat, stirring frequently. Cover and immer 5 minutes, or until pears are just tender, stirring several times. Serve warm or cold.

Each serving provides: 109 Calories, 1 g Fat, 0 mg Cholesterol, 27 g Carbohydrate, 1 mg Sodium, 1 g Fiber, 1 g Protein

Cherries Amandine

The flavor of cherries and almonds seem to be made for each other. In this easy fruit dish, I've blended the two flavors and added an almond-laced creamy topping.

Makes 4 servings

1 1-pound can pitted red tart cherries, packed in water
1 tablespoon plus 1 teaspoon cornstarch
1 teaspoon almond extract
3 tablespoons sugar

Topping:

3/4 cup plain nonfat yogurt (or Greek yogurt)
¼ teaspoon almond extract
2 teaspoons sugar
2 tablespoons sliced almonds (½ ounce)

Drain cherries, reserving liquid. Place reserved liquid in a small saucepan. Add cornstarch, 1 teaspoon almond extract, and 3 tablespoons sugar. Mix until cornstarch is dissolved.

Add cherries to saucepan and cook over medium heat, stirring, until mixture comes to a boil. Continue to cook, stirring, 1 minute.

Place in a bowl and chill.

In a small bowl, combine yogurt with remaining almond extract and sugar. Mix well and chill.

To serve:

Divide cherries evenly into 4 serving bowls or sherbet glasses. Divide yogurt topping evenly and spoon over cherries. Garnish with sliced almonds.

Each serving provides: 144 Calories, 2 g Fat, 1 mg Cholesterol, 28 g Carbohydrate, 41 mg Sodium, 1 g Fiber, 4 g Protein

Rosy Glow Apples

Cooking apples in cranberry juice cocktail gives them a rosy glow as well as a delicious flavor. These apples can be served hot or cold, and make a light dessert or a tasty topping for cottage cheese.

Makes 4 servings

4 small, sweet apples, peeled and cored
(Golden Delicious are a good choice.)
2/3 cup cranberry juice cocktail
1 tablespoon sugar
1 tablespoon cornstarch
1/16 teaspoon ground cinnamon
1/16 teaspoon ground nutmeg
3 tablespoons water
½ teaspoon vanilla extract
1/8 teaspoon lemon extract

Cut apples into quarters, then slice thin.

In a medium saucepan, combine apples, cranberry juice cocktail, and sugar. Bring to a boil over medium heat, stirring frequently.

Cover, reduce heat to low, and simmer 3 to 5 minutes or until apples are just tender.

While apples are cooking, combine cornstarch, cinnamon, and nutmeg in a small bowl. Add water and extracts. Mix until cornstarch is dissolved.

Add cornstarch mixture to apples.

Cook, stirring gently, 3 minutes, until juice has thickened slightly and turned clear.

Serve warm or cold.

Each serving provides: 103 Calories, 0 g Fat, 0 mg Cholesterol, 26 g Carbohydrate, 1 mg Sodium, 1 g Fiber, 0 g Protein

Grape Nutty Baked Apples

My favorite way to serve these cinnamony apples is warm, alongside a scoop of light vanilla ice cream.

Makes 4 servings

4 small apples
(Winesap, York, Rome, or Golden Delicious make good choices.)
¼ cup plus 2 tablespoons Grape Nuts® Cereal (1 ½ ounces)
1 tablespoon firmly packed brown sugar
½ teaspoon ground cinnamon
1/16 teaspoon ground nutmeg
Ground cinnamon for topping

Preheat oven to 375°.

Partially core apples, removing core to ½ inch of bottoms. (Make holes about 1-½ inches wide.) Peel top half of apples.

Place apples in a shallow 1-quart baking dish.

In a small bowl, combine Grape Nuts®, brown sugar, cinnamon, and nutmeg.

Divide mixture evenly into apple centers. Sprinkle apples with additional cinnamon.

Place water in bottom of baking dish to a depth of ½-inch.

Bake, uncovered, 45 to 60 minutes, or until apples are just tender.

Baste frequently while cooking.

Remove from oven and baste again.

Serve warm or cold.

Each serving provides: 115 Calories, 0 g Fat, 0 mg Cholesterol, 28 g Carbohydrate, 63 mg Sodium, 2 g Fiber, 1 g Protein

Rummy Figs and Apples

I love this delicious fruit combo warm or cold over light vanilla ice cream, cottage cheese, or even oatmeal. It's a real high-fiber treat and it "mellows" as it sits. After 2 days in the refrigerator, it's at its best.

Makes 6 servings

8 large figs, cut into quarters
1 small apple, unpeeled, coarsely shredded
1-1/3 cups water
½ teaspoon ground cinnamon
1/8 teaspoon ground nutmeg
1 tablespoon firmly packed brown sugar
½ teaspoon rum extract

In a small saucepan, combine all ingredients, ***except*** rum extract. Bring to a boil over medium heat. Reduce heat to low, cover, and simmer 5 minutes.

Remove from heat and stir in rum extract. (Taste and add a few more drops of extract, if desired.)

Serve warm or chill for later servings.

Each serving provides: 85 Calories, 0 g Fat, 0 mg Cholesterol, 21 g Carbohydrate, 3 mg Sodium, 4 g Fiber, 1 g Protein

Fried Bananas Melba

You'll have enough sauce for a double batch of bananas. If you choose, use it to top light ice cream or other types of fruit. Let your imagination be your guide.

Makes 4 servings

Raspberry sauce:

1 10-ounce package frozen raspberries (unsweetened), drained (If unsweetened raspberries are unavailable, choose those packed in light syrup.)

2 tablespoons frozen orange juice concentrate, thawed

Bananas:

2 teaspoons butter

2 medium, ripe bananas, cut in half lengthwise, and then crosswise.

Place raspberries in a blender container. Blend until smooth. Press through a sieve or strainer. Stir in orange juice concentrate. Set aside. (Makes 2/3 cup sauce.)

Melt butter in a nonstick skillet or griddle over medium-high heat.

Add bananas. Cook 3 to 5 minutes, until bananas are heated through and are beginning to brown.

Divide bananas into 4 serving bowls.

Top each serving with 1½ tablespoons of sauce.

Serve right away.

Each serving provides: 123 Calories, 3 g Fat, 0 mg Cholesterol, 27 g Carbohydrate, 23 mg Sodium, 2 g Fiber, 2 g Protein

Banana Roll-Ups

Flour tortillas make excellent roll-ups for my unusual version of baked bananas. This is a delicious dessert or a unique brunch dish.

Makes 4 servings

1 tablespoon plus 1 teaspoon butter, melted
4 6-inch flour tortillas
2 tablespoons plus 2 teaspoons reduced-sugar strawberry jam or fruit-only strawberry jam
2 medium, ripe bananas, sliced in half, lengthwise
Ground cinnamon

Preheat oven to 400°.

Spread ***half*** of the butter in the bottom of an 8-inch square baking pan.

To soften tortillas, moisten them lightly on both sides with wet fingers. Stack them on a piece of aluminum foil, wrap them tightly, and bake 10 minutes.

Spread 2 teaspoons of jam on each tortilla, staying about 1-inch away from edges. Place a banana half in the center of each tortilla. Roll up tortillas and place them, seam side down, in prepared pan.

Brush tops of roll-ups with remaining butter.

Sprinkle generously with cinnamon.

Bake, uncovered, 15 minutes.

Serve hot.

Each serving provides: 172 Calories, 6 g Fat, 0 mg Cholesterol, 29 g Carbohydrate, 185 mg Sodium, 2 g Fiber, 3 g Protein

Apricot Fruit Bowl

This is a wonderfully refreshing fruit salad. Because I suggest canned and frozen fruit, you can make this all year round. For a special presentation, serve in tall-stemmed sherbet glasses, either plain or sprinkled with granola or Grape Nuts® if desired and it adds a special touch.

Makes 6 servings

1 1-pound can apricot halves (unsweetened), drained
1 teaspoon vanilla extract
2 cups frozen strawberries, cut in quarters
(There's no need to thaw strawberries.)
1 6 oz. container light yogurt
1½ cups canned pineapple chunks (unsweetened), drained

Place apricots in a blender container and blend until smooth. Pour into a bowl and stir in sugar and vanilla.

Add remaining fruit, mixing well.

Add in 1 – 6 oz. container of light yogurt. Stir well into blended ingredients.

Chill several hours.

Stir and divide into 6 sherbet glasses to serve.

Each serving provides: 110 Calories, 0 g Fat, 0 mg Cholesterol, 18 g Carbohydrate, 5 mg Sodium, 4 g Fiber, 3 g Protein

November Compote

The tastes of autumn make this hot fruit dish a real comfort food. Serve it alongside your favorite entrée or for dessert atop light vanilla ice cream.

Makes 6 servings

- 1 cup cranberries, coarsely chopped
- 3 small, sweet apples, peeled, chopped into ½-inch pieces
- ½ cup raisins
- 1 tablespoon all-purpose flour
- ¼ cup firmly packed brown sugar
- ½ cup apple juice

Preheat oven to 375°.

Lightly oil a 1-½-quart casserole or spray with a nonstick cooking spray.

In a medium bowl, combine cranberries, apples, and raisins. Add flour and brown sugar. Mix well. Place in prepared casserole. Stir in apple juice.

Cover and bake 35 minutes, until apples are tender. Stir once during cooking time.

Serve warm. (Leftovers are also delicious cold.)

Each serving provides: 122 Calories, 0 g Fat, 0 mg Cholesterol, 31 g Carbohydrate, 5 mg Sodium, 3 g Fiber, 1 g Protein

GOOD HEALTH ALERT:

Blueberries, strawberries and raspberries contain plant nutrients known as anthocyanidins, which are powerful antioxidants. Berries help to protect against heart disease and cancer.

Pineapple Cranberry Fruit Cup

This is a perfect fall fruit cup, great for an appetizer, dessert, or even for breakfast. For a special touch, top with a few chopped nuts or a sprinkling of Grape Nuts® cereal just before serving.

Makes 4 servings

- 3/4 cup plain nonfat yogurt or plain Greek yogurt
- ½ cup whole-berry cranberry sauce
- 1 teaspoon vanilla extract
- 1 tablespoon sugar
- 1 cup canned pineapple tidbits (unsweetened), drained

In a medium bowl, combine yogurt, cranberry sauce, vanilla, and sugar. Mix well.

Stir in pineapple.

Chill.

To serve, divide evenly into 4 serving bowls or sherbet glasses.

Each serving provides: 129 Calories, 0 g Fat, 1 mg Cholesterol, 30 g Carbohydrate, 43 mg Sodium, 3 g Fiber, 3 g Protein

Rhubarb Fruit Sauce

Instead of applesauce, why not try this deliciously tangy alternative? Rhubarb lovers will be especially pleased.

Makes 8 servings

- 2 cups rhubarb, cut into 1-inch pieces
- 2 medium peaches, peeled, cut into ½-inch chunks
- 1/3 cup sugar
- 1 teaspoon grated fresh orange peel
- ½ cup orange juice
- 2 cups strawberries, cut in half
- 2 teaspoons cornstarch

In a small saucepan, combine rhubarb, peaches, sugar, orange peel, and ***half*** of the orange juice. Bring to a boil over medium heat. Reduce heat to medium-low and cook until rhubarb falls apart, about 15 minutes.

Add strawberries. Cook until berries are soft, about 5 minutes.

In a small bowl or custard cup, combine cornstarch and remaining orange juice. Stir to dissolve cornstarch. Add to rhubarb mixture.

Cook, stirring, 2 minutes.
Cool slightly, then chill.
Serve cold.

Each serving provides: 69 Calories, 0 g Fat, 0 mg Cholesterol, 17 g Carbohydrate, 2 mg Sodium, 3 g Fiber, 1 g Protein

Strawberry Kiwi Sorbet

This quick, easy dessert is so cool and refreshing, and the riper the fruit, the sweeter the sorbet will be. This recipe can easily be doubled to serve 4.

Makes 2 servings

2 ripe kiwis
1 cup strawberries
3 tablespoons water
1 tablespoon sugar (You may need more or less, depending on the sweetness of the fruit.)

Peel kiwis and cut each one into sixths. Arrange kiwis and strawberries on a plate in a single layer, cover, and place in the freezer for at least 1 hour, until frozen solid. Place frozen fruit in a food processor with remaining ingredients. Using the steel blade, process until smooth. Serve right away. (This can also be made in a blender, but you'll need to add enough water for it to blend, and it will have the consistency of a very thick fruit drink.)

Each *serving provides: 93 Calories, 1 g Fat, 0 mg Cholesterol, 23 g Carbohydrate, 5 mg Sodium, 2 g Fiber, 1 g Protein*

GOOD HEALTH ALERT:
Improve your chances of getting a good night's sleep: relax for an hour or so before getting into bed. Read, listen to music or take a warm bath. Don't take work to bed with you. Avoid strenuous exercise within a couple of hours of bedtime. Keep your bedroom quiet, dark and cool (60° to 65° is best). Don't drink caffeinated beverages after dinner. Try to establish a regular sleep schedule.

Citrus Brûlé

Serve this broiled citrus dish hot and bubbly for a delicious appetizer or dessert. *Makes 4 servings*

1 medium grapefruit, peeled and sectioned (Discard white membrane.)
2 small oranges, peeled and sectioned (Discard white membrane.)
2 tablespoons firmly packed brown sugar
Ground cinnamon

Preheat broiler. Lightly oil a 9-inch pie pan or spray with a nonstick cooking spray. Arrange citrus sections in prepared pan. (Be creative and arrange the fruit in pretty circles.) Sprinkle with brown sugar and then sprinkle lightly with cinnamon. Broil until the brown sugar melts and the edges of the fruit are delicately browned.

Serve right away. (Leftovers can be chilled and eaten cold.)

Each serving provides: 73 Calories, 0 g Fat, 0 mg Cholesterol, 19 g Carbohydrate, 2 mg Sodium, 2 g Fiber, 1 g Protein

Minted Grapes

This unusual combination of flavors makes a most refreshing dish. Serve it as an appetizer, a snack, or as a delicious, light dessert.

Makes 4 servings

3/4 cup plain nonfat yogurt or plain Greek yogurt
1 tablespoon sugar
½ teaspoon vanilla extract
1/16 teaspoon coconut extract
1 drop peppermint extract (A little goes a long way!)
1½ cups seedless green grapes, cut in half
1½ cups seedless red grapes, cut in half

In a medium bowl, combine yogurt, sugar, and extracts. Add grapes,mixing well.

Chill several hours to blend flavors.

Each serving provides: 102 Calories, 1 g Fat, 1 mg Cholesterol, 23 g Carbohydrate, 34 mg Sodium, 3 g Fiber, 3 g Protein

Desserts

Ah, dessert! Who doesn't love dessert? In fact, many people will turn to this section of the book first. Whether you are one of them or whether you have patiently reaped the rewards of my other delicious chapters, I welcome you to my world of lean and luscious desserts.

Most people think that desserts have to be high in calories and fat in order to be tasty. Not so! I have found that if I use lots of spices and extracts, and sweet additions such as fruits and fruit juices, I can eliminate much of the fat and still have tasty results. I have greatly reduced the amount of sugar in my desserts and have found that increasing the vanilla extract seems to compensate for the loss.

I've added fiber to my desserts by using whole wheat flour in most of my recipes, and by adding other whole grains, such as brown rice and oats. The many fruits I use provide fiber, vitamins, and minerals.

Whenever I use oil in these desserts, I use it in moderation and choose canola oil, which is a monounsaturated oil. The use of moist ingredients, such as honey, applesauce, and nonfat yogurt, enables me to use smaller amounts of oil.

To reduce the amount of cholesterol in these desserts, I use egg whites in place of whole eggs, and only nonfat or lowfat dairy products. I replace cream with evaporated skim milk and substitute nonfat yogurt for sour cream. I love the taste and texture of nuts and coconut, and have found that a little can go a long way, so reduce the fat content of these recipes by using only small amounts of these high-fat items.

So, indulge! I offer you cakes, pies, puddings, crisps, cookies, and more. Also, for lots of other dessert ideas, be sure to check Breakfast Ideas, Salads and Salad Dressings, Breads and Muffins, Fruits, and Sauces and Toppings. Here are just a few of my other dishes that also make delicious desserts – see index for page numbers:

- Cranberry Crunch Salad – Cool and crunchy.
- Tofu Crème Topping – Doubles as a creamy pudding.
- Rum n' Raisin Muffins – You'll love them warm.
- Cherries Amandine – Cherries with almond crème topping.

Applesauce Orange Spice Cake

Spicy, sweet, and oh, so moist, this tasty cake is a real crowd pleaser.

Makes 12 servings

1¼ cups all-purpose flour
1 cup whole wheat flour
1 teaspoon ***each*** baking powder and baking soda
1 teaspoon ground cinnamon
¼ teaspoon ground cloves
1/8 teaspoon ground allspice
¼ cup plus 2 tablespoons raisins
3 tablespoons orange juice
2 tablespoons canola oil
½ cup sugar
2 egg whites
1 teaspoon ***each*** vanilla extract and orange extract
1 teaspoon grated fresh orange peel
1½ cups applesauce (unsweetened)

Topping:

2 teaspoons sugar
¼ teaspoon ground cinnamon

Preheat oven to 350º.

Lightly oil a 10-inch tube pan, or spray with a nonstick spray.

In a large bowl, combine both flours, baking powder, baking soda, and spices. Mix well. Add raisins.

In another bowl, combine remaining cake ingredients. Beat with a fork or wire whisk until blended. Add to dry ingredients, mixing just until all ingredients are moistened.

Spoon batter into prepared pan. Combine sugar and cinnamon and sprinkle evenly over top of cake. Bake 35 minutes, until a toothpick inserted in the center of the cake comes out clean.

Cool in pan on rack 5 minutes; remove to rack to finish cooling.

Each serving provides: 172 Calories, 3 g Fat, 0 mg Cholesterol, 34 g Carbohydrate, 115 mg Sodium, 3 g Fiber, 4 g Protein

Banana Ring Cake

Tender and moist, the riper the bananas, the sweeter this cake will be.

Makes 12 servings

1¼ cups all-purpose flour
1 cup whole wheat flour
1½ teaspoons baking powder
1 teaspoon baking soda
2 tablespoons canola oil
½ cup sugar
2 egg whites
3 tablespoons skim milk
2 teaspoons vanilla extract
3 medium, ripe bananas, mashed (1½ cups)

Preheat oven to 350º.

Lightly oil a 10-inch tube pan, or spray with a nonstick cooking spray.

In a large bowl, combine both flours, baking powder, and baking soda. Mix well.

In another bowl, combine remaining ingredients, ***except*** bananas. Mix with a fork or wire whisk until blended. Add bananas and whisk again.

Add banana mixture to dry ingredients. Mix just until all ingredients are moistened. Place in prepared pan. (Mixture will be shallow in pan.)

Bake 30 to 35 minutes, until a toothpick inserted in the center of the cake comes out clean.

Cool in pan on wire rack 5 minutes, then remove cake to rack.

Serve warm for best flavor.

Each serving provides: 167 Calories, 3 g Fat, 0 mg Cholesterol, 33 g Carbohydrate, 134 mg Sodium, 3 g Fiber, 4 g Protein

GOOD HEALTH ALERT:

To protect your voice and/or recover from hoarseness, keep your vocal cords well lubricated. Increase the humidity in your surroundings. Up your fluid intake. Avoid alcohol and cigarettes. Glycerin throat lozenges may be helpful, but decongestants or antihistamines may dry your throat.

Chocolate Mousse Cake

You'll love the light, airy texture and deep chocolate flavor plus the unusual look of the cake.

Makes 12 servings

9 egg whites
¼ teaspoon cream of tartar
½ cup plus 2 tablespoons sugar
1/3 cup cocoa (unsweetened)
2 tablespoons canola oil
1 teaspoon vanilla extract

Preheat oven to 350º.

Lightly oil a 9-inch cake pan or spray with a nonstick cooking spray. Then dust the pan lightly with flour.

Place 6 of the egg whites in a large bowl. Beat on high speed of an electric mixer until foamy. Add cream of tartar and continue to beat until egg whites are stiff. Gradually beat in ½ cup of the sugar, 1 tablespoon at a time, beating well after each addition.

In a small, deep bowl, combine remaining 3 egg whites, remaining 2 tablespoons of sugar, cocoa, oil, and vanilla. Beat on low speed until smooth.

Using a folding motion, fold cocoa mixture into egg whites, gently but thoroughly. Place mixture in prepared pan. Smooth the top with the back of a spoon.

Bake 30 minutes. (Cake will puff up high, then sink down while cooling.)

Cool on a wire rack then cover and chill.

Serve cold.

Each serving provides: 81 Calories, 3 g Fat, 0 mg Cholesterol, 12 g Carbohydrate, 41 mg Sodium, 2 g Fiber, 3 g Protein

GOOD HEALTH ALERT:

If you're susceptible to urinary tract infections (UTIs), try cranberry juice. A study at Harvard showed that women who drank 10 ounces of cranberry juice cocktail daily significantly reduced infection rates over a six-month period. The researchers noted that cranberry juice should be used as an adjunct to medical treatment – not a substitute for it. If a UTI is serious enough to cause symptoms, it requires medical attention.

Apple Gingerbread Bars

These moist, spicy, cake-like bars are topped with sliced apples and filled with flavor. I sometimes call them Magic Bars because they disappear so fast!

Makes 16 servings

Topping:

Ground cinnamon
1 small, sweet apple, unpeeled, cut in half, then sliced 1/8-inch thick

Cake:

3/4 cup all-purpose flour
1 teaspoon baking powder
1 teaspoon ground ginger
1 teaspoon ground cinnamon
1 teaspoon vanilla extract
2 tablespoons plus 2 teaspoons canola oil
1-½ cups applesauce (unsweetened)
3/4 cup whole wheat flour
½ teaspoon baking soda
1/8 teaspoon ground cloves
2 egg whites
¼ cup molasses

Preheat oven to 350°.

Lightly oil a 9 x 13-inch baking pan, or spray with a nonstick cooking spray. Sprinkle cinnamon liberally in bottom of pan. Arrange apple slices evenly over cinnamon.

In a large bowl, combine both flours, baking powder, baking soda, and spices. Mix well.

In another bowl, combine remaining ingredients. Beat with a fork or wire whisk until blended. Add to dry mixture, mixing just until all ingredients are moistened. Spread batter evenly over apple slices.

Bake 25 minutes, until a toothpick inserted in the center of the cake comes out clean.

Cool in pan on a wire rack 3 minutes, then invert onto a serving plate.

Serve warm for best flavor.

Each serving provides: 92 Calories, 3 g Fat, 0 mg Cholesterol, 16 g Carbohydrate, 61 mg Sodium, 3 g Fiber, 2 g Protein

GOOD HEALTH ALERT:

Microwaving tends to destroy fewer vitamins than conventional cooking methods. To get the most from microwaving, add as little water as possible to the food. A teaspoonful may be enough to prevent burning. Always cover food while microwaving; this reduces cooking time and thus nutrient loss.

Angel Cake

I took my favorite angel food cake, cut out half of the sugar, and added more vanilla. It's still my favorite angel food cake! It's great by itself, or as a base for shortcake or trifle.

Makes 16 servings

3/4 cup all-purpose flour
1 cup sugar
12 egg whites
1 teaspoon cream of tartar
1/16 teaspoon salt
1½ teaspoons vanilla extract
½ teaspoon almond extract

Preheat oven to 350°.

Have an ungreased 10-inch tube pan ready.

Sift flour with 3/4 cup of the sugar. Sift again.

Place egg whites in a large, deep bowl. Beat on medium speed of an electric mixer until foamy. Add cream of tartar and salt. Beat on high speed until stiff.

Beat in extracts.

Add remaining sugar, a tablespoon at a time, beating after each addition.

Sift ¼ of the flour mixture over egg whites. Fold in lightly. Repeat, folding in remaining flour, ¼ at a time.

Turn into tube pan.

Bake 45 minutes, until cake springs back when lightly touched.

Invert cake in pan to cool. Cool completely, then run a knife around the edges of the cake and remove from pan.

Each serving provides: 84 Calories, 0 g Fat, 0 mg Cholesterol, 17 g Carbohydrate, 50 mg Sodium, Less than 1 g Fiber, 3 g Protein

GOOD HEALTH ALERT:

Highly nutritious foods are often low in cost. Among them are potatoes, bananas, carrots, rice, whole wheat flour and dried beans – the sort of high fiber, lowfat foods that nutritionists now recommend. They also tend to come with minimal packaging – an environmental plus.

Raspberry Nut Torte

This luscious torte can be topped with any flavor jam you like. The ingredients do seem a little unusual, so follow your curiosity and try it!

Makes 8 servings

- 12 saltine crackers (individual squares) (Saltines with unsalted tops will work, but the original saltines add a wonderful zing to the torte.)
- ¼ cup chopped walnuts (1 ounce)
- 3 egg whites
- ½ cup sugar
- 1¼ teaspoons vanilla extract
- 1 teaspoon white vinegar
- 1 teaspoon baking powder
- 3 tablespoons reduced-sugar raspberry jam or fruit-only raspberry jam

Preheat oven to 350°.

Oil a 9-inch pie pan or spray with a nonstick cooking spray.

Place crackers and walnuts in a plastic bag. With a rolling pin, crush them until crackers are in the form of fine crumbs. Set aside.

Place egg whites in a large bowl and beat until stiff, using the high speed of an electric mixer. Slowly add sugar, 1 tablespoon at a time, beating well after each addition. Beat until egg whites hold stiff peaks.

Beat in vanilla, vinegar, and baking powder.

Sprinkle cracker mixture over egg whites and, on low speed, beat for just a few seconds, until crumbs are just incorporated into the mixture. Spread mixture evenly in prepared pan.

Bake 35 to 40 minutes, until golden brown.

Cool in pan on wire rack. When cool, run a knife around the edges of the torte and gently remove from pan. Spread with jam. Chill.

Each serving provides: 108 Calories, 3 g Fat, 0 mg Cholesterol, 19 g Carbohydrate, 121 mg Sodium, 2 g Fiber, 2 g Protein

GOOD HEALTH ALERT:

Most of us eat a lot more protein than our bodies require. Protein needs can be easily met by eating a variety of grains, vegetables, nuts, seeds and fruits.

Pineapple Apricot Coffee Cake

You really must serve this cake warm – that is, if you want to taste one of the most tender, flavorful coffee cakes ever.

Makes 8 servings

Topping:

2 tablespoons firmly packed brown sugar
½ teaspoon ground cinnamon
2 tablespoons chopped walnuts (½ ounce)

Cake:

½ cup whole wheat flour
1 teaspoon baking soda
2 egg whites
2 teaspoons vanilla extract
2 tablespoons canola oil
½ cup plus 2 tablespoons all-purpose flour
½ teaspoon ground cinnamon
1/3 cup sugar
¼ teaspoon orange extract
1 cup orange juice
1 cup canned apricot halves (unsweetened), drained, cut into quarters
1 cup canned pineapple tidbits (unsweetened), drained

Preheat oven to 350°.

Lightly oil a 9-inch pie pan or spray with a nonstick cooking spray.

In a small bowl, combine topping ingredients, mixing well. Set aside.

In a large bowl, combine both types of flour, baking soda, and cinnamon. Mix well.

In another bowl, combine egg whites, sugar, extracts, oil, and orange juice. Beat with a fork or wire whisk until blended. Stir in apricots and pineapple. Add to dry mixture. Mix until all ingredients are moistened. Place in prepared pan.

Sprinkle topping evenly over cake.

Bake 25 minutes, until a toothpick inserted in the center of the cake comes out clean.

Serve warm.

Each serving provides: 204 Calories, 5 g Fat, 0 mg Cholesterol, 37 g Carbohydrate, 120 mg Sodium, 2 g Fiber, 4 g Protein

GOOD HEALTH ALERT:
Recognize your "trigger foods" (foods you start eating and can't stop). Clear them from your house and car, and keep an "in defense of" snack at the office.

Orange Raisin Coffee Cake

Serve these delicious, cinnamony cake squares warm with a cup of coffee or tea for a coffee break they won't forget.

Makes 16 servings

- 1 cup all-purpose flour
- ½ cup whole wheat flour
- 1 teaspoon baking powder
- 1 teaspoon baking soda
- ½ teaspoon ground cinnamon
- ½ cup sugar
- ¼ cup butter, softened
- ½ cup skim milk
- 3 egg whites
- ½ cup raisins
- ½ cup frozen orange juice concentrate, thawed

Topping:

- 1 tablespoon sugar
- 1 teaspoon ground cinnamon

Preheat oven to 350º.

Lightly oil an 8-inch square baking pan or spray with a nonstick cooking spray. Dust the pan lightly with flour.

In a large bowl, combine both flours, baking powder, baking soda, and cinnamon. Mix well.

Reserve and set aside 2 tablespoons of the orange juice concentrate. In a large bowl, combine remaining concentrate with sugar, butter, skim milk, and egg whites. Beat on low speed of an electric mixer until combined. Add dry mixture, 1/3 at a time, beating after each addition. Beat on medium speed 3 minutes.

Gently fold raisins into batter. Pour into prepared pan.

Bake 40 minutes, until a toothpick inserted in the center of the cake comes out clean.

Spread remaining orange juice concentrate over hot cake. Combine sugar and cinnamon and sprinkle evenly over cake.

Cool in pan on a wire rack.

Cut into squares to serve. Serve warm for best flavor.

Each serving provides: 128 Calories, 3 g Fat, 0 mg Cholesterol, 23 g Carbohydrate, 127 mg Sodium, 2 g Fiber, 3 g Protein

GOOD HEALTH ALERT:

The larger the number of people at a meal, the more each person tends to eat. This suggests that social factors may provide powerful eating cues. So, if you're trying to lose weight, be extra careful when eating with others.

Yes Chocolate Cake!

How can healthy taste so good? This cake gets its wonderful, moist texture from maple syrup, applesauce, and apple juice. There's lots of added fiber from the oat bran.

Makes 12 servings

Cake:

3/4 cup whole wheat flour
¼ cup cocoa (unsweetened)
1 teaspoon baking soda
½ cup pure maple syrup
½ cup applesauce (unsweetened)
2 teaspoons vanilla extract
2/3 cup oat bran (3 ounces)
1 teaspoon baking powder
2 egg whites
2 tablespoons canola oil
2/3 cup apple juice
¼ teaspoon almond extract

Topping:

2 tablespoons chocolate chips (or carob chips)
2 tablespoons chopped walnuts (½ ounce)

Preheat oven to 325°.

Lightly oil an 8-inch square baking pan or spray with a nonstick cooking spray.

In a large bowl, combine flour, oat bran, cocoa, baking powder, and baking soda. Mix well.

In another bowl, combine remaining cake ingredients. Beat with a fork or wire whisk until blended. Add to dry mixture, mixing until all ingredients are moistened.

Place in prepared pan. Sprinkle nuts and carob chips evenly over cake, pressing them lightly into the cake.

Bake 35 minutes, until a toothpick inserted in the center of the cake comes out clean.

Cool in pan on wire rack. Cut into squares to serve.

Each serving provides: 134 Calories, 4 g Fat, 0 mg Cholesterol, 24 g Carbohydrate, 117 mg Sodium, 3 g Fiber, 3 g Protein

Blueberry Kuchen

Adapted from a traditional German dessert, this one uses yogurt in place of the usual sour cream topping. Just pour a cup of coffee or tea and enjoy!

Makes 8 servings

Crust:

3/4 cup whole wheat flour

½ teaspoon baking powder
2 tablespoons sugar
2 tablespoons plus 2 teaspoons butter
¼ cup skim milk

Filling:
2 cups fresh or frozen blueberries (If using frozen berries, thaw and drain before using.)
2 tablespoons sugar (Use less if berries are very sweet.)
2 teaspoons cornstarch

Topping:
1 cup plain lowfat yogurt or plain Greek yogurt
2 egg whites
1½ teaspoons vanilla extract
3 tablespoons sugar

Preheat oven to 400°.
Have a 6 x 10-inch baking pan ready.

To prepare crust:
In a medium bowl, combine flour, baking powder, and sugar, mixing well. Add butter. Mix with a fork or pastry blender until mixture resembles coarse crumbs. Add milk. Mix with a fork, then with your hands, until mixture holds together in a ball.

Press dough evenly into bottom of pan to form a crust. Wet your fingers slightly as you work to prevent sticking.

To prepare filling:
Place blueberries in a medium bowl. Sprinkle evenly with sugar and cornstarch, tossing until evenly distributed. Spoon berries evenly over crust.

To prepare topping:
In a small bowl, combine all topping ingredients, mixing well. Spoon evenly over berries.

Bake, uncovered, 25 minutes, until topping is set.
Cool slightly, then cut into squares and serve warm.

Each serving provides: 147 Calories, 3 g Fat, 2 mg Cholesterol, 28 g Carbohydrate, 112 mg Sodium, 3 g Fiber, 4 g Protein

Raspberry Almond Couscous Cake

Couscous is a grain that is available in most supermarkets as well as in health food stores. This recipe turns a grain into a unique dessert. It's not really a cake, but a molded dessert that looks and cuts like one.

Makes 8 servings

2 cups water
¼ cup honey
1 tablespoon cornstarch
2 teaspoons vanilla extract
¼ cup sliced almonds (1 ounce)
1 cup couscous, uncooked (6 ounces)
¼ cup apple juice
¼ teaspoon ground cinnamon
3/4 teaspoon almond extract
¼ cup raisins
3 tablespoons reduced-sugar raspberry jam (8 calories per teaspoon), or fruit-only raspberry jam
Almond slices to garnish

Bring water to a boil in a small saucepan. Stir in couscous, cover, remove from heat, and let stand 5 minutes.

In another small saucepan, combine honey, apple juice, cornstarch, cinnamon, and extracts. Bring to a boil over medium heat, stirring. Boil 1 minute, or until thick, stirring.

Fluff cooked couscous with a fork and drain if any water remains. Stir honey mixture into couscous along with almonds and raisins. Mix well.

Line an 8-inch round cake pan with waxed paper or aluminum foil. Spoon couscous mixture into pan and press in place with the back of a spoon. Cover and chill several hours, or overnight, until cold and firm.

To unmold, invert cake onto serving plate and gently remove paper.

Place jam in a small bowl and stir until smooth. Add a few drops of water, if necessary. Spread evenly over top of cake. Sprinkle with additional almonds to garnish.

Serve cold.

Each serving provides: 168 Calories, 2 g Fat, 0 mg Cholesterol, 34 g Carbohydrate, 4 mg Sodium, 3 g Fiber, 4 g Protein

GOOD HEALTH ALERT:

When you stretch, ease your body into position until you feel the stretch and hold it for about 25 seconds. Breathe deeply to help your body move oxygen-rich blood to those sore muscles. Don't bounce or force yourself into an uncomfortable position.

French Apple Pancake with Vanilla Creme Sauce

This is truly a dessert experience. It can also be topped with light vanilla ice cream in place of the Creme Sauce.

Makes 8 servings

Pancake:

2	egg whites	¼ cup sugar
2	teaspoons vanilla extract	2 tablespoons whole wheat flour
½	teaspoon baking powder	2 tablespoons chopped walnuts (½ oz)
2	small, sweet apples, unpeeled, coarsely shredded (1½ cups)	

Topping:

1	teaspoon sugar	¼ teaspoon ground cinnamon

Vanilla Creme Sauce:

1	cup skim milk	2 tablespoons sugar
2	teaspoons vanilla extract	1 tablespoon plus 1 teaspoon cornstarch

Preheat oven to 350°.

Lightly oil a 9-inch pie pan or spray with a nonstick cooking spray.

To prepare pancake:

In a medium bowl, combine egg whites, sugar, and vanilla. Beat with a fork or wire whisk until blended. In a small bowl, combine flour and baking powder. Mix well. Stir into egg mixture. Add nuts and apples. Mix well. Spread mixture in prepared pan.

Combine topping ingredients and sprinkle evenly over pancake.

Bake 30 minutes.

While pancake is baking prepare sauce:

In a small saucepan, combine milk, sugar, and cornstarch. Stir to dissolve cornstarch. Cook over medium heat, stirring, until mixture comes to a boil. Continue to cook 2 more minutes, stirring. Remove from heat and stir in vanilla.

To serve, cut warm pancake into pie-shaped wedges. Place each piece on an individual serving plate and top with 2 tablespoons of warm sauce.

For pancake: *Each serving provides: 68 Calories, 1 g Fat, 0 mg Cholesterol, 13 g Carbohydrate, 41 mg Sodium, 2 g Fiber, 1 g Protein*

For Vanilla Creme Sauce: *Each serving provides: 32 Calories, 0 g Fat, 1 mg Cholesterol, 6 g Carbohydrate, 16 mg Sodium, Less than 1 g Fiber, 1 g Protein*

Apricot Almond Cheese Pie

This creamy, rich-tasting pie will satisfy even the sweetest of sweet tooths. For another variation, substitute canned peaches for the apricots.

Makes 8 servings

Crust:

3/4 cup graham cracker crumbs (3 ounces, or twelve 2-½-inch graham crackers, crushed)
3 tablespoons butter, melted

Filling:

1-3/4 cups part-skim ricotta cheese
3 egg whites
1 1-pound can apricot halves (unsweetened), drained well on towels
1/3 cup sugar
2 tablespoons cornstarch
1 teaspoon vanilla extract
3/4 teaspoon almond extract

Preheat oven to 350°.

Combine graham cracker crumbs and butter in a 9-inch pie pan. Mix well, until crumbs are moistened. Press crumbs onto bottom and sides of pan, forming a crust. Bake 8 minutes.

Cool slightly.

In a blender container, combine filling ingredients. Blend until smooth. Pour into prepared crust.

Bake 35 minutes, until set. (Center will be a little looser than edges, but will set as pie chills.)

Chill.

Each serving provides: 233 Calories, 9 g Fat, 17 mg Cholesterol, 28 g Carbohydrate, 208 mg Sodium, 2 g Fiber, 9 g Protein

Dreamy Orange Ice Cream Pie

I've used light ice cream in place of regular ice cream in this scrumptious frozen delight. Ice cream lovers will be in heaven!

Makes 8 servings

Crust:

3/4 cup graham cracker crumbs (3 ounces, or twelve 2-½-inch graham crackers, crushed)

¼ teaspoon ground cinnamon

3 tablespoons butter, melted

Filling:

1 quart light vanilla ice cream

½ cup frozen orange juice concentrate, thawed

½ teaspoon ground cinnamon

Topping:

1 tablespoon graham cracker crumbs (¼ ounce, or one 2-½-inch graham cracker, crushed)

Ground cinnamon

Combine crust ingredients in a 9-inch pie pan. Mix well, until crumbs are moistened. Press crumbs onto bottom and sides of pan, forming a crust. Place in freezer 1 hour or longer.

Let ice cream stand at room temperature until softened. (Do not let it turn to liquid.) Place in a large bowl and add orange juice concentrate and cinnamon. Mix well.

Spoon ice cream into chilled crust, swirling the top with the back of a spoon.

Sprinkle evenly with graham cracker crumbs and cinnamon. Cover pie with aluminum foil and return to freezer.

To serve, let pie stand at room temperature for a few minutes, then cut with a sharp knife that has been dipped in hot water.

Each serving provides: 207 Calories, 8 g Fat, 9 mg Cholesterol, 30 g Carbohydrate, 176 mg Sodium, 1 g Fiber, 4 g Protein

Magic Orange Custard Pie

This smooth, custardly delight actually makes its own crust while it bakes. Just throw everything into the blender and then into the oven and presto!

Makes 8 servings

2 cups skim milk
¼ cup frozen orange juice concentrate, thawed
6 egg whites
1 tablespoon plus 1 teaspoon canola oil
2 teaspoons vanilla extract
1/8 teaspoon orange extract
1/3 cup sugar
¼ cup plus 2 tablespoons all-purpose flour
2 teaspoons baking powder

Preheat oven to 350º.

Lightly oil a 9-inch pie pan or spray with a nonstick cooking spray.

In a blender container, combine all ingredients. Blend 1 full minute. Pour mixture into prepared pan. Let stand 5 minutes.

Bake 30 minutes, until puffed and golden.

Cool slightly, then chill.

Each serving provides: 126 Calories, 2 g Fat, 1 mg Cholesterol, 20 g Carbohydrate, 180 mg Sodium, 1 g Fiber, 6 g Protein

Tater Pum Pie

This glorious pie combines sweet potatoes, pumpkin and all the traditional spices for a dessert that will definitely win you rave reviews.

Makes 16 servings

Crust:

3/4 cup graham cracker crumbs (3 ounces, or twelve 2-½-inch graham crackers, crushed)
3 tablespoons butter, melted

Filling:

1 1-pound can pumpkin
1-1/3 cups nonfat dry milk
½ cup frozen orange juice concentrate, thawed
¼ cup plus 2 tablespoons all-purpose flour

1 cup plus 2 tablespoons firmly packed brown sugar
2 teaspoons vanilla extract
2½ teaspoons ground cinnamon
¼ teaspoon ground nutmeg
½ teaspoon ground ginger
½ teaspoon ground cloves
1 18-ounce can sweet potatoes (vacuum packed)
1½ cups water
6 egg whites

Preheat oven to 350°.

Have a 10-inch springform pan ready.

In the bottom of the pan, combine graham cracker crumbs and butter. Mix well, until crumbs are moistened. Press crumbs firmly into bottom of pan and about ½ inch up the sides.

Bake 8 minutes.

In a blender container, combine pumpkin, dry milk, orange juice concentrate, flour, brown sugar, vanilla, and spices. Blend until smooth. Spoon into a large bowl.

In the blender, combine ***half*** of the sweet potatoes with ***half*** of the water and ***half*** of the egg whites. Blend until smooth. Add to pumpkin mixture. Then blend remaining sweet potatoes with remaining water and egg whites and add this to pumpkin mixture. Mix very well, until thoroughly combined.

Pour mixture into prepared crust.

Bake 50 minutes, or until set.

Serve cold or at room temperature. Just before serving, run a knife around the edge of the pie and carefully remove outer ring of pan.

Each serving provides: 193 Calories, 3 g Fat, 1 mg Cholesterol, 37 g Carbohydrate, 134 mg Sodium, 4 g Fiber, 5 g Protein

GOOD HEALTH ALERT:
Opt for 1% or skim milk. Lowfat milks are not created equal. A cup of 2% milk contains 5 grams of fat and thus derives 35% of its calories from fat. A cup of 1% milk contains less than 3 grams of fat and gets 22% of its calories from fat. Whole milk contains about 3.5% fat by weight, yet this fat supplies 50% of its calories. Skim milk, of course, has virtually no fat and contains just as much calcium as whole milk.

Raspberry Glazed Apple Pie

I've saved calories and fat by using a fruit glaze in place of a top crust in this scrumptious pie.

Makes 8 servings

Apple filling:

6 small, Golden Delicious apples, peeled, quartered, and sliced 1/8-inch thick (6 cups)

1 tablespoon lemon juice

¼ teaspoon ground nutmeg

1/3 cup sugar

2 tablespoons water

½ teaspoon ground cinnamon

2 tablespoons cornstarch

1 teaspoon vanilla extract

Crust:

½ cup all-purpose flour

2 tablespoons plus 2 teaspoons butter

3 tablespoons plus 2 teaspoons ice water

¼ cup whole wheat flour

¼ teaspoon baking powder

Raspberry glaze:

1 10-ounce package frozen raspberries (unsweetened), thawed (If unsweetened berries are not available, choose the ones packed in light syrup.)

1 tablespoon cornstarch

2 tablespoons sugar

Preheat oven to 450°.

Have a 9-inch pie pan ready.

To prepare filling:

In a large bowl, combine apples with remaining filling ingredients. Mix well. Set aside while preparing crust.

To prepare crust:

In a medium bowl, combine both flours and baking powder, mixing well. Add butter. Mix with a fork or a pastry blender until mixture resembles coarse crumbs.

Add water. Mix with a fork until dry ingredients are moistened. Work dough into a ball, using your hands. (Add a little more flour if dough is sticky, or a little more water if dough is too dry.) Roll dough between 2 sheets of waxed paper into an 11-inch circle. Remove top sheet of waxed paper and invert crust into prepared pan. Fit crust into pan leaving an overhang. Carefully remove remaining waxed paper. Bend edges of crust under and flute dough with your fingers or a fork.

Stir apples and spoon into crust, layering the apples so that they lie flat. Pour any remaining liquid over apples.

Bake 10 minutes at 450 degrees, then reduce temperature to 350 degrees. Place a sheet of aluminum foil loosely over pie and continue to bake 45 more minutes.

Cool pie on a rack, still covered loosely with foil, for 1 hour.

To prepare glaze:

Drain berries, reserving liquid. Add water to liquid to equal 1 cup. In a small saucepan, combine liquid with cornstarch and sugar, stirring to dissolve cornstarch.

Cook over medium heat, stirring, until mixture comes to a boil. Boil 1 minute, stirring.

Remove from heat and stir in berries.

Spoon glaze evenly over cooled pie.

Chill.

Each serving provides: 200 Calories, 5 g Fat, 0 mg Cholesterol, 40 g Carbohydrate, 59 mg Sodium, 3 g Fiber, 2 g Protein

Tropical Fruit Betty

Here's a great use for leftover bread. I've added the tastes of the tropics for a delicious and very easy, layered dessert that also makes a healthy breakfast.

Makes 6 servings

- 4 slices whole wheat bread (1-ounce slices), crumbled
- ¼ cup plus 2 tablespoons Grape Nuts® cereal (1-½ ounces)
- 1 teaspoon ground cinnamon
- 2 tablespoons firmly packed brown sugar
- 1 medium, ripe banana, very thinly sliced
- 1 cup canned crushed pineapple (unsweetened), drained slightly
- 1 cup orange juice
- 1 teaspoon vanilla extract
- ¼ teaspoon coconut extract

In a large bowl, combine bread, Grape Nuts® cereal, cinnamon, and brown sugar. Mix well.

Place ***half*** of the bread mixture in a shallow 1-quart baking dish. Press firmly in place.

Spread banana slices evenly over bread. Top with crushed pineapple.

Top with remaining bread mixture. Press firmly in place.

In a small bowl, combine orange juice and extracts. Spoon evenly over dessert. With the back of a spoon, pack mixture in place.

Chill several hours or overnight.

Serve cold.

Each serving provides: 156 Calories, 1 g Fat, 1 mg Cholesterol, 35 g Carbohydrate, 166 mg Sodium, 2 g Fiber, 3 g Protein

Graham Cracker Creme Torte

Layers of cinnamon graham crackers and vanilla pudding make a dessert reminiscent of Mom's graham cracker cream pie. The only thing missing is the cream!

Makes 12 servings

- ¼ cup plus 2 tablespoons cornstarch
- ½ cup sugar
- 4 cups skim milk
- 1 tablespoon vanilla extract
- 18 2-½ x 5-inch cinnamon graham crackers

In a medium saucepan, combine cornstarch and sugar. Gradually add milk, stirring until cornstarch is completely dissolved. Cook over medium heat, stirring constantly, until mixture comes to a boil. Boil 2 minutes, stirring.

Remove pudding from heat and stir in vanilla extract.

Place 4 graham crackers in the bottom of a 6 x 10-inch baking pan. Spread with 1 cup of pudding. Alternate layers, adding 3 more layers of graham crackers and 3 more layers of pudding.

Crush remaining 2 graham crackers* and sprinkle on top.

Chill several hours, until completely cold.

Cut into squares to serve.

*An easy way to crush graham crackers is to place them in a plastic bag and crush with a rolling pin.

Each serving provides: 171 Calories, 2 g Fat, 2 mg Cholesterol, 33 g Carbohydrate, 164 mg Sodium, 1 g Fiber, 4 g Protein

Pineapple Brown Betty

The riper the pineapple, the sweeter this dessert will be. I love it served warm and topped with light vanilla ice cream.

Makes 8 servings

½ cup all-purpose flour
¼ cup whole wheat flour
1 teaspoon ground cinnamon
¼ teaspoon ground nutmeg
1/3 cup sugar
¼ cup butter
2 cups fresh pineapple, cut into ½ inch pieces
4 slices whole wheat bread (1-ounce slices), cut into cubes
½ cup water

Preheat oven to 350º.

Lightly oil an 8-inch square baking pan or spray with a nonstick cooking spray.

In a small bowl, combine both flours, cinnamon, nutmeg, and sugar, mixing well. Add butter. Mix with a fork or pastry blender until mixture resembles coarse crumbs.

In another bowl, toss together pineapple and bread cubes.

Sprinkle the bottom of the prepared baking pan with ½ cup of the flour mixture. Top with the pineapple mixture, then sprinkle evenly with remaining flour mixture.

Drizzle water evenly over surface of dessert.

Bake, uncovered, 40 minutes.

Serve warm for best flavor.

Each serving provides: 179 Calories, 7 g Fat, 0 mg Cholesterol, 28 g Carbohydrate, 158 mg Sodium, 2 g Fiber, 3 g Protein

Orange n' Raisin Rice Pudding

There's no milk or eggs in this unique rice pudding. Instead, I've used orange juice, cinnamon, and raisins. The smooth, sweet pudding doubles as a nutritious breakfast.

Makes 4 servings

2 cups orange juice
¼ teaspoon ground cinnamon
1 teaspoon vanilla extract
2 cups cooked brown rice
2 tablespoons cornstarch
2 tablespoons firmly packed brown sugar
¼ teaspoon lemon extract
¼ cup raisins

In a medium saucepan, combine orange juice, cornstarch, cinnamon, and brown sugar. Stir to dissolve cornstarch.

Cook over medium heat, stirring, until mixture comes to a boil. Boil 2 to 3 minutes, stirring. Remove from heat.

Stir in remaining ingredients, mixing well.

Transfer mixture to a 1-quart shallow bowl or baking dish.

Cover and chill.

Serve cold.

Each serving provides: 238 Calories, 1 g Fat, 0 mg Cholesterol, 54 g Carbohydrate, 10 mg Sodium, 3 g Fiber, 4 g Protein

Tofu Rice Pudding

This easy no-bake pudding is a favorite in my house. It's what I always do with leftover rice.

Makes 6 servings

- 9 ounces soft tofu
- ¼ cup honey or confectioners sugar
- 2 teaspoons vanilla extract
- ½ teaspoon ground cinnamon
- 1½ cups cooked brown rice
- ¼ cup plus 2 tablespoons raisins

In a blender container, blend tofu until smooth. Spoon into a bowl and add remaining ingredients. Mix well. Chill several hours to blend flavors.

Each *serving provides: 153 Calories, 2 g Fat, 0 mg Cholesterol, 32 g Carbohydrate, 7 mg Sodium, 3 g Fiber, 4 g Protein*

Vanilla Fruit Couscous Pudding

The fine texture of couscous makes this pudding smooth and creamy. The chopped fruit adds a wonderful sweetness.

Makes 4 servings

2 cups skim milk
3 tablespoons sugar
½ cup plus 1 tablespoon chopped mixed dried fruit (3 ounces)
2 cups cooked couscous (Cook according to package directions.)
Ground cinnamon
2 tablespoons cornstarch
2 teaspoons vanilla extract

In a small saucepan, combine milk, cornstarch, sugar, and dried fruit. Stir to dissolve cornstarch. Bring mixture to a boil over medium heat, stirring. Boil 1 minute, still stirring. Remove from heat. Stir in vanilla and couscous. Place pudding in a shallow bowl and sprinkle generously with cinnamon. Let cool slightly, then cover and chill. Serve cold.

Each serving provides: 254 Calories, 0 g Fat, 2 mg Cholesterol, 54 g Carbohydrate, 72 mg Sodium, 3 g Fiber, 8 g Protein

Very Berry Bread Pudding

Unlike most bread puddings, this unique no-bake version has no eggs or milk – just lots of fruit and flavor. It's delicious plain or topped with light vanilla ice cream.

Makes 8 servings

8 slices whole wheat bread (1-ounce slices), cut into cubes
2 cups fresh strawberries, coarsely chopped
2 cups fresh or frozen blueberries (If frozen, there's no need to thaw.)
¼ cup sugar or honey
¼ cup frozen orange juice concentrate, thawed
2 tablespoons water
1 teaspoon vanilla extract
¼ teaspoon ground cinnamon

Place bread cubes and strawberries in a large bowl. Set aside.

In a small saucepan, combine blueberries with remaining ingredients. Bring to a boil over medium heat. Reduce heat to low and simmer gently 5 minutes.

Pour blueberry mixture over strawberries and bread. Mix well until bread is completely moistened. Transfer to an 8-inch square baking pan. Press pudding down into pan with the back of a spoon.

Cover and chill.
Serve cold.

Each serving provides: 141 Calories, 2 g Fat, 1 mg Cholesterol, 30 g Carbohydrate, 183 mg Sodium, 3 g Fiber, 3 g Protein

Cinnamon Raisin Bread Pudding

This unusual bread pudding is not baked and contains no eggs. The brown sugar and raisins make it wonderfully sweet.

Makes 4 servings

- 2 cups skim milk
- 2 tablespoons cornstarch
- ¼ teaspoon ground cinnamon
- 3 tablespoons firmly packed brown sugar
- 2 teaspoons vanilla extract
- 4 slices whole wheat bread (1-ounce slices), cut into cubes
- ¼ cup raisins

In a medium saucepan, combine milk, cornstarch, cinnamon, and brown sugar. Stir to dissolve cornstarch. Cook over medium heat, stirring, until mixture comes to a boil. Continue to cook 2 to 3 minutes, stirring.

Remove from heat and stir in vanilla. Add bread cubes and raisins and mix well.

Spoon into a 1-quart shallow baking dish.

Cover and chill.

Serve cold.

Each serving provides: 201 Calories, 1 g Fat, 3 mg Cholesterol, 40 g Carbohydrate, 249 mg Sodium, 2 g Fiber, 7 g Protein

GOOD HEALTH ALERT:
Don't eat carbohydrates for a least an hour after exercise. This will force your body to break down body fat, rather than using the food you ingest. Stick to fruit and fluids during that hour, and avoid beer.

Pineapple Soufflé

For the full effect of this elegant dessert, it has to be served right away. Soufflés lose their "puff" rather quickly. I always have the ingredients ready and mix it up after dinner, while the coffee is brewing.

Makes 4 servings

2/3 cup nonfat dry milk
¼ cup sugar
½ teaspoon cream of tartar
¼ teaspoon lemon extract
½ teaspoon ground cinnamon
3 egg whites
½ teaspoon vanilla extract
¼ teaspoon coconut extract
1 1-pound can crushed pineapple (unsweetened), drained well (Place pineapple in a strainer and squeeze out the liquid with the back of a spoon.)

Preheat oven to 350°.

Lightly oil a 1¼ quart soufflé dish or spray with a nonstick cooking spray. Dust sides and bottom of the pan with flour.

In a small bowl, combine dry milk, cinnamon, and sugar. Mix well. Set aside.

Place egg whites in a large bowl and beat on medium speed of an electric mixer until frothy. Add cream of tartar and beat on high speed until mixture forms stiff peaks.

Add dry mixture, a fourth at a time, to egg whites, beating well after each addition. Beat in extracts.

Add pineapple and fold it in quickly with just a few quick strokes.

Place mixture in prepared pan.

Bake 25 minutes, or until puffed and golden. Serve right away.

Each serving provides: 174 Calories, 0 g Fat. 2 mg Cholesterol, 37 g Carbohydrate, 105 mg Sodium, 1 g Fiber, 7 g Protein

Steamed Christmas Pudding with Apple-Brandy Sauce

Add a special old-time note to any holiday or family get-together with this warm, "down-home" dessert. Don't let the cooking time scare you. Just start it steaming and enjoy your guests. Then, when dinner is finished, so is your wonderful, hot dessert.

Makes 8 servings

Pudding:

1 cup plus 2 tablespoons whole wheat flour
1 tablespoon baking soda
¼ teaspoon ground cloves
1 teaspoon ground cinnamon

½ teaspoon ground nutmeg
1/8 teaspoon salt
½ cup raisins
½ cup chopped dried fruit (3 ounces) (Use any combination you like, such as figs, prunes, apricots, or even more raisins.)
¼ cup honey
¼ cup molasses
¼ cup orange juice
2 tablespoons plus 2 teaspoons canola oil
1 teaspoon vanilla extract
1 cup finely shredded carrots
1 cup finely shredded potato, unpeeled, (6 ounces)

Apple-Brandy Sauce:
1 cup apple juice
2 tablespoons sugar
1 tablespoon plus 1 teaspoon cornstarch
1 teaspoon brandy extract (If you prefer rum sauce, substitute rum extract.)

Lightly oil the top of a double boiler or spray with a nonstick cooking spray. Fill the bottom with 2 inches of water and place over medium heat.

In a large bowl, combine flour, baking soda, spices, and salt. Mix well. Stir in raisins and other dried fruit.

In another bowl, combine honey, molasses, orange juice, oil, and vanilla. Mix well. Stir in carrots and potato. Add to dry mixture, mixing until all ingredients are moistened. Place in top of double boiler. Cover and simmer 2½ hours, or until set.

Remove top pan from double boiler and let pudding stand for 15 minutes, then invert onto a serving plate.

To prepare sauce:
Combine all sauce ingredients in a small saucepan. Stir to dissolve cornstarch. Cook over medium heat, stirring, until mixture comes to a boil. Continue to cook, stirring, 2 minutes.

Spoon 2 tablespoons of warm sauce over each serving of pudding.

For Christmas Pudding: *Each serving provides: 237 Calories, 5 g Fat, 0 mg Cholesterol, 48 g Carbohydrate, 355 mg Sodium, 3 g Fiber, 4 g Protein*

For Apple-Brandy Sauce: *Each serving provides: 34 Calories, 0 g Fat, 0 mg Cholesterol, 8 g Carbohydrate, 1 mg Sodium, 0 g Fiber, 0 g Protein*

Celestial Lemon Custards

Similar to a caramel-topped flan, what could be more heavenly than a rich lemon custard topped with pure maple syrup?

Makes 4 servings

4 egg whites
1 cup nonfat dry milk
1-2/3 cups water
1 teaspoon vanilla extract
¼ teaspoon lemon extract
2 tablespoons plus 1 teaspoon sugar
1 teaspoon finely grated fresh lemon peel
2 teaspoons pure maple syrup

Preheat oven to 325°.

Lightly oil 4 six-ounce custard cups or spray with a nonstick cooking spray.

In a medium bowl combine all ingredients, ***except*** maple syrup. Beat with a fork or a wire whisk for several minutes until well blended. Pour mixture into prepared custard cups.

Place cups in a baking pan and pour enough hot water into the larger pan to come halfway up the sides of the cups.

Bake 55 minutes, until set.

Cool slightly, then chill.

To serve, run a sharp knife around the sides of the custard and unmold onto 4 individual serving plates. Spoon ½ teaspoon of maple syrup onto the top of each custard.

Each serving provides: 119 Calories, 0 g Fat, 3 mg Cholesterol, 19 g Carbohydrate, 149 mg Sodium, 0 g Fiber, 9 g Protein

Double Orange Pudding

My favorite time to make this refreshing, sweet pudding is when navel oranges are in season. Serve it in tall-stemmed sherbet glasses for an easy yet elegant dessert.

Makes 4 servings

1 cup orange juice
1 teaspoon grated fresh orange peel
3 tablespoons sugar
2 tablespoons cornstarch
6 small oranges, peeled and sectioned (Discard white membrane.)

In a small saucepan, combine all ingredients, ***except*** orange sections.

Stir to dissolve cornstarch.

Bring to a boil over medium heat, stirring. Boil 2 minutes, stirring. Remove from heat.

Add orange sections and mix gently.

Pour into 1 bowl or 4 individual serving bowls.

Chill.

Each serving provides: 165 Calories, 0 g Fat, 0 mg Cholesterol, 41 g Carbohydrate, 1 mg Sodium, 1 g Fiber, 2 g Protein

Creamy Chocolate Pudding

This smooth, rich pudding has many variations. For chocolate almond, chocolate rum, or chocolate mint pudding, simply add either ¼ teaspoon almond or rum extract, or 2 drops of peppermint extract along with the vanilla. Yum!

Makes 4 servings

- 2 tablespoons cornstarch
- 2 tablespoons cocoa (unsweetened)
- ¼ cup sugar
- 2 cups skim milk
- 1 teaspoon vanilla extract

In a medium saucepan, combine cornstarch, cocoa, and sugar. Mix well.

Gradually add milk, stirring to dissolve cornstarch and cocoa. Cook over medium heat, stirring, until mixture comes to a boil. Continue to cook 2 to 3 minutes, stirring. Remove from heat and stir in vanilla. Spoon pudding into 4 custard cups. Chill.

Each serving provides: 117 Calories, 1 g Fat, 2 mg Cholesterol,, 24 g Carbohydrate, 64 mg Sodium, 1 g Fiber, 5 g Protein

GOOD HEALTH ALERT:
Do regular self-examinations of your breasts. Breast cancer is the most common cancer among women. The best time to examine your breasts is in the week after your period.

Banana Soft Serve

As rich as ice cream and as smooth as frozen custard, this dessert is a real prize. Why not keep a few extra bananas in the freezer so you can prepare this in an instant?

Makes 4 servings

2 medium, ripe bananas, sliced crosswise into ¼-inch slices
½ cup part-skim ricotta cheese
½ teaspoon vanilla extract
1 tablespoon sugar

Place banana slices on a plate lined with waxed paper. Cover and freeze until firm.

In a food processor, combine frozen bananas with remaining ingredients. Using a steel blade, process until smooth. Divide into 4 individual serving bowls and serve right away.

Each serving provides: 109 Calories, 3 g Fat, 10 mg Cholesterol, 18 g Carbohydrate, 39 mg Sodium, 2 g Fiber, 4 g Protein

Mocha Crème Filled Meringue Nests

What an elegant dessert! Both the pudding and the nests can be made ahead and filled just before serving. For lots of other variations, the pudding can be made and eaten separately, and the nests can be used to hold any type of cold pudding or fruit.

Makes 6 servings

Mocha Creme Pudding:

1 cup nonfat dry milk
3 tablespoons cornstarch
2 tablespoons cocoa (unsweetened)
1/3 cup sugar
1½ teaspoons instant coffee (regular or decaffeinated)
2 cups water
1 teaspoon vanilla extract

Meringue Nests:

3 egg whites
1/8 teaspoon salt
¼ teaspoon cream of tartar
1/3 cup sugar
½ teaspoon vanilla extract

To make pudding:

In a small saucepan, combine dry milk, cornstarch, cocoa, sugar, and coffee. Mix well. Gradually stir in water. Bring mixture to a boil over medium heat, stirring constantly. Boil 2 minutes, stirring. Remove from heat and stir in vanilla.

Place pudding in a bowl and cover with waxed paper, placing waxed paper directly on the surface of the pudding. (This will keep a crust from forming.)

Chill.

To make Meringue Nests:

Preheat oven to 275°.

Line a baking sheet with waxed paper.

Place egg whites in a large bowl. Beat on medium speed of an electric mixer until frothy.

Add salt and cream of tartar. Beat on high speed until stiff.

Slowly beat in sugar, a tablespoon at a time, beating well after each addition.

Beat in vanilla extract.

Mocha Crème Filled Meringue Nests – continued:

Divide mixture evenly and drop onto prepared sheet, making 6 mounds. Using a teaspoon, shape each mound into a circle 4 inches in diameter. Then build up the sides 1½ inches, making a nest.

Bake 1 hour.

Turn oven off and leave nests in oven to cool. (Do not open oven door.)

At serving time:

Place nests on a serving platter or on individual serving plates. Mix pudding well and spoon into nests, using 1/3 cup of pudding for each nest.

Serve right away.

(Meringues can be made a day ahead and stored in an airtight container or plastic bag until needed, and pudding can be stored in the refrigerator. Unfilled shells will keep for several days.)

For Mocha Creme Pudding: *Each serving provides: 106 Calories, 0 g Fat 2 mg Cholesterol, 22 g Carbohydrate, 63 mg Sodium, 1 g Fiber, 4 g Protein*

For Meringue Nests: *Each serving provides: 52 Calories, 0 g Fat, 0 mg Cholesterol, 11 g Carbohydrate, 74 mg Sodium, 0 g Fiber, 2 g Protein*

Crème Filled Spice Cakes

Delicious creme filling between 2 cake-like spice cookies makes this a unique treat. Enjoy these for dessert, snacks, or even breakfast.

Makes 12 servings

Cakes:

½ cup all-purpose flour
½ cup plus 2 tablespoons whole wheat flour
1 teaspoon baking powder
1 teaspoon baking soda
1 teaspoon ground cinnamon
¼ teaspoon ground cloves
¼ teaspoon ground allspice
½ teaspoon ground nutmeg
¼ cup plus 2 tablespoons raisins
2 egg whites
1½ teaspoons vanilla extract
½ cup plus 2 tablespoons plain nonfat yogurt
2 tablespoons canola oil
3 tablespoons sugar

Creme filling:

3/4 cup part-skim ricotta cheese
1½ teaspoons vanilla extract
1 tablespoon sugar

Preheat oven to 400°.

Lightly oil a large baking sheet or spray with a nonstick cooking spray.

In a large bowl, combine both flours, baking powder, baking soda, and spices. Mix well. Add raisins.

In another bowl, combine remaining cake ingredients. Beat with a fork or wire whisk until blended. Add to dry mixture, mixing until all ingredients are moistened.

Drop batter onto prepared baking sheet, using 1 scant tablespoon for each cake, making 24 cakes. (Make them as round as possible and keep them several inches apart.)

Bake 8 minutes. Remove to a rack to cool completely before filling.

While cakes are cooling, prepare filling:

In a small bowl, combine all filling ingredients, mixing well.

To assemble cakes:

Place 12 cakes on a serving plate, flat side up. Spread 1 tablespoon of the filling onto each cake. Top each of these cakes with an unfilled one, making a sandwich.

Cover and chill.

Serve cold.

Each serving provides: 126 Calories, 4 g Fat, 5 mg Cholesterol, 19 g Carbohydrate, 143 mg Sodium, 2 g Fiber, 5 g Protein

Oataroons

This unusual variation resembles a macaroon. They're crispy, chewy, and crunchy, all at the same time.

Makes 8 servings

- 1 egg white
- ¼ teaspoon cream of tartar
- ¼ cup sugar
- ½ teaspoon almond extract
- 2 tablespoons finely chopped walnuts (½ ounce)
- ½ cup rolled oats (1½ ounces)

Preheat oven to 350°.

Lightly oil a baking sheet or spray with a nonstick cooking spray.

Place egg white in a small, deep bowl and beat on medium speed of an electric mixer until frothy. Add cream of tartar and beat on high speed until egg white is stiff. Gradually add sugar, beating well after each addition. Beat in almond extract.

Fold walnuts and oats into egg white, gently but thoroughly.

Drop mixture by rounded teaspoonfuls onto prepared baking sheet, making 24 cookies.

Bake 12 minutes, until bottoms of cookies are lightly browned.

Remove to a wire rack to cool.

Each serving provides: 59 Calories, 1 g Fat, 0 mg Cholesterol, 10 g Carbohydrate, 7 mg Sodium, 2 g Fiber, 2 g Protein

Sir Isaac's Fig Bars

These plump, fig-filled cookies are full of flavor and fiber.

Makes 10 servings

Filling:

11 large dried figs, cut in half (8¼ ounces)
1 teaspoon grated fresh orange peel
½ cup apple juice

Dough:

¼ cup sugar
½ teaspoon baking powder
1 cup all-purpose flour
3 tablespoons plus 1 teaspoon butter
½ cup plus 2 tablespoons water
3/4 cup plus 2 tablespoons whole wheat flour

Preheat oven to 350º.
Lightly oil a baking sheet or spray with a nonstick cooking spray.

To prepare filling:

In a blender container, combine all filling ingredients. Blend until figs are in the form of a thick purée.

To prepare dough:

In a large bowl, combine both types of flour, baking powder, and sugar. Mix well. Add butter. Mix with a fork or pastry blender until mixture resembles coarse crumbs. Add water. Stir until ingredients are moistened. With your hands, form dough into a ball. Add additional water, ½ teaspoon at a time, if necessary, until dough holds together.

Place dough on a lightly floured surface and knead a few times. Shape into a log. Roll log into a 12 x 14-inch rectangle. Cut the rectangle lengthwise into 3 long strips.

To assemble:

Divide filling evenly and spoon down the center of each strip. Fold dough over lengthwise and seal the edges by crimping with a fork. Place rolls on prepared baking sheet. Flatten them slightly with your hand.

Bake 20 to 25 minutes, until bottoms are lightly browned.

Remove to a wire rack to cool.

When cool, trim the ends and, using a sharp knife, cut each log into 10 bars, 1¼ inches wide.

Each serving provides: 200 Calories, 4 g Fat, 0 mg Cholesterol, 39 g Carbohydrate, 70 mg Sodium, 4 g Fiber, 3 g Protein

Fruit n' Nut Candy Balls

Kids of all ages love these sugar-free confections. If you wish, the flavor can be varied by substituting other varieties of dried fruit and other extracts. (How about dried apricots with coconut extract?)

Makes 16 servings (2 candies each serving)

- 8 large dried figs, cut into quarters (6 ounces)
- 1 cup raisins
- 1½ cups rolled oats (4½ ounces)
- ¼ cup plus 2 tablespoons sliced almonds (1½ ounces)
- ½ teaspoon vanilla extract
- 1/8 teaspoon almond extract

Combine all ingredients in a food processor. Using a steel blade, process until mixture is uniformly ground and holds together.

Divide mixture evenly and roll into 32 one-inch balls. Wet your hands slightly as you work to keep mixture from sticking.

Place candies on a plate, cover, and store in the refrigerator.

Each serving provides: 101 Calories, 2 g Fat, 0 mg Cholesterol, 20 g Carbohydrate, 3 mg Sodium, 3 g Fiber, 2 g Protein

GOOD HEALTH ALERT:

Showering or bathing in water that's too hot will dry out your skin and cause it to age prematurely. Warm water is much better. Apply moisturizer while your skin is still damp – it'll be absorbed more easily. Adding a little olive oil to your bath will help keep your skin moisturized, too.

Razzleberry Crisp

You can use any combination of berries for this crispy delight. Serve it warm, topped with light vanilla ice cream for a dessert fit for royalty.

Makes 8 servings

1 cup fresh or frozen raspberries, unsweetened (If frozen, thaw and drain before using.)
1½ cups fresh or frozen blueberries, unsweetened (There's no need to thaw blueberries.)
1½ cups fresh or frozen dark sweet pitted cherries, unsweetened (There's no need to thaw cherries.)
¼ cup sugar
2 tablespoons cornstarch

Topping:
1 cup rolled oats (3 ounces)
3 tablespoons whole wheat flour
1 teaspoon ground cinnamon
3 tablespoons firmly packed brown sugar
2 tablespoons plus 2 teaspoons butter
2 tablespoons orange juice

Preheat oven to 350°.

Lightly oil a 9-inch pie pan or spray with a nonstick cooking spray.

Place berries in a large bowl. Sprinkle with sugar and cornstarch. Toss to coat berries. Place in prepared pan.

In a medium bowl, combine oats, flour, cinnamon, and brown sugar, mixing well. Add butter and orange juice. Mix until all ingredients are moistened. Distribute evenly over berries.

Bake, uncovered, 35 to 40 minutes, until topping is crisp and berry mixture is thick. (Frozen berries may take a little longer to cook than thawed ones.)

Serve warm or cold.

Each serving provides: 162 Calories, 3 g Fat, 0 mg Cholesterol, 33 g Carbohydrate, 49 mg Sodium, 4 g Fiber, 3 g Protein

GOOD HEALTH ALERT:
Hang around with positive people.

Chocolate Oatmeal Meringue Cookies

You can whip these up on the spur of the moment and enjoy them before you know it.

Makes 12 servings

2 tablespoons cocoa (unsweetened)
1/3 cup sugar
2 egg whites
¼ teaspoon cream of tartar
1 teaspoon vanilla extract
1½ cups rolled oats (4-½ ounces)
2 tablespoons chopped walnuts (½ ounce)

Preheat oven to 350º.

Lightly oil a baking sheet or spray with a nonstick cooking spray.

In a small bowl, combine cocoa and sugar. Set aside.

In a medium, deep bowl, beat egg whites on medium speed of an electric mixer until frothy. Add cream of tartar and beat on high speed until egg whites are stiff.

Add cocoa mixture 1 tablespoon at a time, beating well after each addition. Beat in vanilla. Fold in oats and chopped nuts.

Drop mixture by tablespoonfuls onto prepared baking sheet, making 24 cookies.

Bake 12 to 14 minutes, until bottoms of cookies are nicely browned.

Remove to a wire rack to cool.

Each serving provides: 76 Calories, 2 g Fat, 0 mg Cholesterol, 13 g Carbohydrate, 10 mg Sodium, 1 g Fiber, 3 g Protein

GOOD HEALTH ALERT:

Improve your circulation and help your lymph glands to drain by the way you towel off. Helping your lymph glands function can help prevent them becoming infected. When drying off your limbs and torso, brush towards the groin on your legs and towards the armpits on your upper body. You can do the same during gentle massage with your partner.

Molasses Raisin Spice Cookies

These crunchy cookies can easily be varied by using different dried fruits in place of the raisins.

Makes 16 servings

1½ cups whole wheat flour
1½ teaspoons baking soda
½ teaspoon ground cinnamon
¼ teaspoon ground nutmeg
1/16 teaspoon ground allspice
1/16 teaspoon ground cloves
½ cup raisins
¼ cup chopped walnuts (1 ounce)
2 tablespoons plus 2 teaspoons canola oil
1/3 cup molasses
¼ cup orange juice
1 teaspoon vanilla extract

Preheat oven to 375°.

Lightly oil a baking sheet or spray with a nonstick cooking spray.

In a large bowl, combine flour, baking soda, and spices. Mix well. Stir in raisins and walnuts.

In a small bowl, combine remaining ingredients, mixing well. Add to dry mixture, mixing until all ingredients are moistened.

With your hands, work dough into a ball. Break off pieces of dough and, wetting your hands slightly to keep dough from sticking, roll it into 32 balls, about 1 inch in diameter. Place on prepared baking sheet, 1½ inches apart.

Place a sheet of waxed paper over cookies and flatten them to ¼ inch thick, using the bottom of a glass. Carefully remove paper.

Bake 10 to 12 minutes, until bottoms of cookies are lightly browned.

Remove cookies to a wire rack to cool.

Each serving provides: 103 Calories, 4 g Fat, 0 mg Cholesterol, 17 g Carbohydrate, 79 mg Sodium, 2 g Fiber, 2 g Protein

Sauces and toppings

This chapter came about when I realized that many of the delicious toppings and sauces that I use in my recipes can also be used on other dishes to create new and exciting menus. I have added some new sauces to this chapter, too, and offer suggestions for their use. When most people think of sauces and toppings, they think of them as high-calorie, fat-laden foods. Well, they can be, and they often are, but I have kept the calories, fat and cholesterol very low in my recipes. I have accomplished this by using fruit juice, skim milk, nonfat yogurt, and tomato sauce as bases. I have one that is made predominately from tofu.

I invite you to be creative with this chapter. Change the flavors of the sauces by changing the extracts and using different fruit juices. Change the use of the sauces by serving them over different dishes. Be sure to check the chapter "Salads and Salad Dressings." Many of my dressings can double as sauces. For example, my Tahini Dressing (see index for page #) is delicious spooned over steamed broccoli and my Tofu Russian Dressing (see index) makes a meatless burger taste just like a fast-food favorite. Here are some ideas for adding my sauces and toppings to dishes from other chapters of the book – see index for page #:

- Tofu and Cheese Blintzes – Top with Piña Colada Sauce or Raspberry Melba Sauce.
- Whole Wheat Waffles – Top with Vanilla Creme Sauce or Almond Yogurt Topping and add fresh raspberries.
- Beany Burgers – Top with Herbed Tomato Sauce.
- Carrot and Potato Pudding – Top with Apple-Brandy Sauce.
- Angel Cake – Top with Orange Creme Whip and fresh orange sections.
- Pineapple Brown Betty – Top with Vanilla Creme Sauce.

Herbed Tomato Sauce

I use this basic recipe all the time, over lots and lots of dishes. Spoon it over cooked rice, omelets, steamed vegetables, pizza, etc. Its uses are endless.

Makes 4 servings

1 8-ounce can salt-free (or regular) tomato sauce
¼ teaspoon dried basil
¼ teaspoon dried oregano
1/8 teaspoon garlic powder

Combine all ingredients and heat.

Each serving provides: 21 Calories, 0 g Fat, 0 mg Cholesterol, 4 g Carbohydrate, 12 mg Sodium, 1 g Fiber, 1 g Protein

Chinese Barbecue Sauce

I serve it as a condiment with grilled or broiled tofu slices. It also adds a wonderful zip to cooked rice, steamed vegetables or baked potatoes.

Makes 4 servings

2 tablespoons honey
1 tablespoon plus 1 teaspoon hoisin sauce (Look for this condiment in jars or cans in the Oriental section of most large grocery stores.)
1 tablespoon plus 1 teaspoon reduced-sodium (or regular) soy sauce
2 teaspoons ketchup
2 teaspoons canola oil
2 teaspoons sesame oil
¼ teaspoon garlic powder
¼ teaspoon ground ginger

Combine all ingredients in a small saucepan, mixing well. Heat and serve.

Each serving provides: 87 Calories, 5 g Fat, 0 mg Cholesterol, 12 g Carbohydrate, 400 mg Sodium, 0 g Fiber, 1 g Protein

Currant-Spice Sauce

This spicy, sweet sauce is delicious over my Tofu Croquettes (see index for page #), or my Raggedy Rice Patties (see index for page #). Be creative and try it over cooked grains, waffles, or anything else you want to "dress up."

Makes 4 servings

½ cup water
3 tablespoons currant jelly
1/8 teaspoon ground allspice
½ cup orange juice
1 tablespoon plus 1 teaspoon cornstarch

Combine all ingredients in a small saucepan. Stir to dissolve cornstarch. Cook over medium heat, stirring, until mixture comes to a boil. Continue to cook 2 more minutes, stirring. Remove from heat. Serve warm.

Each serving provides: 63 Calories, 0 g Fat, 0 mg Cholesterol, 16 g Carbohydrate, 3 mg Sodium, 0 g Fiber, 0 g Protein

Apple-Brandy Sauce

Warm and wonderful, this sauce, in addition to adding a crowning touch to my Steamed Christmas Pudding (see index for page number), will turn any pancakes into gourmet delights. If you prefer rum sauce, substitute rum extract for the brandy extract. *Makes 8 servings*

1 cup apple juice
1 teaspoon brandy extract
2 tablespoons sugar
1 tablespoon plus 1 teaspoon cornstarch

Combine all ingredients in a small saucepan. Stir to dissolve cornstarch. Cook over medium heat, stirring, until mixture comes to a boil. Continue to cook, stirring, 2 minutes. Serve warm.

Each serving provides: 34 Calories, 0 g Fat,0 mg Cholesterol, 8 g Carbohydrate, 1 mg Sodium, 0 g Fiber, 0 g Protein

Raspberry Melba Sauce

Serve this quick blender sauce over any type of fresh fruit, or for a delectable Peach Melba, spoon it over sliced peaches and light vanilla ice cream.
Makes 4 servings

1 10-ounce package frozen raspberries (unsweetened), thawed
3 tablespoons confectioners sugar

Place raspberries and their juice in a blender container. Blend until puréed.

Pour through a strainer into a small bowl. Add sugar, stirring until it dissolves.

Serve right away or chill for later servings.

Each serving provides: 75 Calories, 1 g Fat, 0 mg Cholesterol, 19 g Carbohydrate, 0 mg Sodium, 1 g Fiber, 1 g Protein

Vanilla Creme Sauce

This creamy sauce is served warm over coffee cakes or pancakes. I've used it to top my French Apple Pancake (see index for page #). Also, try it over my Apple Gingerbread Bars (see index for page #).

Makes 8 servings

1 cup skim milk
2 tablespoons sugar
1 tablespoon plus 1 teaspoon cornstarch
2 teaspoons vanilla extract

In a small saucepan, combine milk, sugar, and cornstarch. Stir to dissolve cornstarch.

Cook over medium heat, stirring, until mixture comes to a boil. Continue to cook 2 more minutes, stirring. Remove from heat and stir in vanilla.

Serve warm.

Each serving provides: 32 Calories, 0 g Fat, 1 mg Cholesterol, 6 g Carbohydrate, 16 mg Sodium, 0 g Fiber, 1 g Protein

Piña Colada Sauce

Originally used to top my Piña Colada French Toast (see index for page #), this sauce has lots of other uses. Try it warm, over light ice cream, pancakes, angel cake, cooked rice or sliced bananas.

Makes 4 servings

2/3 cup pineapple juice
2 teaspoons sugar
2 teaspoons cornstarch
1/8 teaspoon coconut extract

In a small saucepan, combine pineapple juice, cornstarch, and sugar, mixing well to dissolve cornstarch. Cook over medium heat, stirring constantly, until mixture comes to a boil.

Boil 1 minute, stirring. Remove from heat and stir in coconut extract.

Serve warm.

Each serving provides: 35 Calories, 0 g Fat, 0 mg Cholesterol, 9 g Carbohydrate, 1 mg Sodium, 0 g Fiber, 0 g Protein

Almond Yogurt Topping

This easy topping is delicious over fruit or angel cake, or both together!

Makes 4 servings

3/4 cup plain nonfat yogurt or plain Greek yogurt
¼ teaspoon almond extract
2 teaspoons sugar
2 tablespoons sliced almonds (½ ounce)

In a small bowl, combine yogurt, almond extract, and sugar. Mix well. Chill.
To serve, spoon topping over fresh fruit or angel cake.
Sprinkle with almonds.

Each serving provides: 54 Calories, 2 g Fat, 1 mg Cholesterol, 6 g Carbohydrate, 33 mg Sodium, 1 g Fiber, 3 g Protein

Orange Creme Whip

Serve this fluffy delight over fresh fruit or make a delicious shortcake by spooning it over berry-topped angel food cake.

Makes 4 servings

½ cup orange juice
2-½ teaspoons sugar
1 teaspoon vanilla extract
2/3 cup nonfat dry milk

Place a medium, deep bowl and the beaters of an electric mixer in the freezer. Chill at least 1 hour.

Place orange juice in a measuring cup. Add ice water to equal 2/3 cup liquid. Place all ingredients in the chilled bowl. Beat on high speed of electric mixer 5 minutes, until thick and creamy.

Serve right away.

Each serving provides: 69 Calories, 0 g Fat, 2 mg Cholesterol, 12 g Carbohydrate, 63 mg Sodium, 1 g Fiber, 4 g Protein

Tofu Creme Topping

This creamy topping, spooned over fresh fruit, makes an elegant dessert. My favorite is fresh berries, or make a quick Peach Melba by spooning it over peaches and raspberries.

Makes 4 servings

9 ounces soft tofu
¼ cup honey or confectioners sugar
2 teaspoons vanilla extract

In a blender container, combine all ingredients. Blend until smooth. Chill several hours, or overnight, to blend flavors.

Each serving provides: 106 Calories, 2 g Fat, 0 mg Cholesterol, 20 g Carbohydrate, 5 mg Sodium, 2 g Fiber, 3 g Protein

Index

Entrees

ETCETERA, ETCETERA. ETCETERA 154

GRAINS 173

VEGETABLES 186

STARCHY VEGETABLE 214

Breads and Muffins 235

Fruits 256

Desserts 271

Millie Snyder

For forty-four years, Millie Snyder has devoted the majority of her time and interest to helping people with weight control problems. In her leadership role with a major weight control service, she expressed her belief that it is not that people don't want to change, they simply don't know how. To that end, she has made a professional life for herself as a public speaker encouraging people with weight problems to "listen up, lighten up," and fix what can be fixed. Because of her concern for people, Millie has established a reputation for helping men and women enhance the quality of their lives by learning how to change.

Millie has also managed, amidst a busy schedule, to create a large line of low-calorie foods. She is always looking for new ways to spread the word about good health.

As her *Lean and Luscious* series becomes available with its incredibly delicious meatless recipes, Millie is excited about this new way of eating.

Millie believes that humor is a necessary requirement for change. Her hobby, she says, is LIFE! "After all," she says, "there's hardly any time for much else." Her personality, both serious and humorous, is one reason why she has become a much sought-after public speaker on the subject of self-image and weight control.

Millie is the mother of two grown children, Craig and Jennifer, and the proud grandmother of five grandchildren, Allison, Jack, Holden, Aubrey and Hunter.

With over 1.5 million copies of her hit book series *Lean and Luscious* sold, Millie has shown generations of families how to not only live a healthful life but how to enjoy it, too! Her books show you how to transform your body. She will show you how to transform your mind.